MOODY

To Val, Jason, Janine and Dickie Moody
for turning back the years so bravely.

MOODY

THE LIFE AND CRIMES OF
BRITAIN'S MOST NOTORIOUS HITMAN

WENSLEY CLARKSON

MAINSTREAM
PUBLISHING
EDINBURGH AND LONDON

First published in Great Britain in 2003 by
MAINSTREAM PUBLISHING COMPANY (EDINBURGH) LTD
7 Albany Street
Edinburgh EH1 3UG

ISBN 1 84018 744 1

A catalogue record for this book is available from the British Library

Typeset in Caslon and Gill
Printed and bound in Great Britain by
Mackays of Chatham plc

One, two! One, two! And through and through
The vorpal blade went snicker-snack!
He left it dead, and with its head
He went galumphing back.

'Jabberwocky'
Lewis Carroll (1832–98)

Contents

Author's Note

However I word this note I'm going to upset somebody. One of my main sources put it bluntly: 'There are people who will be fuckin' angry that I've talked to you. Jim's mates are hard characters and I don't want to upset *any* of them.'

Obviously there are few readily available written records covering much of Jimmy Moody's activities, so I have had to trust the judgement and recollections of numerous individuals, many of whom would rather not have their names reproduced in this book. It has been dependant on the memories of men – people who are fallible, contradictory, touched by pride and capable of gross omission. But I believe them because there are no hidden agendas in this story. I make no apologies for the strong language, either.

Much of the structure of this book rests on the results of a long series of interviews, conversations and recollections supplied, at times unwittingly, by dozens of individuals. I've spent many hours in formal conversations with them. Of course some vital names are missing and that will frustrate those who were involved in the eras mentioned here. But ultimately, I've tried to re-create a life story that twists and turns from the mean streets of London, through even harsher prison corridors to the confusing world of Irish terrorism before returning to the capital's underworld. It's been a fascinating journey which I hope you are going to enjoy and relish as much as I have.

Wensley Clarkson, 2003

Prologue

'He's been shot, Jason,' said the voice. *'You better get down there, quick.'*

It was at 10:30 p.m. on Monday, 1 June 1993, that Jason Moody heard the words he'd been dreading for years. He put down the phone and immediately called his friend John, who raced round to his flat in Poplar, East London, to pick him up. They headed straight for his father's favourite pub, The Royal, on the edge of Victoria Park, in nearby Hackney. Thunder was rumbling overhead and the moonlight, peeping through the cracks in the grey sky, was drenching everything in shades of black and white.

Flashing blue lights, yellow scene-of-crime tape and a crowd of rubbernecks greeted Jason as his friend's silver BMW pulled up at The Royal. Word was already spreading fast.

'Fella's been shot.'

'Must be a contract job.'

'What is the world comin' to?'

Jason jumped out of the Beemer before it had even come to a halt.

'Where is he?' he asked a young PC standing outside the main entrance to the pub.

'Who're you?'

'Is he all right?'

'You family?'

'Just a friend. Is he gonna be OK?'

'You better ask that lot,' said the PC, nodding towards two plain-clothes detectives, standing with notebooks just inside the entrance area.

Jason later explained: 'I didn't want to tell 'em who I was in case the old man got up and made a run for it. Then they'd have nicked me.'

Jason stepped inside the doorway next to the detectives. 'Is he gonna make it?'

'Who wants to know?'

Just then the double doors to the saloon bar swung open and paramedics pushed past Jason carrying his father on a stretcher. Jason blinked his eyes to try and take it all in, gulping for air as a nauseous feeling rose from his throat. He later recalled: 'The old man looked bad. One of his arms was hanging down the side of the stretcher. All the colour had drained out of his face. I knew he was in trouble.'

'Is he all right?' Jason asked again, as he moved alongside the stretcher.

The paramedics didn't respond. Were they expressing an air of disapproval connected to the violent nature of his father's gunshot injuries? All the figures standing and staring in his direction from behind the crime-scene tape blurred into the blue-and-white flashing lights sweeping the parking area outside the pub.

Just then a finger of lightning shot out of the sky and illuminated the gothic wrought-iron gates of nearby Victoria Park.

Jason struggled to keep up with the paramedics as they approached the ambulance.

'Which hospital?' he asked.

'The London.'

Jason turned and broke into a run towards his friend's car. Suddenly, alongside him was one of the young detectives from earlier.

'You're his son, aren't you?'

Jason ignored the copper and pulled open the passenger door to the BMW just as his friend was firing-up the two-litre engine.

'Sir, I need to talk to you . . .'

The BMW swerved off the kerb, leaving the rookie detective watching its departure and furiously writing down the registration number.

'Stay behind the ambulance,' Jason told John.

He punched out a number on his mobile phone. 'It's not lookin' good, Mum. Meet you at the hospital.'

The ambulance got caught up in late-night traffic at the junction with Cambridge Heath Road and the Mile End Road. Drinkers were spilling out of pubs just as other, younger clubbers were pouring into the East End nightclubs Jason and his father knew so well. The ambulance slowed down to a snail's pace, its flashing blue light hardly meriting a glance from the passing crowds.

'For fuck's sake, MOVE IT!' screamed Jason, leaning across and blasting John's horn angrily. 'Why the fuck ain't he got his siren on?'

It was here, in the heart of the East End, that Jason's father had made and lost so much of his fortune. It was on these dangerous streets that he'd spent his final years, ducking and diving until he couldn't take it any more. It was here his father had caused havoc and made friends and enemies who would haunt him, adore him and ultimately betray him. He'd moved into his final hideout near The Royal because he couldn't stand to run anymore, but it was a miserable little place with no personal possessions, no reminders of his beloved wife and kids. There was nothing there of all the good times that he'd somehow fitted in between the dark deeds that overshadowed him from such an early age.

'Let the fuckers come and get me,' Moody had told his son Jason just a few hours earlier. 'I don't fuckin' care. I'll 'ave 'em all. They're the ones who're shittin' themselves. Tell 'em Jimmy Moody wants a word. I'm waitin' for 'em.'

Just then the ambulance turned off the Whitechapel Road into the London Hospital, slowing down as it approached the entrance to the Accident and Emergency department. As John slung the BMW up on a kerb, Jason flew out of the car so quickly he left the door swinging open behind him. Just then the double back doors of the ambulance swung open and paramedics gingerly began lifting the stretcher carrying his father.

'Is he all right?' asked Jason, his voice quivering with fear for the first time as the events of that awful evening started to dawn on him. Jason later described it as 'like being in a dream. None of it seemed real'.

Neither of the paramedics answered as they descended the two steps from the back of the ambulance.

'Please, he's my fuckin' dad.'

'He's gone, son.'

The paramedics disappeared through the plastic swing doors into the A & E department, leaving Jason standing alone on the forecourt. He put his head in his hands. He was too confused to cry. Too angry to shout. Just then he heard a male voice. He glanced through the hazy plastic see-through doors at the blurred image of an elderly man speaking to one of the nurses.

'You know who that was, don't ya? That geezer Moody who bunked out of Brixton with some IRA bloke. He was a hero round these parts. Pity they got 'im in the end.'

Thirty minutes later, Jason Moody walked into the ice-cold morgue in the basement of the London Hospital to find his father lying on a slab of marble. He forced himself to look down at the body because he had to be sure it really was him. Everything still seemed such a blur since he'd taken that phone call.

Jason took a deep breath and stood over the body silently. His eyes were watering and he felt a mixture of pain and anger, a sense of relief and also of dread. He felt relief because the nightmare of life was finally over for his father. Dread because Jason feared his father's death would unleash yet more violence. He wished nothing more than for it all to finish, especially for his family. Let all the pain and bloodshed die with him.

After 13 years on the run, Britain's most notorious hitman was officially back in the East End – in a mortuary with a tag around his toe: '*James Alfred Moody, 52, address unknown. Cause of death, gunshot wounds.*'

What goes around, comes around.

ONE

Born to Die

To attractive, young mother Rosina Moody the seaside village of Looe, in Cornwall, must have seemed a paradise – albeit a lonely one – in 1941. Her husband Richard Moody was serving with one of the hundreds of merchant navy ships making the perilous crossings to and from North America. She'd been evacuated from bombed-out south-east London for a safer haven. Rosina was 22 years old, heavily pregnant and already the mother of a boy called Richard, whom she'd had to leave behind with her own mother in the capital.

Rosina never forgot her first impressions of the town as she got off the train after being persuaded by Hitler's bombs to head for the safety of the countryside. The first thing she noticed on walking out of the station was the old bridge next to the post office where numerous fishing boats were tied up, their crews unloading catches and checking the conditions of their vessels.

Then Rosina looked down at the written instructions from the family she was to lodge with, and turned left towards Market Street where the buildings were close to the street. Chimneys bellowed out smoke and occasionally someone would come out of a shop, give her a brief glance and then look the other way. She was a stranger who longed to be back home in the slums.

Within a month of her arrival in Looe – on 27 February 1941 – Rosina gave birth at the local hospital to a beautiful bouncing boy called James Alfred. Soon she was pushing baby Jimmy in his pram down to watch Looe's fishing fleet of more than 50 vessels set sail for the same dangerous waters where her husband's ship was being shadowed by German U-boats in the north Atlantic.

Yet Rosina longed for the day when she could return with baby Jimmy to the grey, familiar streets of Camberwell Green in south-east London. Her spell of loneliness in Cornwall was only broken by an occasional visit from a friend or relative from 'The Smoke'. Thankfully, Looe was well served by the Great Western Railway which passed through Liskeard, where you could change for all stations to Looe.

It was that very same train line which brought the worst news of all for Rosina when one of her brothers arrived in early 1942 to tell her that her husband Richard's cargo ship, *The Galateer*, had been torpedoed by a U-boat 400 miles west of Cornwall. All on board were presumed lost. Now a widow in her early 20s, life for Rosina seemed destined to be an uphill struggle.

Rosina and Jimmy returned to London during the closing days of the war and were reunited with her eldest son, Dickie. But the three years Rosina and Jimmy had spent together in Cornwall helped form a special bond between them that was never broken. As Dickie later explained: 'I was the annoying one compared with Jimmy. He was the apple of her eye. No doubt about it.' Being back on the mean streets of south-east London brought even harder times for Rosina. Rationing, Jimmy Moody's aversion to school and the chaotic atmosphere of post-war London would all combine to cause upheaval in the Moody family.

As they grew up, Rosina's sons Dickie and Jimmy would worship the ground their mother walked on. She sacrificed everything for them and they would forever be indebted to her. But then Jimmy Moody wasn't the first London criminal to adore his mum and he certainly wouldn't be the last.

On V-E Day in May 1945, Rosina and her two young children hit the streets of Camberwell Green in celebration like everyone else. People were in a frenzy preparing street parties. Many even dragged out the timber they'd been saving and a huge bonfire was lit. Residents were up ladders hanging out bunting and Union Jacks. In Rosina's mother's street, a piano had been pushed out in front of the terraced houses and low-rise redbrick blocks of flats. Bells rang out and, as it got dark, the street lights came on for the first time since the Blitz had begun five years earlier; over at the local town hall, fireworks exploded in the sky above as searchlights danced in the moonlight. People sat in the street or stood over bonfires as effigies of Hitler roasted. The war was over. And Rosina knew it was time to find another husband. Someone who could look after her and her two boys, and give them the sort of paternal influence they both needed so desperately.

Areas like Camberwell Green were decades away from disbanding the stench of real poverty. The combined efforts of Hitler's bombing raids and the economic realities of life in post-war Britain might have effectively flattened some of the slums, but little or nothing was being built in their place. For children like Dickie and Jimmy it was the norm to live in a virtual shanty town on the edge of vast craters where they and other children played in the mud and grime, unaware that unexploded bombs lay just yards from them.

Rosina Moody had no choice but to live with her two boys at her mother Annie's tiny terraced house opposite a block of flats in a narrow Camberwell street. Sharing the house with them were uncles Teddy, Frankie and Bob. Explained Dickie: 'Everyone round those parts called my granny "Pawnshop Annie" because she was always down the pawnshop with her boys' suits on a Monday.' Neither of the Moody boys remembered much about their grandfather Tom, except that he didn't say much. He later died from the fumes that wafted across London in the great fog of the '50s which prompted the then government to ban all fire materials, apart from smokeless fuel.

Dark-haired Rosina Moody was caught between two worlds; she was young enough to go out and meet other young people but had to balance that with the responsibilities of being a mother to two small boys. It was only a matter time before she met Freddie Mills, a well-paid newspaper printer who was a 'good catch' for any single girl. After Rosina married Mills, they all set up home together with his daughter in a house in Lancaster Avenue, in the suburb of West Norwood. Rosina even insisted the two boys adopt the surname 'Mills' so that they all felt part of one big, happy family.

Dickie and Jimmy's antenna for bad people had developed through their own ability to survive on the cracked pavements and rundown streets of Camberwell Green and they believed stepfather Mills was 'a bad 'un'. The boys were protective towards their mother and sensed that Mills would bring her nothing but unhappiness in the long run. 'He was tight with his money and violent towards us,' explained Dickie. The boys – who were about eight or nine by then – also loathed the suburbs. Even their own relationship began to suffer. Dickie recalled: 'There was a lot of rivalry between Jimmy and me due to our unhappiness with Mum's situation with Mills. He was a fuckin' bastard.'

Jimmy Moody was haunted for the rest of his life by the smell and density of cigarette smoke, thanks to Freddie Mills' virtual non-stop tobacco consumption which Jimmy believed influenced his mum Rosina to take up smoking as well. Freddie Mills would blow rings of smoke in young Jimmy's direction whenever the family sat down at mealtimes. Mills *never* waited for the boys to finish their food before he lit up. But it was Jimmy whom Mills clashed with the most. The contempt it bred inside the youngster was there for all to see.

Most weekends the two boys went to the Saturday-morning matinee at their local cinema. As Dickie later recalled: 'One of us would pay and then let the other in through the back door. We'd also usually go into the local Woolworths and nick gear out of there. Every kid did that. It was the normal thing back then.'

In post-war London virtually everything was available from street-corner spivs who'd managed to get hold of goods which had 'fallen off the back of a lorry'. To kids of Jimmy Moody's age, it seemed that most laws were there to be broken. So, even before he'd reached his teens, Jimmy Moody was having problems with authority. Dickie lays much of the blame at the door of 'evil' stepdad Freddie Mills. 'Jim hated him so much. He'd try and fight him and then end up getting a slapping for his troubles and go out and fight another kid to burn off all that hatred.'

Jimmy Moody even joined the Lin Boxing Club, back in their old home territory of Camberwell Green, to try and work off all that fury. The well-built youngster was soon knocking out boys more than two years his senior and was very happy to be back in London instead of the boring, lifeless suburbs. But then Jimmy's drive to be the fittest and best fighter was fuelled by a determination to win the biggest battle of his life so far.

Jimmy Moody's relationship with his disciplinarian stepfather had led to a strained atmosphere in the house which encouraged the emergence of Moody's self-destructive personality. As a child, Moody did not receive the kind of attention he needed from his family and increasingly found it difficult to establish a boundary between himself and the world beyond his caring mother and Dickie. He was becoming more individually minded and self-assured, with his own ideas about the world around him. Other family members noticed how fearless Moody could be and the way he would try to manipulate situations to suit himself and no one else. He also seemed incapable of appreciating when he had hurt other people's feelings. He felt little remorse and certainly no sympathy for his victims.

There was clearly an inner sadness in Moody that was demonstrated in his reluctance to take part in any childlike preoccupations. An ideal childhood is supposed to be a pleasurable experience in which the developing individual learns how to be happy and derive happiness from as many situations as possible. But Moody's few childhood friends soon concluded that he was not capable of enjoying things in a way typical of other children.

Moody's development had its own twisted symbolism – one steeped in the terror of unpleasant memories and fears permanently stored in his mind. Young Jimmy Moody told himself he'd never struggle financially in the way his own family had done. He vowed to only marry when he was wealthy. He had no intention of repeating history.

By the time Jimmy Moody reached 13, he was a striking-looking boy, almost 6 feet in height with a well-defined face, strong eyebrows and deep, dark, narrow, green eyes. At school, Moody possessed an aggressive streak, which made him appear more bad tempered than his classmates. He said little to anyone outside of his own circle of associates, but his photographic memory surprised many of his friends and teachers. 'He never forgot anyone's name and recognized people's faces before they even had a chance to introduce themselves,' recalled one childhood friend.

One day, the teenage Moody came home from school to find stepfather Mills shouting at his mother Rosina in an argument over housekeeping money. 'Mills was being a tight bastard as usual,' explained Dickie. 'He was always keeping Mum short of money for the shopping and stuff. We used to call him "Herod, King of the Jews" because he was so tight. He liked to keep control over her that way. Anyway, Jim started having a right go at him. Mills was outraged and they had a scrap. Jim went crazy and floored him. He demolished that bastard Mills. He deserved it.'

Dickie and Rosina Moody eventually dragged Jimmy Moody off his stepfather because he was in danger of killing him. When Rosina refused to even discipline Jimmy, Mills demanded that she and her two boys move out of his house immediately. 'Mum chose us,' recalled Dickie. 'That made us feel a lot better about ourselves, but Mills had already caused a lot of damage by then. Thank God we never saw him again.'

Jimmy Moody's hatred of Freddie Mills was so intense he insisted on changing his name back to Moody and his mother and brother soon followed suit. Rosina, Dickie and Jimmy moved to a small, rundown council flat in the Brixton area of south London. Moody, though, was expelled from his new school for fighting within weeks; teachers said he was uncontrollable. The family eventually got a transfer to a newly built council flat in Rosendale Road, Dulwich. Young Rosina Moody had already survived Hitler's bombs, single motherhood, widowhood, marriage to a bully and now she was back on her own with two hungry, growing tearaways to bring up.

Dulwich basked in relatively smoggy air close to the even more smoke-ridden industrial docklands of Bermondsey and Rotherhithe. Inside that flat in Rosendale Road, Jimmy Moody was rarely disciplined by his mother, who did nothing to curb his energetic and erratic behaviour, which sometimes bordered on the psychopathic. When Moody got caught stealing apples from a neighbour's tree, Rosina didn't even attempt to tell him what he'd done was wrong. And young Jimmy Moody constantly boasted about what he'd do when he grew up. 'Earn a packet,' he pledged to anyone who would listen. 'I'm gonna be the richest kid in the world.'

Jimmy's mother was greatly impressed by her younger son's pledges. One family friend never forgot the day he was at the Moody home and Rosina turned around and said proudly: 'My Jimmy's gonna make a success of his life. He's gonna to be very rich, I know it.'

There was a corner sweetshop at the end of Rosendale Road where Jimmy and his brother Dickie loitered most afternoons after school. Frequently they'd steal empty bottles of Tizer by slipping through the shop's side gate, where all the empties were stored. Then Jimmy and his brother would walk brazenly in the front door and claim back the penny per bottle, and buy sweets with it. Jimmy Moody was alert to all around him and his perceptiveness, even at that young age, was noticed by many of his contemporaries.

Back at home, Rosina kept the family's cramped two-bedroomed flat spotlessly clean and seemed to be forever clearing up after her two sons. 'If a crumb was dropped on the lounge carpet she'd appear with a dust pan and brush it up within seconds. It did make it a little tense for visitors,' explained one family friend.

Young Jimmy Moody always remembered to give his mother birthday cards, gifts and Mother's Day cards. Their closeness was noticeable to many relatives and friends.

Moody also developed a virtual obsession with clothes. Even in his early teens, he somehow managed to afford to buy one new shirt every month. And he constantly changed the style of his thick, dark hair. By the age of 14, Moody had a paper round and was occasionally handling stolen bicycle parts. He even boasted to one friend that he'd earn more money than some of the dads of his schoolmates by the time he was 15.

Undoubtedly, many of Jimmy Moody's problems related to his hatred for his stepfather Freddie Mills. At school, for example, he'd take on bullies because he felt sorry for their victims after the way Mills had treated him. Moody was expelled from two more local schools before he walked away from all formal education at 14. Dickie explained, 'Jim didn't like school. He was never there. We also both used to get a lot of stick from the teachers and kids who were cruel to us because we didn't have a real dad.'

Even sports – apart from boxing – proved an outlet for Moody's frustrations for all the *wrong* reasons. Dickie explained: 'Jim played football a lot back then but was lethal because he used to chop everyone from behind.' The teenager – now an inch over six-feet tall and a physical match for any adult – was about to hit the outside world with a vengeance.

In those days, it was easy to blur the line between right and wrong. Rationing and the black market helped spawn a new breed of villain. That was how the classic phrase 'fell off the back of a lorry' came to be invented. Moody took to ducking and diving like many others in south-east London at the time. Jimmy Moody might not have been academically bright, but all his friends and enemies from those far-off days say he never lacked cunning. There were only two real career paths for teenagers like Jimmy – a life of crime or the police. He'd already decided which one he was going to take.

Jimmy Moody was soon regularly stealing from local shops and selling items for a pittance to local spivs. Moody even nicked a load of plants from a nearby nursery which he brought home as a gift for his cash-strapped mother. Dickie recalled: 'That was Jim's way of being thoughtful, but of course all it did was get him in more trouble.'

The teenage Jimmy was bulking up into an extremely hefty individual, thanks to constant weight training as well as boxing adults at a new south London boxing club, just off the Walworth Road. But outside the ring, Moody's brooding temper was leading to weekly showdowns. At one stage when he was 14 or 15 his family persuaded him to register as an out-patient at the Maudsley Hospital, opposite King's College Hospital and just up the road from where the Moodys lived in Dulwich. Doctors were so worried about his temper, they put him on sedatives – which deeply disturbed Moody, who found that the drugs made him feel even less in control. He eventually threw the pills away and simply stopped turning up for hospital appointments.

Dickie Moody was undoubtedly the quieter of the two brothers, although that might have been because he never considered himself to be his mother's favourite son. Jimmy Moody was over-indulged by Rosina and that seemed to give him an air of cold invincibility. But the two brothers looked very similar, which caused much confusion on the streets of south-east London. Dickie explained: 'It was quite handy for Jim if he was up to mischief, but it was a right pain for me because I was always bein' pulled in by the law for things I never done.'

Jimmy Moody nursed a fascination for cars, mainly because no one in his immediate family could afford one. For Moody a car was to become the ultimate status symbol. With war rationing and low wages, cars were still considered a special luxury. That made them an object of great curiosity – and envy – to the teenager. This obsession would grow into a much more serious habit. One time Moody was even caught inside a neighbour's car as he tried to steal it.

Soon, brothers Jimmy and Dickie were regularly going down to the seaside resort of Brighton at weekends. Dickie explained: 'Jim'd nick a motor and we'd drive down with a couple of girls. He loved nickin' cars.'

Back in south-east London, it was hardly surprising that a life of crime was beckoning for Jimmy Moody. The spivs he regularly came into contact with encouraged him to start burgling houses and fencing the loot through them. Moody began targeting houses in the expensive streets of nearby Greenwich. It was only a matter of time before he was arrested climbing out of the window of one house. Moody got two years in a borstal at a place called Usk, in Wales.

The saddest aspect of Moody's incarceration was that neither Dickie nor their mother Rosina ever went to visit him in borstal. Dickie explained: 'It was too far and we didn't have the money to pay for the train journey.' Moody felt a sense of rejection at never having any visitors. Inside borstal, other young criminals concluded there was no other career path to follow. Moody and his new 'family' would spend hours every day planning robberies to commit when they got out.

Dickie explained: 'Jim became even more angry and frustrated inside borstal. He was set on a path to crime. When he got out he'd changed so much. He even walked in a different way. He had an attitude.' Moody had learned in borstal that you never grassed up your mates and you hated 'pervs' such as child molesters. Recalled Dickie: 'He'd go crazy at the very mention of a grass's name or details of a child molester.' That's when Moody got a new nickname: 'Hateful Jim'.

On Jimmy's release from borstal, Rosina Moody tried to divert her son by persuading him to join the merchant navy, just like his father before him. This appealed to Moody because he was very proud of his father's wartime service and also because he wanted to please his mother. Soon he was off travelling the world. Going straight wasn't going to be easy, though, because Moody found it difficult to take orders from anyone and was constantly being reprimanded for fighting.

There were some moments of light relief in the merchant navy. One time Moody's ship was in an Egyptian port alongside an American vessel packed with the latest fashion item, denim jeans. As Moody's son Jason explained years later: 'They drew straws on who would dive into the water, swim across to the Yankee ship and barter for some jeans. Dad lost so he dived in, swam over, climbed straight up the ladder and then came back with a load of jeans in a plastic bag on his back. But as he was swimming back a fin came out the water and the crew were all shouting "Shark! Shark! Shark!" Dad was terrified and began frantically swimming towards his ship. Just then the "shark" leapt out of the water and it turned out to be a dolphin. He loved telling that story because he got all those jeans on to his boat and flogged them for a fortune.' One of Moody's favourite ports of call was the tropical island of Madagascar in the Indian Ocean where he picked up a couple of tattoos, of a Geisha girl on one arm and an eagle on the other.

The merchant navy was an important part of Moody's development as an adult. He was proud of serving and having a 'straight job'. But when Moody was transferred to tankers with smaller crews and much harder conditions, his temper got the better of him. Brother Dickie recalled: 'He got what they call double DR for violence. That's a "Declined Report". He knocked out a chef in a fight about the food. In the end, Jim held the merchant naval record for six warnings after having fights. Usually it was two marks and you're out and he had six. He fought with the blacks, whites, Chinese, Latins, you name it.'

So, after two complete trips around the globe, Jimmy Moody left the merchant navy. Dickie Moody then persuaded his short-tempered brother to accompany him on a working holiday to the seaside resort of Paignton, in Devon, where the local Pontin's holiday camp had jobs available for dishwashers. Jimmy and Dickie got down to Devon on the Sunday and within a day Moody was causing havoc. It all started when Dickie helped himself to a bottle of milk from the kitchen fridge and was reprimanded by a senior member of staff.

Dickie later recalled: 'That set Jim off and he went bananas. It turned into a free-for-all. He completely laid this other bloke out. We all ended up bein' nicked by the law and he got three months when he came up in court the following week.'

Jimmy Moody served his time, then got back to south London and was soon stealing cars again for joyriding, committing burglaries and causing mayhem. If Moody was hard up and wanted a new suit he'd walk into a branch of the men's outfitters, Burton's, wearing an old pair of jeans and a tatty shirt, put on a new suit in the changing-room and run out of the shop at high speed.

Many of Moody's friends at this time took and sold drugs, such as purple hearts, but Moody refused to touch any substances. To him, drugs were a menace to society and he didn't trust them, especially after those doctors had forced him to take sedatives when he was a schoolboy. They'd made him feel depressed and 'weird'.

Jimmy Moody became a familiar face to the Dulwich Police, who'd earmarked him as a troublemaker. 'He was pulled in almost every time anythin' happened on the manor,' explained Dickie. 'He soon started not to care at all. It's what happens to so many kids involved in crime.'

TWO

Den of Thieves

Many south-east London pubs were hotbeds for local villains and Jimmy Moody – observant and perceptive as ever – soon separated out the real winners and losers. Often he'd slide into bars and sit in a corner listening to the 'dodgy deals' going down. He was fascinated by these tough, edgy characters in their sheepskin coats and mohair suits who seemed to carry endless bundles of five-pound notes around in their pockets.

In the gritty dockland areas of south-east London near where Jimmy Moody grew up, petty thieves were still stealing tea chests off lorries and selling every commodity they could lay their hands on. Sometimes truck drivers were even kidnapped while their loads were stolen, but usually no one was actually harmed. Everything was fair game: cigarettes, spirits and clothing. Often railway containers were raided at night and their contents would end up on local street markets the following day.

Moody and his brother Dickie started nicking lead off roofs and collecting scrap to sell down at the yards which had sprung up where Hitler's bombs had flattened buildings. Moody was soon making ten to fifteen shillings a day from local fences. Being a 'fence' seemed to Moody a very profitable and crafty way of making good money out of crime. Fences were well-organised and respected 'businessmen' in the community. Everyone – even the youngest children – noticed the aura surrounding them. As former Kray twins' henchman and one-time south-east London resident Freddie Foreman explained: 'They got great respect because of their mannerism and their obvious affluent lifestyle.

They always looked smart. They knew how to dress well. They'd have a little business going, they'd drive a decent car and they'd spend their money wisely.'

As post-war dockworkers on both sides of the Thames – east and south – lost their jobs, they had to find ways of replacing the high wages (and bungs) they'd been earning over the years. High-earning print jobs were rare, so the fast-emerging heroes were the pavement artists – robbers – who'd scoop a few thousand pounds on a couple of 'jobs'. True, they'd sometimes get caught by police, stand trial at the Old Bailey and go down for a stretch. But at least they lived in style.

In the 1950s, bank raids were usually carried out in the dead of night, with master safecrackers pitting their wits against whatever security arrangements happened to be in operation at the time. But as lock design and other security improved, tackling a safe itself became an increasingly difficult task. Even the use of gelignite was no longer a sound bet: a device had been developed that, if triggered by the force of an explosion, simply threw extra bolts across the safe door.

The armed-robbery scene developed as wages increased and firms had to hire companies to transport their cash to factories and offices on wage day – Thursdays. There were no security companies in those days. More often than not two or three trusted workers in a company would be given a few extra bob to pick up the cash from a nearby bank, armed with a cosh if they were lucky.

Inevitably some workers began informing their friends of this transportation of relatively large sums of money and robberies became commonplace. As one robber from those days explained: 'It was easy pickings because these 'guards' were just ordinary workers and they didn't want to get bashed up or put up a fight to protect the firm's money.'

Often the takings from such crimes would be re-invested into honest businesses. 'The objective was to get enough money to retire from crime and then go into a straight business,' explained one old villain. 'Then you could afford to bring up your kids, buy your own home and get a decent motor, even manage a holiday now and again.'

The other reward for a career as a robber – besides the cash – was underworld fame – picking up the evening paper and seeing a banner headline and knowing that most people inside the criminal community would know who'd carried out the job. Many in south-east London were even incensed by the long sentences on such criminals, who were seen as latter-day Robin Hoods. And in the middle of this environment, prison became the natural breeding ground for bigger and bigger robberies as inmates linked up with new partners in crime while they served their sentences inside. A stretch in prison was like attending university or college.

And Jimmy Moody was about to graduate.

Moody's early girlfriends later complained that he was constantly disappearing in the middle of dates. One old friend explained: 'Jimmy was a very smooth operator. He never tried hard, but the girls used to flock around him. He had a twinkle in his eye and because he'd been brought up by a single mother he knew how to talk to women. But there wasn't anyone serious and Jim was always up to mischief, disappearing to do a deal and make some money.'

Jimmy Moody may have enjoyed a discipline-free home life, but he had a very big chip on his shoulder about his childhood. He found it difficult to express his true feelings and rarely confided in his friends or family about the problems of his upbringing. That attitude manifested itself in a complete and utter disregard for rules and regulations, almost a complete contempt for society. Moody didn't like people having better cars than he did, owning flashier suits or going out with prettier girls. It really grated with him that he didn't have as much money as the wealthiest people in what was then a very class-ridden society. He made up for it by avoiding paying for most things if he could.

By the age of 19, Jimmy Moody, 6 ft 1 in. tall, muscular and intimidating, was a regular at the legendary clubs and bars in and around the Old Kent Road, in the heart of south-east London. Moody was known as a useful strong-arm man who dealt in scrap metal – lead pipe, copper sheeting, cast iron and steel – old and new. Moody also started to distance himself from his family because he didn't want to get them involved in his activities.

Jimmy Moody even got himself a flashy two-tone grey-and-blue Ford Zephyr with a 2.8 V6 engine that throbbed like a purring cat. Most villains at the time preferred Zephyrs or Zodiacs, which were fast and held the road well, but were less conspicuous than Jags. Cars had a lot of different uses for characters like Jimmy Moody. Some were potential changeover vehicles for robberies, although these tended to be less flash than the big Fords. And then there was the good old Bedford van, a favourite south of the river because of its sliding doors, which meant robbers could jump out even before the vehicle came to a halt.

The robber's number-one car for 'work' was a Rover 90, built like a tank and often used for stopping post-office vans. East End robber Bernie Khan recalled: 'You could never use a Jag for ramming but the Rover took a whack. They've never been the same since that model stopped being made.'

Jimmy Moody was frequently to be found tinkering with the engine of his beloved Zephyr parked outside the family home in Rosendale Road. He loved buffing up the chrome bumpers with his mum's Silvo Polish. And when he went out in that car he felt as if he was *someone* for the first time in his life.

As Jimmy Moody's circle of acquaintances grew, so did all his criminal habits. One friend from his school days got himself a job in a meat warehouse and immediately became involved with Moody in smuggling out carcasses of beef on lorries. Jimmy Moody had numerous such 'little earners' on the go. He also decided he wouldn't leave home until he'd saved enough money to buy 'a proper place'. In any case, Rosina Moody always had a meal on the table for her beloved son Jimmy. She kept his room immaculately clean, ironed his shirts and even took his suits to the dry-cleaners.

Rosina never directly tackled her son about his criminal activities. South-east London had always been a law unto itself, so why shouldn't a lively youth like Jimmy Moody be mixed up in a bit of ducking and diving?

South-east London's reputation as the nation's epicentre for robbery could be traced back to a subculture of which Jimmy Moody knew a great deal. Many of the high-profile robberies of the '50s, leading up to and including the Great Train Robbery in 1963, featured robbers from south-east of the river. The heroic status those criminals achieved in the eyes of many was nowhere more evident than on the streets where they grew up. Armed robbery had already taken on a romantic hue all of its own. Now it was in danger of being positively glamorous.

When one armed police officer shot dead two gun-totting robbers in Peckham, south-east London, and wounded a third as they tried to snatch £50,000 from a security van, extra police had to be drafted into the area to prevent a riot. Women shouted abuse at police officers from the balconies of their flats; children taunted them in the street; and seven people at a pub frequented by the robbers were arrested on charges ranging from threatening behaviour to assault. Many pubs in south-east London had become places where guns could be obtained relatively easily. Those taverns were, from the '50s onwards, considered virtual no-go areas by the police.

Jimmy Moody had hung around enough villains to know that if he was going to infiltrate the upper echelons of the south-east London underworld he'd have to enjoy a lot of warm pints of bitter in the company of some hard characters.

As Freddie Foreman later explained: 'You'll meet a certain person and you'll get a rapport with them, you'll like them and the best way to know that they're OK is through the belly of that man. You get drunk with them. You have a night out and then you see the way they perform and handle themselves: if he doesn't get soppy and start running off at the mouth, or get insulting to women or in company, and if he can conduct himself with or without a drink. Then you know he's a good guy.'

Jimmy Moody believed that once you formed a relationship with another criminal he would have your unquestioned loyalty. You got involved with other criminals because they were, in a twisted way, completely trustworthy. You knew they wouldn't turn you over. You had their trust and they had yours. These were the kind of values that appealed to Jimmy Moody.

Moody was still in his teens when control of what the popular newspapers liked to call London's 'underworld' switched to a new kind of villain in the mid to late '50s. After the Second World War, the capital fell into the hands of a few characters who Fleet Street crime reporters dubbed as 'King of the Underworld' and 'King of the Dog Dopers'. Amongst them were the infamous Jack Spot Comer and his bitter rival Billy Hill. They organised protection, minders, thieves, hitmen and hardmen who then gravitated towards Soho and other sections of the West End, mainly from east and south London.

Jimmy Moody briefly encountered the two legendary figures when he was called up west for some debt-collecting work through a well-known face in south-east London. Hiring freelance hardmen was not unusual – even back in those days – and Moody impressed all who met him. 'He was a first-class soldier. Did the job that was required. No questions asked,' one old-time villain recalled.

But after the eclipse of the ageing Comer and Hill in the late '50s there was a vacuum left in Soho and the West End. Step forward the Kray Twins: young, suave, savvy and extremely ruthless East Enders. They were followed closely by their rivals from south of the river – the

Richardsons. At first these two family-led gangs formed 'a loose cross-London alliance' with the help of a third family – the Nashes from Islington, who were described by many as 'the wickedest brothers in England'.

Harry Wilkins – who was later to lead the hunt for Moody's own killer – was an inexperienced Scotland Yard constable at this time, with only two years' service. But he soon learned what the Krays and Richardsons were up to. He later recalled: 'People like the Krays and Richardsons felt they were above the law. They felt they were leading a charmed life.' While the Krays ran clubs, hobnobbed with showbiz celebrities and ostentatiously donated money to charity, the Richardsons moved between scrap metal in Camberwell to mines in South Africa. The Krays even invited journalists to pen their autobiographies and boasted of their contributions to certain charities. They and the Richardsons were becoming the open, supposedly acceptable, face of modern crime.

THREE

Taking a Shirt from Charlie

It was no surprise that Jimmy Moody's involvement in the scrap-metal business brought him into contact with the Richardson brothers, already the crime kings of south-east London. Every manor had its hierarchy; Charlie and Eddie Richardson, from Camberwell, were running Peckford Scrap Metal Limited. They were also making a small fortune fencing other people's stolen goods, including a large proportion of the watches and jewellery Moody had just started to accumulate from smash 'n' grabs raids in the West End of London. All this helped swell the Richardson's coffers, who had also spread into West End drinking clubs and even gold mines in South Africa. Boss Charlie Richardson impressed all he met with his ability to be socially acceptable anywhere he went – either at up-market West End clubs or on the back streets of south London, whose marks he never tried to rub off. Many later described him as a likeable character, despite being incomprehensibly sadistic. Big Jimmy Moody, obsessed with fitness and retaining a sailor's self-discipline, was the 'ideal handyman' for the Richardsons. Today he'd be called an enforcer or minder.

The Richardsons had much in common with Jimmy Moody, including a father who'd served in the merchant navy. Mum Eileen had run a sweetshop and brought up her children in a 56-shilling-a-week council flat on an Dulwich council estate near where Jimmy Moody lived. Both Richardson brothers – like Jimmy Moody – had been excellent boxers. At the tender age of 14, Charlie Richardson found himself the head of his family when his father walked out on his mother, two younger brothers and a sister. The age gap between Charlie and Eddie Richardson was virtually the same as that between Jimmy and Dickie Moody. When the school-leaving age was raised from 14 to 15, Charlie went 'AWOL' – he'd been planning his adulthood for years.

By the time Jimmy Moody met the Richardsons they'd moved into Soho with a very profitable fruit-machine business called the Atlantic Company. The brothers shrewdly made the notorious Mad Frankie Fraser a partner in Atlantic after he'd earned a fearsome reputation in the '50s as London's premier hardman, having notched up a list of victims headed by Jack Spot, whom Fraser 'punished' after Spot dared to challenge the criminal superiority of Fraser's then boss, the even more legendary Billy Hill. Fraser was as mad as his nickname, capable of terrifying bouts of violence and fearless of other criminal faces. Jimmy Moody was impressed by Fraser and the two men went through a lot together, although something about Fraser always slightly troubled him. Moody later told one associate: 'Fraser was one of those typical, chippy, midget types. Small and violent 'cause he thought the whole world was against him. But he was up for *anything*. Evil little dwarf!' By the early 1960s, Charlie Richardson had a string of companies and an office in London's swish Park Lane, with nearly 100 employees. On paper, he was a millionaire and he'd gathered round him a fearsome gang consisting of some of the toughest faces in the country.

With Charlie Richardson expanding his operations, it only seemed natural that a tough young tearaway like Jimmy Moody would find a place within the 'firm'. Charlie prided himself on his talent for spotting 'real hardmen'. As one of his team later explained: 'Charlie sucked people's brains dry. When he'd got all he could, he discarded them.'

In south-east London pubs like The Frog and Nightgown, The Connoisseur, The Prince of Wales and The Beehive in Peckham, young Jimmy Moody soon found himself mixing with some of the hardest gangsters in London. And Moody made it clear he was up for anything, including 'going across the pavement', as robbery was known in those days. He wasn't scared. The thrill of doing more 'street work' filled him with excitement.

By 1963, Charlie Richardson was raking in so much money he could afford one of the biggest houses on Denmark Hill, south-east London, a house which had once been owned by Canon William Fenton Morley, the rural Dean of Leeds. No wonder many on his manor referred to Charlie in virtually royal terms. He was the king of his very own castle. He even got himself a Doberman Pinscher to guard his impressive house and kept a well-stocked bar in the lounge for Jimmy Moody and the rest of his team whenever they popped round for a chat. The wallpaper was blood red and the furniture surprisingly tasteful and traditional. Whenever Moody had a meeting with Charlie, the dog – which he was terrified of – would pad impatiently outside the French windows.

Charlie, chubby faced, always in a neatly pressed 50-guinea suit, dreamt of being another Al Capone. He led an empire built on fear. Richardson and his gang meted out their own brutal rough justice and created their own set of laws. 'Trials' were held in shabby warehouses they called 'courtrooms' and sadistic punishments included electric-shock treatment, tooth pulling, beatings, stabbings and burnings.

Jimmy Moody and other members of the team often stood around laughing and jeering as punishments were handed out. The process became known as 'taking a shirt from Charlie' because of Richardson's practise of giving a bruised and bleeding victim a clean shirt so that he could go back home without arousing too much attention.

Charlie Richardson was happy to tell anyone who'd listen that he and his gang 'kept crime in our area down and controlled what people got up to. We performed a social service.' Brothers Charlie and Eddie believed in the so-called 'good old days' when 'you could leave your door open when you went out. We had no muggings and no local burglary. If there was any, I would find out who did it and give them a smack in the mouth before the Old Bill ever heard about it.'

Jimmy Moody became a regular at the Richardson's favourite watering hole – The Astor Club, Grosvenor Square, in London's West End – where the brothers adored mixing with celebrities and wheeler-dealers. One night Moody gave a Krays henchman a hiding for daring to attack one of the Richardson's best pals inside the club. Moody pinned the man to a wall with an axe and told him not to be a naughty boy *ever* again. The axe didn't even merit a raised eyebrow on the premises.

So, Jimmy Moody was now a successful up-and-coming young hood, with a love of pricey suits and flashy motors. It was time to find himself a serious girlfriend.

When losing one's virginity, said Queen Victoria, one must close one's eyes and think of England. Attaching a little more lyricism to the act, the great romantics, from Cervantes to Byron, saw virgins as roses and their deflowering a poem to passions that would saddle lions. Jimmy Moody had already tasted plenty of passion by the time he reached his early 20s, but his most important experience of romance came when he went on a blind date with 21-year-old blonde Valerie Burns, a friend of the wife of one of his criminal associates, a notorious East End gangster called Mickey Ismael.

Val – who was just six months younger than Moody – agreed to let Moody pick her up at her family's Poplar home for a night out, south of the river at a villains' drinking club called The 191, in Brockley, near Upper Norwood. Val has never forgotten that night. 'He didn't even look up when I walked out of the house to get in his Zephyr. But the moment I laid eyes on him I knew he was the one. In the car, he was lookin' out of the window and in the rear-view the whole time. Typical. Always watching his back in case there was any trouble around.'

As Moody drove Val to the club in Brockley, he almost knocked down an old lady at a zebra crossing. 'His mind just wasn't on the road. He even said: "I'll hit the next one with any luck." I *think* he was jokin'.'

As Val and Moody sat talking over a drink in the club, Moody suddenly leaned his vast frame closer and whispered in her ear: 'I'm going to marry you one day.'

Val recalled: 'I can't honestly say I was surprised because I felt exactly the same way as him. No doubt about it. Jim was handsome – big, flash, not flash-flash, just flash enough. He had a good spirit about him. When he smiled his eyes smiled and you couldn't help but look at him. I laughed so much when he teased me.'

Moody was so smitten he didn't even mind when Val lit up a cigarette – despite the hatred for smoking derived from his stepfather's habit. A few days later Val agreed to go on a daytrip down to the seaside resort of Southend-on-Sea in his Zephyr. Val never forgot Moody turning up at her parents' home to pick her up. 'I was just coming down the stairs when I heard this voice and I looked out the window and there he was leaning against the Zephyr on the other side of the road, tapping his watch and saying "Come on. You ready?"' Moody even bought a carton of 200 cigarettes for Val as a gift. He proudly informed her that he'd bought them earlier from a man who told him that, naturally, they'd fallen off the back of a lorry.

The relationship soon developed. Val explained: 'I used to see him weekends and sometimes I'd go to the pub Saturday lunchtimes where all his mates would tease me because he'd given up his precious lunchtime to see me. They were surprised he was so serious about a woman.'

But the long arm of the law was never far away. Val explained: 'Jimmy was up to no good, even when I first knew him. That was 1962. Then he went into prison for three months for some kind of burglary. Breaking into a shop or something.'

Val promised Moody she'd visit him in prison west of London. She explained: 'I got one of the girls at work to come with me for the weekend, we booked into a bed and breakfast and I went to visit him.' It was impossible for Val not to realise what kind of person she was falling in love with. 'Of course I knew he was up to no good, but I didn't care. I loved him.'

Eighteen months later, Val was pregnant and it seemed only natural that she'd marry Jimmy Moody. He was delighted because he genuinely saw himself settling down happily with her. So Moody and Val Burns married at Poplar town hall, on 23 May 1964. The photos taken at the wedding showed a classic East End bash – lots of smiling and proud faces. Few people who attended that day mentioned what Moody did for a job. But most already knew.

After the wedding, Moody and Val went to live with his protective mother Rosina in the same flat he grew up in, in Rosendale Road, Dulwich. It wasn't easy. Val explained: 'I was always visiting my mum and dad in Poplar, which created problems because Jimmy wanted me to come straight back home from work to him. But I really missed my mum and dad. And my mother-in-law idolised her boys, worshipped the ground they walked on, which made me feel like an intruder.'

After three months, a heavily pregnant Val told Moody she couldn't live in Dulwich any longer. Moody was upset, but prepared to go along with anything that made Val happy. A few weeks later, Moody arrived at Val's parents' home in Poplar with the keys to a nearby flat.

Their first proper family home was in a block called the Grosvenor Buildings, just beside the busy Blackwall Tunnel, slap bang in the middle of the old East End. Val recalled: 'We couldn't live in it at first because it needed so much work.' Moody even managed to drag himself away from his 'job' to help Val redecorate the flat in preparation for their baby.

Val and Jimmy Moody's first child was born on 23 December 1964. The little boy was first called Danny by Val, then Moody decided he preferred the name Jason because Jason was his favourite character on the TV series *Rawhide*.

So Val, Jason and Jimmy Moody moved into their new home a week later, on New Year's Eve, 1964. All Val knew about her husband's 'job' was that he worked with a man called Harry Rawlins who sold soap and washing-up liquid on a market stall and owned a shop. Rawlins was a 'ducker and diver', an active criminal who used Moody as a henchman and driver. Moody told Val he delivered and picked up items for Rawlins.

Life in the Grosvenor Buildings certainly wasn't easy for Moody, Val and baby son Jason. Moody tended to come and go, depending on his criminal enterprises. Those who knew him at the time say these ranged from jewellery-shop smash 'n' grabs to strong-arm work for the Richardsons.

And Val was finding out the hard way what it was like being married to a criminal. As one old friend later explained: 'Val was left mainly on her own to look after Jason while Moody was off committing crimes and hanging out in late-night drinking dens.' Yet Val Moody believed her husband would eventually provide the perfect home and family that he promised her. He said that once he'd got enough money together he'd quit his 'dodgy' work, buy himself a second-hand lorry and do some freelance haulage for companies in south-east London and Kent.

The Great Train Robbery of 1963 and the subsequent capture of the gang was a chilling wake-up call to many south-east London criminals. Moody's brother Dickie explained: 'Everyone on the manor was on about how long they was sentenced. Jim – who'd even been in prison with one train robber, Roy James – saw it as an outrage.' Most villains concluded that they might as well go for a huge payday since the jail terms being handed out were so long. They had nothing to lose.

Jimmy Moody was soon up to his neck in murder and mayhem. In January 1965, the mystery of who killed Krays' associate Ginger Marks remained unsolved despite massive press coverage and police inquiries. The search for Marks started after his wife received an anonymous phone call saying that her husband had been shot in Cheshire Street, Bethnal Green. Police went to the location, found a pool of blood on the pavement, a pair of spectacles belonging to Marks and a .22 bullet embedded in a wall. But there was no trace of Marks himself and no hospital or doctor reported treating a victim of a shooting. Many of the people linked to the Marks killing had close ties to Jimmy Moody.

The Richardsons and their team of associates, including Jimmy Moody, also continued using their own weapon of choice – torture.

Straight and simple. One victim, Benjamin Coulston, who owed the Richardsons money, had all his right toes smashed to pieces by a hammer wielded by Richardson's men and the big toe on his left foot was also damaged for good measure. Miraculously, Coulston was still able to walk with shoes on despite the attacks.

On 18 January 1965, Coulston was attacked again when a Richardson henchman smashed him over the head with a lump of iron outside a pub. Coulston was then bundled into a Ford and driven to offices in Camberwell, where Charlie Richardson placed a gun on a table and ordered Coulston to be stripped, before asking him: 'Where's the £600 you took off 2 of my men?'

Standing in the corner of the dimly lit room was Mad Frankie Fraser, who then moved towards Coulston with a pair of pliers. Coulston later recalled: 'He put them into my mouth and started to try and pull my teeth. He slipped and pulled a lump of my gum out instead. He tried again and pulled part of a top tooth out. I felt the crack.'

Fraser then made way for Moody and another man who punched and kicked Coulston until he was 'bleeding and battered'. Next, Charlie Richardson casually flicked on the switch of an electric fire and Jimmy Moody placed it right up against Coulston's face. Then Moody began moving it down his body. Coulston later said: 'He went down between my legs. Then he stopped.'

Jimmy Moody stubbed cigarettes out on Coulston's arms and chest. 'But by then I didn't have any more pain,' Coultson recalled. Coulston was tied up in a tarpaulin sheet and taken for a ride. Afterwards, back in Richardson's office, Eddie casually announced they'd found out that it was not Coulston who had the £600 and he was very sorry. Coulston spent the following four days in hospital.

Then there was quietly spoken 39-year-old Jewish businessman Bernard Wajcenberg. He later recalled how Charlie Richardson opened a cabinet in his office and demanded £5,000, even though Wajcenberg had visited his office to get £1,000 allegedly owed to him by Richardson. 'I could see there were choppers, hammers and shotguns in that cabinet,' said Wajcenberg.

Richardson then told him: 'Go and make phone calls to your friends and get the money.' Wajcenberg tried to reason with Richardson and explained that he could prove 'in black and white' that he did not owe him any money. He later explained: 'We went through the books for hours. Everyone was satisfied, including Richardson's accountants, that I didn't owe him the money.'

But Wajcenberg still had to promise Richardson he would get the £5,000. 'I had to pretend I was guilty. I could not get out of it any other way.' Wajcenberg then borrowed £5,000 from friends and handed it over to the Richardsons. The following morning he took a plane to Germany and stayed out of Britain for two months.

In July 1965, another man in debt to the Richardsons, James Taggart, was attacked by Jimmy Moody and Mad Frankie Fraser while Charlie Richardson looked on. 'Fraser smashed me across my body and head until a wooden pole he was holding broke,' recalled Taggart. 'My face was a mass of blood.' The walls and floor were also smeared in Taggart's blood. Fraser, Moody and others even broke off to eat sandwiches and drink a couple of beers before attacking Taggart again. He eventually pretended to be unconscious in the hope they might stop. 'I just assumed I would automatically become a dead man,' Taggart later explained.

Then Charlie Richardson got a phone call saying his brother was arriving at Heathrow from South Africa, so the attack stopped and Taggart was instructed to get up, clean off the blood and put on his clothes. He was then helped to his car. The following day he paid the Richardsons more than £1,000.

On another occasion, Jimmy Moody was present when Charlie Richardson brought his heel down hard on the wrist of a man called Derek Harris as he sat in an armchair. Shortly afterwards, a portable generator was brought into the Richardsons' office. Harris later recalled: 'Charlie came up to me, stuck a thumb in each eye and twisted his thumbs round. I felt extreme pain.' Then Richardson told an enforcer called Roy Hall to take off Harris's shoes and socks and attach a lead from the generator to his toes. 'Then the handle of the generator was turned and I got a violent electric shock. I jumped out of the chair and yelled. Charlie gave instructions to bind and gag me and also to remove my clothing. Then the treatment was repeated with the generator and somebody remarked that it did not seem to be working well enough. So a bottle of orange was poured over my feet. The handle of the generator was turned repeatedly. The leads were removed from my feet and were held to different parts of my body. Then I was unbound and my clothes were handed to me.'

As Harris was putting on his shoes, Charlie Richardson walked casually across to him and plunged a knife through his left foot and into the floorboards.

By this time, Jimmy Moody was earning so much money through the Richardsons that he bought himself a sparkling silver 3.8 Mark II Jag, complete with spoked wheels and a walnut dashboard – although his hefty six-foot-plus bulk was quite tricky to get in and out of the Jag's smaller-fitting doors.

FOUR

Casualties of War

Besides working as a henchman for the Richardsons, Jimmy Moody also further enhanced his reputation in south-east London by taking part in a number of daring armed robberies – or 'enforcement actions', as the bigger gangs liked to call them.

But the murder of Krays henchman Ginger Marks threatened to spark a full-scale war between the Richardsons and the Krays. As one-time Krays lieutenant Albert Donoghue later explained: 'Everything on the other side of the Thames was Injun Country to us. If the Richardsons got hold of any of us, we'd have been "cranked up".' Communication between the two firms had been reduced to purely 'ambassadorial' level. Small, meaningless messages passed between them as each tested the water for the inevitable big battles that lay ahead. The Krays and their associates claimed they were about to 'make the Thames foam with blood'. Just what direction this chilling outbreak of violence would come from was anyone's guess.

In February 1966, Eddie Richardson and Mad Frankie Fraser approached the management of Mr Smith's Club in Catford, south-east London, with a proposition that they should 'assist' in keeping order there. Richardson brought some suitable 'employees' to the club on the evening of 7 February for a meeting where the arrangement was rubberstamped. Those 'employees' included Jimmy Moody, the only one to actually bother signing the visitors' book when he entered the club that night. Eddie's older and more powerful brother Charlie was away on business in South Africa, otherwise, many have since insisted, the spiral of violence that was to follow might never have occurred.

It all began on a quiet Sunday a few weeks later, when 39-year-old James Andrews, a known associate of the Krays, was shot and injured from a passing white car outside his home in Rotherfield Street, Islington, north London. Fingers were immediately pointed at the Richardsons.

Eddie Richardson, the impetuous, tinder-box younger Richardson brother, later insisted he wasn't interested in starting a war with the Krays. Certainly, a couple of days after the Andrews shooting, he seemed more concerned with his agreement to 'police' Mr Smith's Club. The Richardsons and Mad Frankie Fraser's company Atlantic Machines had also agreed to put slot machines – 'one-armed bandits' – on the premises. Mr Smith's, one of the largest nightclubs in London, was so named because its low prices catered for the 'Mr Smiths' of this world. The furniture was classy and the lighting as mean and moody as the regulars. Opened in October 1965, with Diana Dors – Britain's answer to Marilyn Monroe – providing the cabaret, Mr Smith's was soon a runaway success and packed out most days of the week. It included a restaurant, bar, dance floor, two bands, a vocalist and cabaret. There were also tables for gaming – boule, blackjack and dice. Police knew the sort of characters the club attracted and regularly opposed the club's drinks licence, albeit unsuccessfully.

As one regular later commented: 'An ugly atmosphere was developing in a good-class gaff. Second-rate teams were making patrons and management uncomfortable. Something had to be done.' By late February 1966, Rosemary Kenny, a 19-year-old receptionist at Mr Smith's Club, had also noticed the tension on the premises. She later explained: 'It was a horrible sort of atmosphere. There were strange faces, new faces.' Many of the staff and customers had already been removed by the management, who felt trouble was brewing. One night, Miss Kenny even spotted a man with a gun in a shoulder holster under his jacket as he used the phone at her reception. That same evening she saw a pistol inside another man's jacket.

A few weeks later – in March 1966 – Mad Frankie Fraser and Eddie Richardson walked into the club at around 10 p.m. with some associates, including henchman Ronnie Jeffreys. All of them noticed a well-known local face, Billy Hayward, drinking in another corner with a man called Henry Botton and one of the notorious Hennessey brothers, Peter. Billy

41

Hayward's boys from Abbey Wood were known as 'a right bunch of nutters' around the Deptford and Lewisham areas. Their henchman Hennessey was dubbed a loud-mouthed braggart. The Krays considered the Haywards to be on their team, even though they came from the wrong side of the river.

Just then Jimmy Moody — another Atlantic employee — strolled into the club with associate Harry Rawlins and approached Fraser and Richardson's table. He told them he was planning to rob the club's casino and had come in to case the joint. Fraser thought Moody was kidding and told him: 'We're gonna be employin' the doormen and we'll be helpin' them, not hinderin' them — forget it.'

Moody immediately backed down and Fraser later admitted he couldn't tell if Moody had been serious about the robbery plan. Meanwhile, Billy Hayward closely watched Moody's movements inside the club and seemed paranoid that something was about to happen. Fraser later insisted this would have been madness, since he and the Richardsons were supposed to be protecting the club, not wrecking it.

By 3.30 a.m., Moody, Fraser, Eddie Richardson and their pals were the only ones left in the club besides Billy Hayward and his associates. Then one of Richardson's team spotted a .410 shotgun strapped inside Billy Hayward's jacket. Within seconds, insults were being traded and trigger fingers started twitching.

The club's owners then asked Eddie Richardson to politely inform Hayward that it was closing time and he should leave. Staff rang a local taxi firm to send several cars to take customers away. Richardson then tried to assert his authority on the proceedings.

Eyeing up Hennesey as he spoke, Richardson spat, 'No one gets another fuckin' drink without my say-so' — he smashed a bottle on the table — 'unless you want some of this.'

Seconds later the two men had ripped off their jackets and steamed into each other for a brutal stand-up fight on the dance floor. Thirty feet away, Hayward's friend Dickie Hart was stroking the trigger of his .45 revolver.

Eddie Richardson was still hammering Peter Hennessey into the floor when Billy Hayward tried to pull out his sawn-off, but the weapon got caught up in his coat. Jimmy Moody then grabbed a heavy glass ashtray and smashed it over Hayward's head, knocking him out. That's when someone shouted, 'Shoot the bastards.' Hart panicked and started firing in all directions. Within seconds, the club was echoing to a hail of gunfire, with men hiding behind tables and others lying injured. Chicago had come to London in 1966.

One blast of the shotgun went off, peppering Eddie Richardson in the buttocks. Another bullet hit a chair leg and another the roof. A fourth shot tore into Moody's mate Harry Rawlins' shoulder, bursting an artery. Staff scrambled for the exits, knocking over tables and chairs, as more screams and shouts rang out. Out through the doors into the street the fight still raged, with firing coming from behind walls and hedges. To the crack of revolvers was added the blast of another sawn-off shotgun. At least eight guns were fired. Detectives responding to a flood of 999 calls later found trails of blood splashed on pavements and walls outside the club exits.

Mad Frankie Fraser yelled at Hart that Rawlins was badly injured and demanded an ambulance be called. Hart agreed, but then saw Jimmy Moody approaching and let off another shot. He missed. Undeterred, Moody leaned down to try and help Rawlins by tying a handkerchief around his arm in a tourniquet to stop the blood leaking out of the wound.

Moody and associate Ronnie Jeffreys then carried Rawlins out of the club, with Fraser walking in front of them as cover. Then came Dickie Hart, following behind with his gun panning nervously in all directions. Suddenly, Fraser punched Hart hard in the mouth, grabbed his wrist, and tried to take the gun, which went off and shot Fraser in the thigh. As bulldog Fraser knocked the gun away from Hart's grasp before collapsing in a heap with a shattered thighbone, another shot rang out.

One of Billy Hayward's men yelled: 'You're fuckin' mad, Frank.'

Fraser was pulled to his feet by another associate and hopped on one leg 300 yards down the street before collapsing in a thick privet hedge. Dickie Hart had caught a bullet from his own gun during the struggle with Fraser and staggered off in the opposite direction.

Housewife Mrs Pat Lowe saw the battle from her bedroom window. She later recalled: 'All the men were running around shouting at each other. I couldn't make out much of what was being said, but I did hear one yell, "Kill him, kill him." One of them had a shotgun. It was fired and one of the men dropped to the ground.' There were also trails of blood splashed on garden walls in nearby Honley Road and pavements were covered with cardboard boxes and dustbin lids.

Another resident watched in astonishment as an injured man was dragged by one arm along the road. A man took a gun from his belt and shouted: 'Let me kill him. Let me kill him.' Someone out of sight shouted: 'Don't do that, that would be murder.' The injured man was then carried round a corner with the assistance of others.

Bricklayer Ken Barnard, from nearby Farley Road, was awoken just before 4 a.m. by the sound of shots. From his bedroom window he saw a man lying outside Mr Smith's Club, being hit over the head with a bottle. Barnard later recalled: 'The whole scene was very confused. There were blokes running about everywhere.' One resident saw a man carrying another man in a fireman's grip and heard him scream at someone else, 'Johnny, give us a fuckin' hand. He's hurt.' The other man replied: 'Drop the cunt and just run!'

Local resident Michael Carver leaned down to feel the pulse of a man lying on the steps into the club, but there was barely anything. Then, as he moved the man onto his side, a 12-inch-long glass gemmy fell out of the man's inside pocket. One prosecutor later described the scene at Mr Smith's as being 'rather like part of a western film'.

As more shots rang out, Jimmy Moody rolled up in his silver Mark II Jag – in the midst of the mayhem. But Moody was oblivious to the danger and headed for his injured pals. By this time more than 20 people were embroiled in a deadly free-for-all. Gunshot victim Dickie Hart even managed to kick a few more people before collapsing on the pavement. Billy Hayward staggered from the scene with his gashed head pumping blood in all directions. Hennessey and another man crawled off into the night.

Jimmy Moody and associate Ronnie Jeffreys bundled Eddie Richardson and the badly bleeding Rawlins into the Jag and pulled away from the scene. A few minutes later Moody dropped an unnamed man off near the Rotherhithe Tunnel, apparently trying to lay a false trail for the police. Then he took the wounded Eddie Richardson and Harry Rawlins to the casualty department at the Dulwich Hospital.

The body of Dickie Hart lay crumpled under a lilac tree outside 48 Farley Road. He'd been shot and then some of the 'opposition' had played football with his head. It wasn't a pretty sight. At first, police mistook his corpse for a sack of old potatoes. A preliminary postmortem later showed he'd died as a result of a .45 bullet wound in his chest, close to his heart.

Meanwhile 42-year-old Mad Frankie Fraser – the most badly injured besides the dead man – lay under a privet hedge, where he'd buried himself for camouflage, in his bloodstained 70-guinea Saville Row suit with an open razor in his top pocket. A police officer called PC David Emberson found Fraser lying facedown. When he tried to turn him over, Fraser yelled out in pain. He was then found to be lying on the gun that killed Dickie Hart.

Over at the Krays' favourite, The Regency Club in the East End, there was a phone call for Ronnie Kray. When he put the receiver down he told all those present – including local criminal Bernie Khan – what had just happened at Mr Smith's. Khan later recalled: 'Ronnie was full of excitement about the shooting and said, "Let's drink to that." He was over the fuckin' moon.'

Flying Squad chief Tommy Butler was outraged by the shooting and swore to track down the culprits. Butler was known as a '24-hour copper with the brain of a don and the memory of an elephant'. He was going to need all his skill and experience to sort out the Mr Smith's shootout before anyone else got hurt. Within hours of the incident, Butler's detectives swooped on numerous addresses. Meanwhile Eddie Richardson, Mad Frankie Fraser and Harry Rawlins remained at Dulwich Hospital suffering from gunshot wounds, alongside Moody's ashtray victim Billy Hayward. The four men were all put under a 24-hour police guard 'for their own protection'.

The day after the Mr Smith's affray, armed detectives swooped on Jimmy Moody at his Aunt Edie's house in Auckland Hill, West Norwood, after an anonymous tipster spotted the gleaming silver Jag parked in the driveway. Moody was so shocked to have been tracked down that he put up little resistance. The detectives cuffed him before putting him in the back of a Black Maria.

However the battle of Mr Smith's was to pale into insignificance next to the war that was just about to erupt. Rumours swept across the Thames of a revenge attack by the remaining Richardson soldiers, who were said to be preparing to hit the Krays outside The Lion pub in Tapp Street, Bethnal Green the following Saturday.

But the guns of gangland came out again even sooner. This time the venue was The Blind Beggar pub in Whitechapel. It was already famed as the favourite haunt of Ginger Marks, whose disappearance after being shot near the pub in January 1965 had first increased tensions between the Krays and the Richardsons.

Drinking gin and tonic in the Beggar a couple of nights after the Mr

Smith's shootout was 38-year-old George Cornell, described as a car dealer from Camberwell, and a known associate of Eddie Richardson. He'd been lured into the pub that night – Wednesday, 9 March – by an urgent message from a criminal associate.

That same evening one of the Krays' 'spies' walked into The Lion – nicknamed 'The Widow's' – and told Ronnie Kray that Richardson-enforcer Cornell was on the manor. There were rumours that Cornell was the man who'd shot down Dickie Hart at Mr Smith's. As Krays henchman Albert Donoghue later recalled: 'To Ronnie this was a diabolical liberty – a provocation, an act of war.'

Ronnie Kray strutted out of the Widow's with henchmen Scotch Jack Dickson and Ian Barrie in tow. A few minutes later Scotch Jack pulled up outside The Blind Beggar in a black Ford Consul. Ronnie Kray and Ian Barrie walked straight into the saloon bar to find Cornell sitting at the end of the bar with three associates. A record was playing, peculiarly enough entitled 'The Sun Ain't Gonna Shine Any More'. Cornell, with drink in hand, saw Kray approaching him from the door of the saloon bar. He just had time to say, 'Look who's here,' before Kray drew a Luger out of his right-hand overcoat pocket, levelled it at Cornell's head and fired a 9 mm bullet squarely into the centre of his forehead. Cornell was dead before he even hit the ground.

Cornell's two associates dived to the floor just as Ian Barrie pulled out an automatic and fired two bullets into the wall above their heads. Then Kray and Barrie strolled back outside to their waiting car.

The Blind Beggar killing has long been part of British criminal folklore because the incident fuelled the war between the Krays and Richardsons. Jimmy Moody wasn't present that evening because at that time he was in the cells at Catford Police Station.

As one senior police officer told the *News of the World*: 'The sinister aspect of it is that if this indiscriminate shooting continues, one day a casual bystander is going to get hurt. Since capital punishment was abolished more gangsters are carrying guns and are prepared to use them.'

Rumours that Cornell's killer was Ronnie Kray ensured that the Krays and the Richardsons brought down the shutters on their so-called glamorous, high-profile lifestyles and returned to what they knew best – cold-blooded intimidation and revenge. Crime reporters started getting threatening phone calls warning them to lay off the two families. Gangster clubs closed down overnight and the celebrities – who'd made it their business to knock round with the villains – suddenly fled all the usual haunts.

On 11 March 1966, police officially confirmed a link between Dickie Hart's death at Mr Smith's and the shooting of George Cornell at The Blind Beggar. Detectives also believed that a third man had been 'marked for murder' by the same gangs. Police were anxiously trying to trace the unnamed man before he was killed.

With Flying Squad chief Tommy Butler at the helm it was clear Scotland Yard would come down hard on the gangsters threatening the peace on London's streets. The police, though, were handicapped by the wall of silence maintained by all involved. Many officers were openly blaming the warfare on changes in the UK laws, which had allowed roulette and other games to be set up in clubs. 'There is so much money in the game that the protection gangs have stepped in. It is like Chicago all over again, but with no death penalty,' said one senior detective.

Ronnie Kray never regretted the death of George Cornell. 'He was a drunkard and a bully. I done the Earth a favour,' he explained many years later. Kray believed he had the 'right' to shoot Cornell dead because this was a battle between soldiers of crime who knew the risks they were taking. Kray explained: 'We never harmed no one on the outside. No "civilians". We kept to our own kind, our own people.' Jimmy Moody's loyal brother Dickie had no idea his kid brother was so heavily mixed up with the notorious Richardsons until armed detectives swooped on the family home in Rosendale Road following Moody's arrest at his aunt's house. It was the first of many such raids over the following 30 years.

Jimmy Moody and his two Mr Smith's co-defendants, Eddie Richardson and Billy Hayward, first appeared before magistrates at Woolwich on 17 March 1966. They were charged with causing an affray and possession of offensive weapons. The badly injured Mad Frankie Fraser was charged with murdering Dickie Hart. Detective Chief Superintendent Tommy Butler said all four should be kept in custody because of the gravity of their offences and fears about their own safety. Moody's criminal associate Henry Rawlins, 35, of Logs Hill, Chiselhurst, Kent faced similar charges as he recovered from his injuries. Ron Jeffrey, 29, described in court as a Covent Garden porter of Ferndene Road, Herne Hill, south-east London, was also charged with causing an affray in the same incident.

Jimmy Moody undoubtedly emerged from the Mr Smith's shootout with an even bigger reputation than before. Dragging Eddie Richardson to safety and saving Rawlins' life earned him a lot of underworld praise. But his main priority at this point was to be acquitted of the Mr Smith's charges.

Shortly after the start of the Mr Smith's trial at the Old Bailey, Charlie Richardson – now back from South Africa – gave his strong-arm boys a list of all the jurors' names. Richardson instructed them to find out where they lived and 'pay them a little visit'. Charlie boasted that one woman witness had already accepted a bribe. The first witness to take the oath in box even had to be ordered to attend court after he refused to give evidence.

Later it was also revealed that a juryman at the same Old Bailey trial was twice approached by different people about giving a false verdict. Before the hearing was resumed on 6 July 1966, the judge and other court officials examined police reports about the attempt to nobble the case. The judge refused to abandon the trial but told the court: 'I wish to stress as strongly as I can that you are here to try the defendants on evidence that you hear in this court and this court alone.' Police guards were immediately put on all the jurors' homes.

In the middle of the Mr Smith's trial, rumours about the torture inflicted by members of the Richardson gang started sweeping London. As Albert Donoghue later commented: 'When Ronnie heard them (rumours of torture) he used to say anyone who tortured somebody must be a coward. That was rich coming from him!' The Richardsons insisted they were being set up by the police, who were desperate to break up their gang, and there were no torture sessions. But as Donoghue pointed out: 'There's people walking or limping around today who'll tell you different.'

When Flying Squad chief Tommy Butler and his hand-picked team of detectives heard from one initial witness about the alleged torture sessions they were determined to track down more witnesses before the Richardsons and their team of gangsters started exerting 'pressure' on anyone brave enough to give evidence against them.

At dawn on 30 July 1966, police investigating the torture allegations swooped on Charlie Richardson's Georgian mansion in south-east London. In all, a total of eight men plus Richardson's common-law wife Jean were arrested – although Jean was later released on bail. There was stunned disbelief in south-east London that 'untouchable' Charlie Richardson had been arrested on these new, much more serious charges. Many believed the entire police force was in the Richardsons' pocket and there'd be no witnesses prepared to speak out against Charlie and his gang. Many also presumed Richardson would buy off the judge in the case. Later that day, Jimmy Moody was informed in prison that he'd also be charged in connection with the torture allegations.

Jimmy Moody's first trial for his role in the Mr Smith's shootout ended with the jury unable to agree on a verdict for him, Henry Rawlins and Ron Jeffrey; all three were acquitted. Moody was told he'd remain in custody on charges connected to the torture allegations. Billy Hayward and an associate were both found guilty of making an affray at Mr Smith's. Hayward was also found guilty of possessing a loaded shotgun. Both got five-year sentences.

An Old Bailey jury found Eddie Richardson – described as a 30-year-old chemist of Mead Road, Chislehurst, Kent – guilty of causing an affray at Mr Smith's. He was also sentenced to five years in prison. Mad Frankie Fraser was acquitted of murder charges, although he was found guilty of fighting and making an affray and also got a five-year sentence.

The police were disappointed about the acquittals of Moody and his two friends, but felt certain they would nail down the entire gang at the torture trial, which was scheduled for early the following year. The Krays were buoyant and even more confident they were now the number-one crime family in London. As henchman Albert Donoghue later recalled: 'We all felt able to relax and move around London more freely. Most of our serious opposition was off the streets.'

In February 1967, while on remand in Brixton Prison, Jimmy Moody got to see his two-week-old daughter Janine for the first time. It was a moving experience. Staff and prisoners applauded Val and her baby when they entered the visitor's area in A-wing. Moody said afterwards that he was almost reduced to tears. Family and crime were now set on an inevitable path to death and destruction.

FIVE

Torture Time

In September 1966, Jimmy Moody, aged just 25, found himself alongside 15 other defendants, all accused of torture, at an initial hearing at Clerkenwell Magistrates Court. They included Charlie and Eddie Richardson plus Mad Frankie Fraser. Bail applications were all opposed with prosecutors pointing out: 'In this case there is a history of extreme violence and some of the witnesses have been subject to this violence. All the other witnesses are fully aware of the violence and are in extreme fear.'

Jimmy Moody – handcuffed to two policemen – was also on a grievous bodily harm charge after he attacked three police officers while in custody the previous day. Moody shouted at the court: 'I was bleedin' from my head in the cells for an hour. I had to have stitches. This is a police state – they can say what they like.'

Moody's lawyer Mr M. Beckman told the court: 'My client was, in fact, violently attacked by the police.' Moody's punch-up with the police did nothing to harm his reputation.

Jimmy Moody got few mentions in the press coverage of the torture-gang arrests because the Richardsons and Mad Frankie Fraser hogged the limelight. But detectives knew Moody was by this time a key member of the Richardson gang. His loyalty in the aftermath of the Mr Smith's shootout had given him an increasingly powerful role within the organisation. As one south-east London criminal later explained: 'Big Jim showed the Richardsons he was a good soldier when he took two of the gang to the hospital, risking his own safety in the process. They owed him, big time.'

Meanwhile, millions of newspaper readers across the nation were gripped by details of the Richardson gang's evil acts of torture. Many were asking how such a barbaric group of men could live and thrive in the middle of a modern, cosmopolitan city like London. And when the trial finally opened at the Old Bailey in early 1967 it hogged the front pages and sparked shock and horror amongst the law-abiding citizens of Middle England.

At the Old Bailey, witness George Green was allowed to write his address on a piece of paper for the court, due to fear of reprisals if his details were announced. Green then told how he himself had been tortured when he was visited by Eddie Richardson and the now-deceased George Cornell after receiving a 'final warning' from Charlie Richardson over money that was owed to him. Green continued that later, when he told one Richardson gang member the police had been in touch with him, Cornell tipped him upside down on a chair and hit him across the head with a pair of pliers. Green told the court: 'Then he started hitting me with chairs and ashtrays, kicking me and punching me.'

The next day Eddie Richardson, conducting his own defence, accused another torture victim, Benjamin Coulston, of being a police informer. Coulston denied the allegation in court. Later that same day Jimmy Moody stood in the witness box to answer questions about Coulston relating to an incident in 1965. Moody told the court: 'If what has been alleged is true, I ought to be in a straitjacket because I would be a Frankenstein.'

Then Mr T. Williams, QC for the defence, asked Moody: 'Were you at the address where the torturing of Mr Coulston took place?'

'No,' Moody replied.

'When you were charged with this offence did you say to the officer in charge of the case, "You must have bribed or blackmailed the witness to give evidence."'

'Yes. I'd been in solitary confinement for six months. I was shocked at being charged with assaulting someone I'd never seen in my life.'

Moody admitted to the Old Bailey he'd refused to go on an identity parade at Brixton Prison because he could not see what the nine other men looked like. Moody was asked by a prosecution lawyer why he had a problem with appearing in the identity parade.

'I was being framed and was too frightened to say anything,' Moody answered. 'I did shout out at the magistrates' court but not while Coulston was giving evidence. I did protest my innocence on two other occasions, however.'

Charlie Richardson remained the boss even during the long hours in the Old Bailey courtroom during the torture trial. He showed little emotion and hardly moved, apart from a gentle easing of his broad shoulders to free himself from an uncomfortable suit. His head never moved, though his eyes would occasionally dart right towards the jury or left towards counsel. Even as the trial drew to a close, he remained alert, self-contained and full of contempt.

But Jimmy Moody and the others sitting in the dock alongside Richardson were not so cool. Brother Eddie sat looking dejected, Frankie Fraser yawned, Moody leaned forward abstractedly with his head on his arms. The others fidgeted, daydreamed and occasionally smiled at each other.

On 7 June 1967, following a nine-week trial, Jimmy Moody was found not guilty of causing grievous bodily harm to alleged torture victim Coulston and not guilty on a charge of assault occasioning in actual bodily harm to Coulston. After the verdict was announced, Moody turned towards the judge, put up his hand and said, 'Sir.'

Moody's acquittal sparked talk of more jury bribery. 'It was a bloody outrage,' recalled one detective from that era. 'We all knew they'd been leaning on the jury, but we couldn't get anyone to admit it.'

All that alleged jury nobbling didn't help big cheese Charlie Richardson, however, and he was convicted on nine charges at the same Old Bailey trial. These included robbery with violence, demanding money with menaces or force, causing grievous bodily harm and assault. Richardson remained expressionless even when Mr Justice Lawton sentenced him to 25 years imprisonment after calling his actions 'vicious, sadistic and a disgrace to society'. Then, just as the police were about to lead him down to the cells, he half-bowed towards the jury. 'Thanks very much,' he said. Brother Eddie, 31, and three other members of their strong-arm team were also found guilty on various charges, including violence.

The end of the Old Bailey torture trial attracted widespread headlines and exhaustive newspaper coverage. Frankie Fraser was even nicknamed 'the dentist' by the tabloids after details of how he would demand money with menaces by trying to pull out people's teeth with pliers. And there were rumours that Jimmy Moody had killed at least one man with his bare hands. Others alleged he'd shot two or three other villains who'd upset the Richardsons. But without the ultimate piece of evidence – a body – the police could do nothing. In any case, as one south-east London detective later explained: 'There was also this attitude that if Moody had knocked off a few pieces of vermin then it made our jobs a lot easier, so why bother getting too steamed up about it?'

Back at the Moody family's extremely modest flat at The Grosvenor Buildings, Jimmy Moody's wife Val had returned home alone after the case as Moody had remained in custody on assault charges relating to the three policemen he was alleged to have attacked. It was a day Val would never forget – for all the wrong reasons.

She explained: 'When I walked into the flat I found a complete stranger in my bed with gunshot wounds. He just looked up at me and said, "Jimmy said I could stay here." I just turned around and walked out of the flat without saying a word.'

The following day Val visited her husband in Brixton Prison and mentioned the incident. 'Oh, don't worry about him, darlin'. He's a pal of mine who was in a bit of trouble and I told him he could stay there. You don't mind, do ya?'

That was when Val decided it was best if she moved herself and the children back to her parents' home in Poplar.

In June 1967, Jimmy Moody pleaded guilty at the Old Bailey to assaulting the three policemen. Just before court got under way, Moody shouted out that he'd been in remand for so long he'd only ever seen his baby daughter inside a prison. Moody had become increasingly frustrated at how slowly the wheels of justice were turning for him. After hearing that Moody had spent the previous 15 months in custody since his arrest in March 1966, Judge Graham Rogers said he would ensure a sentence would mean his immediate release.

Val later heard about her husband's problems at the Old Bailey when she spotted an *Evening Standard* billboard at Marylebone Station: 'MAN'S OUTBURST AT OLD BAILEY TRIAL'. Val immediately turned to a friend she was with and said: 'I bet that's Jimmy.'

Val felt sorry for her husband at this time because he seemed to be getting a lot of rough treatment while in prison awaiting various trials. Val explained: 'In prison he'd been hit by a prison officer who he fought off and he even gave me his jacket with blood on it to show to our solicitor to prove what had happened. They set about him and he fought back and injured them. I knew Jimmy had a violent temper but he didn't deserve this.'

Val and the couple's two small children Jason and Janine were eventually rehoused in a council maisonette in nearby Hackney, which was a vast improvement on that earlier place by the Blackwall Tunnel or being stuck at her parents' home in Poplar.

A few weeks later, the Kray twins lured Jack 'The Hat' McVitie to a party at a flat in Stoke Newington, north London, where Reggie put a gun to his head and pulled the trigger. When it failed to go off, someone passed Reggie a knife and he plunged it into McVitie's face. Then he slashed the small-time villain's face as he lay dying and finished him off by ramming the knife down his throat. That incident marked the beginning of the end for the Krays and shortly afterwards they were arrested and jailed for life.

In the summer of 1967, Jimmy Moody – still in his mid 20s – was at last a free man, but he no longer had the Richardsons to turn to. Their imprisonment was the end of an era for Moody. How was he going to pick up the pieces and start making some money again? Back at the family's new flat in Hackney, Moody made fleeting appearances, citing 'work' as a reason for not hanging around for long. He loved Val and the kids, but found it virtually impossible to stay in one place for more than a matter of days. Moody constantly looked for new criminal opportunities and didn't want to drag his family into that world. However, when Moody was at home, he made an effort to be a normal father. In the evenings, Jimmy Moody would tuck his two children into bed and read them his favourite poem, 'Jabberwocky' by Lewis Carroll. A few years later when his son was old enough to understand what his father did for a job, Moody would place Jason on his knee and regale him with stories of his criminal escapades. Moody's path to criminality was set in stone.

SIX

Earning Respect

Jimmy Moody faced the most fundamental of problems following the disbanding of the Richardson gang: where could he get work – as in criminal activity? Moody was like a soldier without any commanding officers. 'Jim needed guidance, he had to be pointed in the right direction otherwise he was liable to make some grave errors,' explained one old associate from the late '60s.

During this period, Moody became much closer to his older and straighter brother Dickie and began using his mother's flat in Rosendale Road, Dulwich as a useful 'flophouse' whenever committing crimes which he didn't want Val and the children to know about. Moody's mother Rosina was delighted to have him regularly visiting and would lay on special meals, offer to wash and iron all his clothes, and pamper him as if he was still a teenager. Dickie took it all in his stride. 'He was her favourite and she knew he was up to no good, but we didn't ask too many questions,' recalled Dickie. 'Jim didn't volunteer anything because he didn't want to upset mum.'

Jimmy Moody was having a tough time making enough money to support Val and the kids and continue the high-quality lifestyle he'd enjoyed under the Richardsons. He started once again committing off-the-cuff crimes, like jewellery-shop smash 'n' grabs, but often for no more than a few hundred pounds.

Eventually, as word got around that Moody was on the market, more lucrative and 'challenging' jobs started to come in from gang bosses in south and east London. One retired London criminal explained: 'We all knew Jimmy Moody was capable of anything. He'd proved that with the Richardsons. So he was offered contract killings of other criminals.' The work was well paid – usually between £5,000 and £10,000 – and Jimmy Moody had no qualms about killing another man, although his first assignment turned out to be rather close to home.

Scotch Jack Buggy was an American gangster born in Scotland and now living in London. Buggy had real form, as they say, including run-ins with Jack Spot and Billy Hill. The Richardsons hated his guts and there'd been a bullet with his name on it for many years. It was only a matter of time before someone like Jimmy Moody caught up with him.

Buggy was lured into the Lederer's Bridge Club, in Mount Street, Mayfair, with the promise of a money-spinning deal. Lederer's – a small two-room club above the famous Pathfinders Club and Poultry Shop – was a regular haunt of Jimmy Moody from his days with the Richardsons. Once inside the club, Buggy was shot twice in the head before his body was trussed up and transported down to the south coast. A few weeks later his corpse was fished out of the sea by two off-duty police officers near Seaford, Sussex. It then emerged that Buggy owed other villains more than £30,000.

Another contract killing linked to Moody following his release from prison provided some harsh lessons on how *not* to pull off a successful hit. In August 1967, a 26-year-old Camberwell car dealer called Tony Turnhill was driving through the Kent countryside when three men in a Jaguar tried to ram his vehicle. Turnhill knew immediately what was happening and tried to lose his pursuers through a maze of twisting and turning narrow country lanes. He then turned into Lavender Lane, a cul-de-sac in the village of West Malling. A man fitting Moody's description stepped out of the Jaguar and aimed his .38 – a hitman special because it didn't spit out bullet casings like a 9 mm – at Turnhill's head and body. Moments later the Jaguar reversed at high speed out of Lavender Lane, the team believing they had completed their job. But despite being badly injured, Turnhill then staggered half a mile to an isolated house called Broadwater Farm and called for help.

Police mounted an armed guard at Turnhill's bedside after one of the .38 bullets was removed from his head at the specialist Atkinson Morley's Hospital in Wimbledon, south London. The other bullet miraculously failed to penetrate Turnhill's body because of an obstruction in his jacket. Although Turnhill refused to help police with their inquiries despite recovering from his injuries, rumours of Moody's involvement were fuelled by a witness who provided descriptions of the three men. The contract was cancelled, costing the hit team a lot of cash, as well as pride.

Crime in the late '60s was heading for epidemic proportions. Tens of millions of pounds worth of stolen property changed hands illegally every week. Violent offences were up by more then 10 per cent each year from 1965 and the number of drug convictions rose from 3,190 in 1967 to 4,836 in 1968.

Many believed that the jailing of the Krays and the Richardsons would help destroy the menace of organised crime. They couldn't have been more wrong. New, better organised crime networks, often run by cold-blooded individuals rather than families, were emerging. They financed everything from bank robberies to drug deals. Hijacked goods lorries were also a particularly popular source of income at the time.

No amount of police activity could stem the tide of crime that was sweeping the nation. The new crime bosses were happy to hide behind hard-core do-or-die villains like Jimmy Moody. Moody was prepared to carry out the orders of wealthy individuals in order to thrive. Moody's son Jason explained many years later: 'My dad was a soldier taking orders from his bosses and most of the time he didn't question those orders.'

The police were constantly on Jimmy Moody's tail following his recent double acquittals at the Old Bailey. 'There was a feelin' that Jim should have been sent down, that he was livin' on borrowed time,' explained his brother Dickie many years later.

Dickie Moody was working hard as a scaffolder back in those days, but he remained close to his younger brother. 'We used to drink a lot at Freddie Foreman's pub, The Red Sails in Clapham. There was no all-day drinking back in them days so we then used to go on to drinking clubs where a lot villains were regulars. The so-called chaps.' And Moody – always the most generous man in any bar and now once again earning good money – made a point of keeping his brother financially afloat. 'We all knew he was in with the heavy mob. He'd come up here and bung me and Mum a few quid. Treat her to a few clothes and stuff,' explained Dickie. Jimmy Moody never admitted his cash was also coming from the occasional contract killing. Dickie explained: 'I knew he was up to no good, but not exactly what he was doing. Jim was the type of fella everyone wanted to keep on the right side of. In those days people used to line up to buy him a drink.'

But Moody's alcohol intake was becoming a problem, as Dickie recalled: 'He started drinkin' a hell of lot with the Richardsons and just carried on after they'd gone. His favourite tipple was whisky, but it didn't half make him aggressive.' But that aggression did fuel the respect he craved. Explained Dickie: 'Jim got quite a reputation after those two court cases. He'd walk in a boozer and the place would go quiet. You could hear a pin drop. People were that impressed.' Or terrified.

However, in those days following the Mr Smith's and torture trials, Dickie also noted a different Jimmy Moody emerging: 'He was havin' more and more rucks with punters all the time. Those bottles of Scotch set him right off.' Jimmy Moody's ever-growing sense of isolation from the normal world and a penchant for heavy drinking had turned him into a tinderbox.

And the police raids kept coming. Dickie explained: 'Different cops would call round here once or twice a week. Sometimes we'd get raids at two or three in the morning. There'd be an almighty bang on the door; we always knew it was Old Bill before they hollered, "Open up, police!", but Jim was never round here with us when they came bangin'.'

That's when Rosina Moody, hands on hips, would start yelling at the police for harassing her boy. 'What you want with my son? He ain't done nothin'. You hear me?'

But the reason the police never found Moody at his mother's flat was because the family had devised a special system just in case he ever turned up when the police were calling. Dickie explained: 'Mum would put a towel out over the balcony so Jim knew we had company. Stupid bastards never worked it out.'

Rosina and Dickie Moody were also paid a few visits by Jimmy Moody's so-called 'friends'. Dickie explained: 'A couple of his mates turned up looking for Jim, but there was no threat to me or my mum – although we could tell they was pretty heavy geezers and they weren't always too happy with Jim.'

On Easter Monday, 15 April 1968, Moody, his brother Dickie and two friends, gate-crashed a party in Ildersley Grove, Dulwich, near the Moody family home in Rosendale Road. It was a lively affair, hosted by the two Day brothers. One of them – William – was celebrating his departure from the merchant navy. As Dickie later recalled: 'There were a whole bunch o' people there, lots o' booze, lots o' birds. We was well happy when we walked in.'

But within minutes of arriving, trouble flared. Dickie recalled: 'One of our friends had a row with William Day about turning the music down. Then Jim hit the roof.' As Dickie explained: 'Anyone who didn't agree with Jim got a slap for their troubles. Everyone was the enemy after he'd had a few whiskies.'

One punch by Moody quickly developed into a fully pitched battle between him and 21-year-old William Day. A man called Vincent Dalton tried to intervene and was punched in the face. Dickie then got dragged into the fight because he felt obliged to help out his brother, although he knew it was going to end seriously. The punch-up spilled into the back garden. Minutes later, Day had suffered two depressed skull fractures after being attacked with bricks and kicked. The Moody boys scarpered over the back wall and headed home to Rosendale Road. Surgeons later fought to save William Day's life, but he died the following day.

Dickie insists to this day that his brother was riddled with guilt about the incident, but not because the other man died. 'He felt I got dragged into it. He always said he should have handled it himself.'

Jimmy Moody had now crossed the boundary from cold-blooded occasional hitman to out-and-out psychotic killer capable of ending a man's life over a small disagreement at a party. He'd lost touch with reality and so-called 'normal' morals. His anger about killing Day was fuelled by his earlier arrest by the 'enemy', the police, not because he felt any remorse for ending another man's life.

In Rosendale Road, Rosina Moody was shocked to hear what had happened and told her two boys to leave before the police turned up. Back at the party, many of the witnesses were too scared to tell detectives much about the six-foot-plus psycho who'd savagely beaten William Day. But officers soon recognised the description.

Next morning, police announced they were hunting for notorious local criminal Jimmy Moody and his older brother Dickie. They also had descriptions of the friends who were with them. Detectives appealed for more witnesses, including four mini-skirted young women who attended the party, to come forward and help them with their inquiries.

Five days later – on 22 April 1968 – Moody's two friends gave themselves up and appeared in court accused of involvement in the death of merchant seaman William Day at the party. Moody later claimed his two friends had given police statements about him and his brother Dickie. 'Those two names will never be forgotten or forgiven,' explained one close friend of Moody only recently. 'Grasses are the lowest form of pond life.'

The following day – 23 April – Moody's mother Rosina, now 49 years old, made a public appeal to her two sons to give themselves up. She told them through journalists: 'For my sake, I ask you to either come home together or both go to West Dulwich Police Station and see Detective Chief Inspector Alan Jones. It is vital you contact the police as soon as you read this appeal.'

Jimmy Moody was angered that the police used his dear old mum as bait. Moody was convinced Rosina would never have done such a thing voluntarily. Dickie later explained: 'Jim thought it was outrageous they used Mum like that.'

Then on 27 April detectives were tipped off that the Moody brothers were in a van due in Rossiter Road, Balham, later that day. In broad daylight, Detective Chief Inspector Alan Jones and his team pounced, but Jimmy Moody wasn't going to be taken that easily. An almighty dust-up ensued between the Moody brothers and police. Eventually Jimmy Moody was brought down by a rugby tackle from a detective who was even bigger than he was.

The two brothers were then escorted under armed guard to West Dulwich Police Station. Later that night they were both charged with the murder of William Day. On 1 May 1968 Jimmy, now 27, and Dickie, 28, appeared before local magistrates handcuffed to police officers, and were remanded in custody.

The police had been after Jimmy Moody for a long time and detectives even tried to get Dickie to make a statement against his brother to further incriminate him. 'They wanted Jim for other things,' recalled Dickie. 'I wouldn't crack so I s'ppose he owed me in a sense, although we never talked about it later. I know he would have done the same for me. That's what bein' brothers is all about, ain't it?'

Both men were kept in custody in Brixton Prison's D-wing and Dickie never forgot how his younger, supposedly tougher brother, came close to tears as he apologised for landing Dickie in so much trouble. 'It was one of the few times I saw Jim looking really emotional,' recalled Dickie. 'He felt so bad about what had happened.'

Then, just before they were due to appear in court for their murder trial, the charge was dropped to manslaughter due to lack of evidence. The two brothers still denied the charges, saying they acted in self-defence. On 4 October 1968, Jimmy and Dickie Moody were found guilty of the manslaughter of William Day as well as assaulting another man called Vincent Dalton. Each got six years. As the sentences were announced, Dickie Moody turned to his one-time friend whom he felt had grassed him up in the public gallery at the Old Bailey and shouted: 'Hope you're satisfied now.' Both brothers were still incensed by who they now saw as their two turncoat friends.

Judge Mr Justice John Stephenson summed up: 'This was an appalling outbreak of violence for which no doubt drink was responsible. But when this conduct is in the garden of a London house it cannot be overlooked.' Jimmy Moody's reputation in south-east London ensured that there were no follow-up problems with the family of victim William Day. Dickie explained: 'When his family found out who Jim was they kept well away from us. People who knew Jim was with the Richardsons always gave him a wide birth.'

So it was back to prison for Jimmy Moody. He wasn't happy about the circumstances behind his incarceration, but he resolved to serve his time and then start earning some real money. Thanks to his profile, Moody had no real problems inside prison, but he greatly missed his family. Val had two young handfuls – Jason and Janine – to contend with as a single mum and Moody felt bad because he knew he should have done more to support them all.

'It cracked him up to have to be away from Val and the kids,' says Dickie. 'Jim adored his family even though he sometimes had a problem showing it. Goin' down for that killin' really hit him hard and he swore that once he got out he'd never be jailed again. He even said he'd rather be dead.'

So when son Jason, by now four years old, sent his father a Christmas card it virtually reduced Moody to tears. The card was the size of a 'wanted' poster and featured a red printed message:

CAUSE IT'S MEANT, DAD, FOR YOU!
MERRY CHRISTMAS AND HAPPY NEW YEAR, DAD!
To My Daddy
Happy Christmas
Lots and lots of love from your boy Jason.
[Numerous 'x' marks everywhere plus two thumbprint-size photos of toddler Jason]

Moody hung it in his cell.

'And no one ever dared take the mickey out of his family or else they'd be dicin' with death,' explained Dickie.

Jimmy Moody began his six-year sentence at Albany Prison on the

Isle of Wight. When Jason, Janine and Val visited Moody, the two children were told: 'Dad's building a bridge on an island.' Jason later explained: 'I had no idea he was in prison. We were told we were jumping on ferries to the Isle of White because Dad was building bridges. Then we'd get there and ask him why he wasn't coming home during a visit and he'd say: "Can't come home at the moment, son. Daddy's still gotta build this bridge. But I'll be back soon."'

Jason still has vivid memories of the Isle of Wight. 'We had to go on the hovercraft, which was quite an adventure. The prison provided a free bus from the port – naturally I thought it was paid for by the construction company employing my dad to build those bridges.' Jason added: 'It was strange because we'd go all over the country visiting him and we was always told by Mum he was on a building job. Long Lartin, Parkhurst, Albany, Gartree places like that. And we never questioned it. Not once.'

Jimmy Moody didn't stay long in any prison before he was transferred because the authorities were determined to try and break his spirit and stop him planning new crimes with other inmates.

The late '60s were a time of great unrest in prisons across Britain. When Moody was in Parkhurst a huge riot erupted after inmates began protesting about conditions.

For 40 terrifying minutes on 24 October 1969, 7 members of staff feared for their lives as riot-crazed inmates held them captive. One prisoner came within a whisker of slitting the throat of an officer. Nine prisoners eventually surrendered including armed robber Stanley Thompson, 22, and Mad Frankie Fraser, both later charged with riotous assembly and given extra time on their sentences. Fraser of course knew Jimmy Moody well from their days with the Richardsons, and Thompson was a 'bolter' – an inmate determined to try and escape.

Moody's main pre-occupation inside was keeping fit; he exercised furiously, narcissistically boosting his already vast physique with a punishing regime that he'd keep up for the rest of his life. Every time he did a press–up he saw it as a mark of defiance against the system. In his mind, they'd never beat him. Ever.

Dickie Moody served his entire sentence away from Jimmy. 'They deliberately kept us apart because they didn't want no trouble, but I know Jim would have been calmer if I'd been around,' explained Dickie. Dickie drew the ultimate short straw when it came to prisons by serving much of his sentence in London's grim Wormwood Scrubs. 'I was no threat so they just left me in the Scrubs to rot.'

The relationship between the two brothers intrigued all who came across them. They were like chalk and cheese in many ways but their loyalty to one another was unswerving. Nothing and no one ever came between them. Yet in other ways they weren't that close; Dickie believed in earning an honest crust, while Jimmy was addicted to crime. But there was never any question of Dickie grassing up his kid brother, even though Moody later said he wished Dickie had walked free because he'd done 'fuck all' and didn't deserve to go to prison for killing Day.

The brothers regularly wrote each other letters in prison and Rosina loyally visited each of her boys at least once a month, however far she had to travel. Possibly she'd learned from the mistakes of the past when no one had visited the teenage Jimmy Moody when he was locked up, causing open resentment and hatred towards society to develop in him.

SEVEN

Domestic Chaos

In late 1970, Parkhurst Prison rioter Stan Thompson, a man who'd attracted the attention of everyone from Mad Frankie Fraser to Jimmy Moody, was transferred to the notorious Dartmoor Prison. Thompson resented being moved because it meant a long journey for any visitors from his east London manor. As a notorious 'bolter', it got Thompson thinking about ways to escape. Slim, fit and popular with other inmates, Thompson had always been a bit of a rebel and had been given an extra 18 months for his part in the Parkhurst riot of October 1969.

At 8.30 p.m. on Sunday, 14 November 1971, Stan Thompson and two pals, Wally MacKenzie and Jim Stevens – complete with a VHF radio to listen to police communications once they were out in the big, bad world – cut through their bars and left their cells through the windows.

The three inmates made a 100-yard dash across the prison exercise yard to the gate they'd earlier noted was usually open at night. Dressed in grey prison uniforms and fawn raincoats, they reached the bottom of the 22-foot-high prison wall where they assembled a home-made ladder and climbed over before the dog patrol even got a sniff of what had happened. Brand new floodlight equipment that had just been installed wasn't operating at the time.

The escape may have been faultless but – as had so often been the case in the past – getting off the notorious moor was a much bigger challenge. Typically, Stan Thompson had gone to the trouble of memorising an Ordnance Survey map and, as one inmate later boasted, knew it better than the inside of his own cell.

Within hours, 300 police officers had set up road blocks and brought in dogs to help in the search. Prison officers searched on horseback, while helicopters buzzed overhead. But as night time fell and mist closed in on Dartmoor, there still wasn't any sign of the three escaped prisoners. The following day's national newspapers were full of front-page headlines about Stan Thompson's 'daring' escape from Dartmoor. 'DANGER MEN OF DARTMOOR ON THE RUN,' screamed the *Daily Express* on 15 November 1971. And, naturally, the police warned the public: 'These men must be regarded as dangerous.'

The night after their escape, Thompson and his mates turned up at an isolated farm in Spreyton, Devon, and demanded a meal from Mrs Elsie Powlesland, a farmer's wife, who called the police immediately after they'd gone. The following day police had their next real break when a stolen Austin A35 car with three men sped away from a police roadblock at Burrowbridge, near Bridgwater, Somerset. Minutes later the car slid to a halt on the outskirts of the town and Thompson and the others hotfooted it through a nearby housing estate. A 3-hour search of the town, involving 150 policemen with 25 cars, 4 dogs and a helicopter, ended when all 3 were arrested.

In prisons across the nation, inmates toasted the antics of Messrs Thompson and co. As inmate Bernie Khan explained: 'There's nothing better for a prisoner's morale than to hear about an escape bid. Makes us realise there is always a way out of the hellhole.'

One of those who listened to the details on the radio with great relish was Jimmy Moody. One day Thompson's skills would become invaluable to him, although neither knew it at the time. As Stan Thompson admitted many years later: 'To some of us, escaping is the only way we can keep our sanity. We gotta know there's a chance to get out otherwise we might as well give up on life.'

Another dramatic escape bid caught Jimmy Moody's attention; 17 prisoners facing charges for a series of bank robberies attempted a breakout from Brixton Prison, in south London. It was a well organised attempt with outside help and Moody – by then incarcerated in Gartree Prison, in Leicestershire – noted with interest how a Ford Transit had been hired and then placed outside the prison. Having a standby vehicle seemed to be a key factor in any successful escape bid, as had been proven by the numerous breakouts organised by the Great Train Robbers over the years.

But the key to this particular escape attempt was the treatment of remand prisoners – long considered a 'joke' by staff and inmates at

Brixton. They were entitled to wear their own clothes, have their own food, radios and newspapers because they had not yet been found guilty in a court of law. Visitors to remand prisoners weren't even separated by a barrier and inmates were allowed in each other's cells. Planning a breakout was something to pass the time and if that scheme could be turned into a practical reality then so be it. The Brixton escape was foiled at the last minute, but the very notion that it could be considered suggested there were a lot of elementary problems about Brixton which could not be fixed overnight.

Dickie Moody was eventually released from prison in 1972. His younger brother had to stay a year longer after losing his privileges when he handed out some brutal punishment to a couple of paedophiles. One former prison mate of Moody explained: 'His speciality was to run into a cell, bash the fuck out of them, set their mattress alight, then bolt their door on the way out in the hope they'd choke. Sometimes he'd even slice 'em up with a homemade chiv made from a razor on a melted-down toothbrush head.'

Jimmy Moody's criminal psyche was irreversible, although he pledged in a letter to his older brother that he'd never touch another drop of Scotch again. 'That bloody fire water's got me in enough trouble as it is,' Moody wrote to Dickie. It was one of the few pledges Moody would ever make in his entire life.

In 1973, Jimmy Moody finally stepped out of Gartree Prison's steel gates, heard them slide shut behind him, and no doubt thought to himself, 'Well, mate, you're on your tod now. No more nice gentle screws to bring you breakfast, dinner and tea and tuck you up in bed at night.' His old windcheater felt cold after the thick prison uniform and like all inmates, he paused for a few seconds outside the building, while looking back at the gates. Then he pledged to get the hell out of that place before they changed their minds and dragged him back inside again.

Two hours later Moody found himself standing outside King's Cross Station, relishing the peace and quiet of early morning London. It was still too early for the main rush hour, but commuters and lorries were already starting to jam up the city streets. The black cabs looked almost the same except some of them were a different shape from before. Luckily they still made that same familiar diesel clunking noise; engines, tyres, exhaust . . . peace and quiet, London style.

Jimmy Moody quickly spotted his driver in a Zodiac waiting across the street from the main station exit. The two men headed to a nearby caff to put away some bacon and eggs. Even though he hadn't eaten anything since his last lousy plate of porridge at five that morning, Moody couldn't get a normal brekky down because the food was so rich. It'd be a few days before he could handle real food again.

Next there was the important matter of Val and the kids. Those children needed security. Val needed a man. For six years, Jimmy Moody hadn't provided anything apart from a few quid here and there. Moody dreaded the idea of Jason and Janine growing up without a dad just like he had. Val was always saying she had to think of the future and Moody feared that one day she would see the future without him. Moody appreciated her point, but begged her to stay married to him in the hope that once he was out things could be different. He'd even promised to steer clear of trouble – although he never actually said what that meant. After the last visit to prison by Val and the kids, Moody's brain had gone AWOL for a while and he'd beaten some poor bastard to a pulp after a row over a plate of spaghetti in the prison canteen. But now Moody was back in the real world and that meant living by a different set of rules. Or did it?

The world that Jimmy Moody had stepped back into was filled with sharp-eyed detectives determined to win back the streets after all those gangster-filled years of the '60s. Scotland Yard's very own crime buster, Detective Chief Superintendent Albert Wickstead, aka 'The Grey Fox', head of the Yard's Serious Crimes Squad, mounted raid after raid in 1973, which resulted in 235 officers taking 93 men and 1 woman into custody. One senior detective even told the *Daily Express* at the time: 'The other side have never been hit so hard.'

The massive Flying Squad operation was based at Limehouse Police Station in the middle of the East End. As Moody read about the raids shortly after his release, he must have wondered what kind of war he'd walked back into. Would he even be able to survive in an environment where all the old gangs had been dispersed?

The Flying Squad had been in existence so long its nickname in rhyming slang, the Sweeney (from Flying Squad/Sweeney Todd, the notorious Fleet Street barber who turned his customers into meat pies), was generally regarded as a cliché. The squad was set up at the end of the First World War, when London experienced a crime wave as large numbers of men recently released from the armed forces emerged onto the streets of the capital, many of them hardened to violence after the carnage on the Western Front.

The Sweeney enjoyed rapid crime-busting success and in 1920 were provided with two motor tenders, capable of a top speed of 35 mph (the speed limit at the time was just 20 mph). Then a *Daily Mail* journalist referred to them as 'a flying squad of picked detectives' and the name stuck. Their exploits went on to figure in a number of British films, and in the mid-1970s the squad would be eulogized in a TV series, *The Sweeney*, starring John Thaw and Dennis Waterman.

But the glamorous, hard-nosed image of the Flying Squad left detectives wide open to accusations of corruption in the form of a detective either turning a blind eye to what was going on in return for a cut of the action or – if the information led to the recovery of stolen property – pocketing some of the reward money that the detective claimed on the informant's behalf. A strategically placed officer could also, for a fee, ensure bail was granted, hold back evidence and details about past convictions from a court, or pass on to people under investigation details of a case being made against them or warnings about police operations in which they could become compromised. Corrupt officers also held onto a proportion of whatever valuables they recovered during an inquiry.

In the mid-1970s – when Jimmy Moody was reviving his criminal career in south and east London – the newly appointed deputy assistant commissioner, David Powis, ordered a crackdown to stop corrupt policemen from creaming off reward money meant for informants. In future, all payments amounting to more than £500 would be handed over by Powis himself.

Jimmy Moody was more interested in scheming the downfall of his rivals than making a few extra bob by informing on them. He had big plans afoot to turn himself into a major-league criminal carrying out really big, meaty robberies.

The good news for Moody was that jury nobbling and interference with star witnesses were still virtually weekly occurrences at London's big courts, including the Old Bailey. The DPP regularly objected to bail applications by villains on the basis that there is a 'strong fear' of interference with witnesses.

But another disturbing new element was creeping into the London underworld – the supergrass. Perhaps the most notorious of all was the controversial passport to freedom that bankrobber Bertie Smalls negotiated from Britain's lawkeepers. Characters like Smalls played their cards close to their chest. His chips were times, places, hauls and christian names. Smalls and other grasses believed that what they had to offer would be enough to win the most important gamble of their lives – freedom. Smalls was one of the most hated men in the criminal underworld and Moody told one criminal associate that he'd 'gladly kill that bastard for nothing. He's vermin and should be wiped off the face of this earth.'

In May 1974, Smalls helped convict seven men at the Old Bailey of robbing the Barclays Bank at Ilford of £237,736 and Barclays Wembley branch of £138,111. After that, he was guarded by 12 armed detectives at a secret hideout 24 hours a day, knowing full well that a £60,000 contract had been put on his head. Back in south-east London, Jimmy Moody and others continued to be outraged. 'This ain't about money. It's about respect and not grassing up people. It's the ultimate sin, ain't it?' he told one associate.

The Flying Squad regularly hauled in villains like Jimmy Moody knowing full well they had committed particular crimes, but aware there was no way of proving their guilt. Moody was even approached by crime bosses to help frame high-ranking police officers, just before they were due to give evidence at major trials. The aim was to smear their names to such an extent that their evidence would be seriously questioned in court. But Moody didn't find the nature of such work appealing; he was happier on robberies and the occasional contract killing. As Jason Moody explained years later: 'If there's one thing my dad would never do, it's frame another person – whether they were a cop or a criminal. It just wasn't his style.'

Detective Bill Forman – who was to later have many Moody encounters – agreed: 'Jimmy Moody was an old-fashioned villain in many ways. He was extremely honourable in that he'd never grass someone up, not even a bent copper. He had standards which might seem strange to an outsider, but those rules were what he lived and worked by.'

But being a professional hitman didn't cross that line. As East End criminal Bernie Khan commented: 'If someone got in Jimmy Moody's way, God help them. If he had a job to do – and by that I mean a murder or a robbery – then there was no stopping him. He was as cold as ice in that respect.'

That reputation led police to suspect Moody had played a part in one of the most shocking professional hits of the mid-'70s – the assassination of haulage contractor George Brett and his 10-year-old son Terence in 1975. Father and son had left their Upminster, Essex, farmhouse accompanied by a man wearing a bowler hat and business suit, and were never seen again. The man drove a Mark II Jaguar – Moody's favourite model. One of his oldest associates later pointed out: 'That was typical of the cozzers. Blame Big Jim for a hit just because the killer used the type of car he liked.' The professional hitman who really carried out the double hit on the father and son would later play a pivotal role in Moody's future.

Another victim of a professional killer around this time was East End crook William Moseley, whose dismembered body was washed ashore in the Thames Estuary in midsummer, 1975. Then in August that year, the body of 37-year-old armed robber Michael Cornwall was found in a grave in a wood in Hatfield, Herts. He'd been shot in the head. One police source who has looked at the files on both murders insists to this day that Jimmy Moody's name was at the top of the suspects' list. 'Both of these had Moody's hallmark stamped all over them. We believe that by 1975 he was taking on contract killings to supplement his income from robberies and other crimes.' East End robber Bernie Khan explained: 'Jim would go wherever the work was – east, west, south, north. It didn't matter. On both sides of the river. He was a hitman first and foremost. All the other work was secondary to that, even the big blaggings.'

Moody's other jobs, such as robbing jewellers in places like Hatton Garden and raiding small banks were, according to Khan, 'what we call the "in and outters". He also did some banks over the counter. A lot of the banks still didn't have glass and shutters at the time.'

Moody wasn't spending much time at the family home in Hackney at this time. He dropped in an average two nights a week because, he told Val, he was worried about the police raiding the property and he wanted to keep her and the children out of trouble. Sometimes Moody showed up in the middle of the night, tapping on a ground-floor back window in the back garden – Jason and Janine cherished such visits. They never forget how their father would sometimes take them for walks before bedtime.

Jason recalled: 'Near where we used to live was a long, dirty canal with a towpath on each side. When I was about nine or ten – Janine was two years younger – Dad would take us down there by going over a wall and then pushing through some overgrowth to the water's edge. It seemed like a real adventure at the time. Then all three of us would sit on a wall and chuck stones and stuff in the canal while Dad told us a story about a tortoise and a goldfish racing up and down the canal. We used to believe him and would rush to the edge to see if we could spot either of them. Dad always made sure you couldn't work out who'd win until the very last moment, and there was always a good reason why one animal beat the other. Now, every time I go near any water I think about the tortoise and the goldfish.' But Val wasn't happy with the state of her marriage. She told Moody she was once again moving back into her parents' home in Poplar because she couldn't cope with his continual absences. As Jason explained: 'We never knew when Dad would appear at home so it wasn't fair on Mum. I think Dad knew this, in his heart of hearts.'

Moody eventually persuaded Val to use their own flat in Hackney whenever he was coming over so they could have some privacy from her parents. The rest of the time Val and the children stayed in Poplar. Yet there were other times when the Moodys seemed like one big, happy and united family. Jason remembered: 'One time he took us all down to the seaside at Margate in Kent for a day out as a family. It was a brilliant day. He was very relaxed. Him and Mum were all over each other; it was lovely. Anyway, in the evening we went out to an Italian restaurant. Dad was flashing his cash, as usual. Then Mum went to the toilet and Dad called the waiter over, chucked a tenner at him and said that when Mum came back he was to tell her we'd run out without paying. The waiter looked at Dad like he was nutty, but he wasn't goin' to argue with him. So the three of us left the restaurant and hid over the other side of the road. We watched in stitches while Mum got more and more angry as the waiter demanded she pay for the meal. The old man was laughing so much I thought he was going to choke. Then he runs over to the restaurant and bursts in and gives her a big cuddle. It was typical Dad.' Back at school in the East End, life wasn't easy for young Jason. 'Other kids kept away from me because of who my old man was.' Then a teacher hit Jason when he was playing up in class. It nearly led to a nasty confrontation. 'I had to beg the old man not to come to the school and sort out that teacher. A few days later he turned up unexpectedly when I was playing in a school badminton tournament. When I'd finished my game I remember coming off the court and catching the old man looking over at all the teachers.'

'Which one belted yer, son?' Moody asked Jason.

'Doesn't matter, Dad.'

'Which one?'

Jason nodded in the direction of the relevant teacher.

As Jason explained: 'My dad gave that teacher the eye for a while and then we left together, but the teacher never caused me any more problems. One look at the old man was enough.'

Another time when Jason was playing a school football game on local parkland in the East End, he suddenly noticed his father on the touchline. He explained: 'Next thing I know he's shouting encouragement like all the other dads and cheering on the team.' At half time, Moody strolled up to Jason and whispered in his ear: 'You need to kick that other bastard's legs away, son.'

'I can't do that, Dad, I'd get sent off.'

'Nah way. Just show him who's boss.'

'Yeah, sure Dad,' nodded Jason, but with absolutely no intention of doing what his father told him.

As Jason later explained: 'That's the way the old man was. He didn't see it like the rest of us. It was him against the rest of the world and God help anyone who got in his way.'

All the old clichés about loving his wife and kids really did seem to apply to Jimmy Moody, despite his long absences from home. One of his oldest criminal associates explained it this way: 'You gotta remember that being a proper crim like Jimmy is a lonely life. You desperately need the security of your family and that's why he tried his hardest to be a good father and husband, although it obviously wasn't easy.'

East End robber Bernie Khan explained: 'Jim loved his wife and kids, but he never knew how long he'd have with them, so he liked to treasure every moment.'

It was inevitable that Jimmy Moody's criminal activities would overlap with his beloved family. One time, Jason and Janine arrived home to find their father sitting at the kitchen table calmly cleaning a shotgun. 'He was as cool as a cucumber and I was so worried I actually said to him: "Are you that scared of somethin', Dad?"'

Moody laughed it off: 'I sleep like a baby every night, son. Straight out. Watch. Out like a light.'

Another time, Janine, then aged about nine, woke up in the middle of the night and noticed her father in a pair of underpants standing in the hallway outside her bedroom, cleaning another gun. 'I just shut my eyes and went back to sleep,' Janine recalled, while admitting that image of her father would haunt her for the rest of her life.

Moody upset Val by buying Jason an airgun for his 11th birthday, when the family were staying in a caravan on the south coast for a rare break together. Later that same day – after the children had gone to bed

– the ever-playful Moody crept up behind his wife and said, 'Watch this,' before aiming the air rifle at her backside and pulling the trigger. Moody tried to laugh off the incident while Val burst into floods of tears.

'Wot you cryin' for, girl? It's only a little bee sting.'

As Val later recalled: 'I wasn't happy. I just didn't understand why Jimmy would do that to me.'

Jimmy Moody's light-hearted response hid a multitude of sins.

EIGHT

Pump Action

Although he maintained that happy-go-lucky, joke-a-minute exterior, Jimmy Moody occasionally let slip the complex nature of his personality – like the time he took Jason and Janine to visit a zoo in Kent. Jason explained: 'Dad was fascinated by all the big cats in their cages and he dragged us over to them virtually the minute we got there.'

Moody's eyes glazed over as he studied three tigers pacing up and down inside their cage. Jason continued: 'He seemed to go into a trance, just standing watching their every movement. His mind was buzzing. He was miles away, engrossed in watching them.'

Moments later, Moody turned to Jason and said: 'If I had my way I'd let 'em all lose. It's a crime to keep creatures like this behind bars.' Then Moody went back to his own thoughts. Janine and Jason ended up wandering around the rest of the zoo unaccompanied while their father stayed at the tiger enclosure. When Jason and Janine returned they found Moody in exactly the same spot.

As Jason later explained: 'I only thought about it afterwards when I realised my dad really related to those tigers. He'd been locked up for much of his life and he was always pacing up and down, even when he was at home. Those tigers were an extension of him.' Like any self-contained outsider, Jimmy Moody was relating to creatures he felt something in common with. The outside world didn't know or care about him so why should he care about it?

When Jason was just 12 years old, Moody took him out for a day in the countryside and introduced him to real firearms. Jason explained: 'We went to the back of a field with a 12-gauge shotgun and he taught me how to shoot with it.'

Jimmy Moody proved a surprisingly patient teacher. 'This is how you load the gun, son,' he said as he popped open the barrel. 'It takes 12 cartridges and then you pump it out like this. . .' Moody went through the motions as if he'd done it a thousand times before. Later, Moody put the gun down on a tree stump, got out a cloth and turned towards Jason: 'And this is how you clean it. That's more important than anything else, son.'

Within half an hour, Jason was blasting live shots at a tree 20 yards from where they were standing. Jason explained: 'I'll never forget how that shotgun kicked my shoulder back after I pressed the trigger. I was black and blue by the end of that first session, but I was just happy to be with him.'

Jimmy Moody even took a Polaroid photo of his son Jason posing with one of his Remington shotguns. 'I was so proud that he let me pose with that gun,' recalled Jason. 'I knew it had been used to do bad things, but all that mattered to me was that he was giving me his approval and I desperately needed that from my dad.'

Val was furious with her husband for teaching their young son how to fire a shotgun, but having firearms in the house irritated her even more. A bizarre incident perfectly illustrated her fears.

One afternoon, Val walked into the family flat in Hackney to find her husband dressed head to toe in black – balaclava, shirt, jacket and his favourite highly polished monkey boots – standing directly in front of a full-length mirror hanging on the back of the bedroom door. Moody briefly looked up as his wife entered.

'Hello, luv. Just tryin' somethin' out,' he said.

Val had been married long enough to Jimmy Moody not to bother asking any awkward questions. She headed for the kitchen.

Back in the bedroom, Moody pulled a .38 revolver out of a shoulder holster. He was getting a proper feel for a new weapon which he'd bought from an ex-copper who'd become one of the biggest suppliers of guns in south and east London. He stood there with his feet pointing forward about a shoulder distance apart. Arms extended but not locked. Then Moody gripped the weapon with his right hand and used the grooves of his right hand for his left hand to grip – always remembering the left hand had more to do with the grip than the right.

Then Moody lined the sights up. There were two on most handguns; the rear sight used to line up the white strip on the front sight. He needed that white strip to go straight across the top of his target.

Moody always used his right eye because it was definitely better than his left. Once he had the target perfectly lined up, he flicked off the safety and squeezed slowly. That way he'd never know exactly when the gun would go off, which meant his body wouldn't tense up in expectation. When that flame jumped out of the barrel and a snort of cordite hit the air, Moody knew he was in business. But of course all that would come later if and when he needed to use live ammunition.

Moody turned back to the bedroom mirror and crouched down, watching himself throughout the move.

'Everyone on the floor!' he yelled.

He looked straight into the mirror, checking out his expression.

'NOW!'

Val continued her household chores in the kitchen as if nothing was happening.

Then Moody panned the gun to his right, still watching himself avidly in the mirror.

'I said, don't fuckin' move!'

Moody swung 180 degrees with the gun aimed, watching all the imaginary people in front of him as he went.

In the kitchen, Val was cutting up carrots for that night's supper when she heard an enormous bang. She rushed towards the bedroom fearing the worst.

'Jesus Christ, Jimmy. What have you done?'

Moody was standing with the smoking gun still grasped tightly in his hand and aimed at the mirror, which was now shattered.

'Don't worry, love, bit of an accident,' sniggered Moody, ripping off his balaclava.

As Val later explained: 'That bullet went right through the mirror, the door and directly through the neighbour's wall. Luckily, the next-door flat was empty at the time. Jim thought it was all a big laugh.'

Following that close shave, Moody tried out all his new weapons at a basement in Hackney belonging to a small-time villain called Mickey. The walls had been padded up with soundproofing material from a recording studio in Chigwell that had been knocked down to make way for a supermarket. Moody went to the basement four or five times a year, even when he didn't have a specific job, to fire off a few rounds from his collection to keep them all in working order. Moody always preferred to try out a new gun with at least three different types of ammo. It was getting more and more difficult to get a reliable supplier in east or south London and many guns were stolen without ammo in them. Moody often went out near Brands Hatch in Kent, to a little ammo man who worked from a barn at his isolated farm.

Whenever Moody carried a weapon around he was in the habit of putting the gun in its holster and dropping the bullets in a plastic bag in a jacket pocket. It was a sort of good-luck thing with him. It also covered him in case he was ever pulled by the law because a loaded gun meant three years longer than if it was empty. Jimmy Moody knew the laws of the land well.

Moody's family say his obsession with guns did to a certain extent take over his life. On one crazy occasion Moody lost the key to their flat and fired off the lock with a revolver so he could get in. 'He loved guns and saw them as his protectors,' recalled Jason. 'Maybe in some ways he was too reliant on them, but they were the only things he trusted.'

Around this time, Jimmy Moody was offered good money by crime bosses from other parts of the UK to do some 'specialist' jobs – murders and beatings – on their behalf. Jobs were set up for Moody by local gangs. He'd then slip into a city, carry out his 'assignment' and be gone before anyone had even worked out he was there in the first place. The key was he wouldn't be recognised. As such he became, in effect, a commuter killer who could melt back into the Smoke before his crimes had been discovered.

This disturbing new 'inter-city' trend amongst criminals led to calls for much closer cooperation between police forces across the UK. Detectives knew that the rent-a-crime network emerged from prisons, where criminals traditionally formed new working partnerships. Jimmy Moody was soon carrying out killings and beatings as far afield as Liverpool, Newcastle and Birmingham. He felt he was only dishing out violence to those who deserved it in the first place.

Moody also continued his 'day job' as a robber. As an old associate explained: 'If you went to Jim and said, "Look, here's 50 grand to go and kill a geezer," or you said, "There's a bank over there, can you do it," he'd go and do the pair of them that same day if he could. Give him an order and Jim would carry it out, simple as that.'

This source, who knew Moody for more than 30 years, went on: 'Jim didn't have a conscience about what he was doing, whether it was a robbery or a killing. There was no self-torture, no guilt. It was all just work to him. His only fear was about being sent down. He couldn't do time again. He hated being caged up and told me he'd never let the cops take him alive again.'

Around this time, Moody was also regularly called upon to intimidate court witnesses. On one occasion, he was paid by a south London gang boss to do a 'knee cap' job on a west Londoner who was about to appear on trial in Winchester Court, Hampshire. His victim was standing with an associate in the bar of a well-known pub in Stoke Newington, east London, when Moody appeared brandishing a shotgun. The victim's face turned a whiter shade of pale and he dived for cover. An innocent bystander was injured as the shot sprayed across the bar in all directions. Nonetheless, the job had the desired effect because the witness withdrew his testimony.

The '70s saw the ethnic make-up of the old London criminal manors completely transformed by the arrival of tens of thousands of immigrants, particularly from Asia. Jimmy Moody was unsettled by the changes taking place around him. He believed in the Tories and the old-fashioned ethos that England was for the English; Asian shopkeepers and West Indian local bus conductors were a source of bemusement to Jimmy Moody.

There had been other large shifts in south and east London society in the two or three years since Jimmy Moody's release from prison. Much of the capital was being gentrified and other areas were being colonised by office blocks. The Krays and the Richardsons had been inside for a while, and many of their old pals had fled to the Costa del Sol. The men who were taking their place were not interested in flashy cars and hobnobbing with the rich and famous. These far more deadly characters were building business empires on a bed of black money by financing major crimes and then pouring that loot into major London building developments, including the Docklands area of Wapping. Many of these characters knew all about Jimmy Moody and his fearsome reputation as a professional villain.

Jimmy Moody was on the lookout to join a 'classy' team of robbers who could challenge the new, supposedly robber-proof security vans that were being built to withstand everything. They were factory tested with pickaxes and cutters, and even gunfire. The idea was to turn the vans into fortresses on wheels, complete with a supposedly sophisticated alarm system. A whole industry had developed around how to stop robbers getting their hands on the money while it was on the move and security firms even copied the military by having their staff wear uniforms.

But the cash-in-transit industry remained vulnerable to robbers with a bit of creativity. And when in the mid-'70s these blaggers began regularly shooting at guards, it seemed the villains had declared war on the police. The main problem was working out how to catch robbers preying on vans, which meant the police spent much of their time chasing their tails. On pay day – traditionally Thursday – many detectives were simply sent out to look for robbers. It was open season for the professional blaggers and the police just weren't prepared or equipped for the latest surge in the crime of robbery. It was a perfect time for Jimmy Moody to join the most notorious gang of highway robbers the underworld and Scotland Yard have ever known.

NINE

Chopper's in Charge

In the summer of 1976, Jimmy Moody was tapped-up by a well-respected armed robber called Charlie Chopper Knight in a pub in south-east London. 'That's how most of us were recruited. A man who knows a man who knows a man,' explained Bernie Khan, who was also enlisted to the same team. Knight asked Moody if he was interested in being the strong-arm man for a team of robbers looking to expand into the lucrative London and south-east England markets. It sounded more like a sales job than a recruitment pitch for a gang of armed blaggers. As Khan explained: 'You'd be chattin' away in the boozer with Chopper and all of a sudden he just says, "You're in." Simple as that.'

Jimmy Moody was delighted because he'd always disliked being a freelancer who had to plan and pull off most jobs either solo or with just one other accomplice. He knew from the size of the team described by Knight that the money could be enormous. Initially, this band of highway robbers would always strike on wages day, Thursday, so they first became known as the Thursday Gang. Their total haul would eventually exceed £2 million, making them the most successful team of robbers in criminal history.

Jimmy Moody wasn't the main creative force behind the gang, but he was to become a highly influential team member, not least because of his ability to enforce decisions and help prevent disasters. 'In other words, he'd kick the shit out of anyone who got in our way,' explained Bernie Khan. 'Someone had to be there with a shotgun covering the lads while they were at work and Jimmy Moody was that perfect hardman. We knew we could depend on him to protect us while we were actually nickin' the money. Jimmy was fearless, reliable, strong and cold.'

The team being assembled by Chopper Knight had first worked as a unit two years earlier under two Scotsmen – Alex Sears and Sammy Benefield. They were the only survivors from the original gang. The idea was to run a group of robbers capable of operating nationwide from London to as far north as Dundee, in Scotland, and from Essex across to the Midlands.

Chopper Knight, 38, wasn't the overall 'Mr Big' as such because a hardcore committee of criminal faces financed and selected the jobs to be done, checked details of layout, security and then suggested the right men for the job. But Knight was the self-acclaimed general – the man who'd pull each job together.

Charles Roland Knight, aka 'Chopper', aka 'The General', aka 'Top Cat', had been robbing since the '60s. Short, well built and with a round, deadpan face that gave little away, Knight got his main nickname when his mother sent him into the garden every day when he was a child to chop wood. The former painter and decorator was such a good organiser that police later said he could have become a millionaire businessman if he'd used his talents more honestly. One detective recalled: 'Chopper was an unpretentious fellow who kept a really low profile. There was no flash car or flash house. God knows what he did with his money, but we never found any of it.'

Other robbers recruited by Chopper Knight included: John William Woodruff, 41, aka 'Big Bad John', who had a classic East End background. This lofty, softly spoken, mousy-haired former builder had been on the robbery scene for years, but had a weakness for 'going on the piss, smashing up boozers and then going back the next day to pay for the damage,' according to another member of the gang. Woodruff was given an eight-year sentence for what was one of the first-ever security van hold-ups in London's Shepherd's Bush in April 1968. When Woodruff got out of prison he headed straight for Chopper Knight's new team.

Then there was Jimmy Moody's great pal Tony Knightly, 36, a highly respected, experienced and utterly dependable villain. Knightly was a very sociable fellow whom, even the police admitted, 'was a good bloke to go and have a beer with'.

Bernie Khan, 34, was an East End robber with a difference: he was half Indian. Small, wiry, a cheeky chappy with an appetite for life, he and Knightly were the self-appointed 'technicians', the men who'd actually grab the loot while heavier characters like Moody waved their weapons in the air. Another gang member was Big John Woodall, 50. Woodall had not long been out of jail when he was recruited by Chopper. Woodall had been a big-name face once, so it was quite a come down for him to be back on the streets.

Scotsman Alex Sears was a driver with a penchant for rally driving. As one robber later recalled: 'Alex was obsessed by cars, especially those fast ones with fat wheels they use in Monte Carlo!'

Other robbers came in and out of the gang as it sparked terror and stole fortunes up and down the country, but these characters were the 'A-team'.

All jobs were meticulously planned during meetings in pubs and clubs where Moody and others often suggested new targets they'd seen on their travels. The team initially had one golden rule: try to pick the most isolated spot for the actual robbery, whether it's a moving target – a van – or at a factory. 'The quieter the better because then we knew the cops would take a lot longer getting there,' explained Bernie Khan.

Vehicles were the most vital preliminary tool for any big robbery and the gang went on to steal literally hundreds during their reign. A well-stocked arsenal of weapons was also essential. There was even a jester-like range of disguises, including ginger wigs, coloured spectacles, false beards and large moustaches. Some robbers said they'd even be prepared to dress up as women to confuse potential witnesses.

Moody and the gang's other strong-arm men were expected not to hesitate to fire their weapons – usually revolvers and shotguns – and would use sledgehammers, hammers and iron bars to shatter windscreens. Gang member Sammy Benefield provided the first arsenal of weapons by breaking into a gun shop in Ingrave, Essex, and stealing one Browning 12-bore semi-automatic shotgun, one Mossberg 12-bore shotgun, one Winchester 101 shotgun, one Manufrance perfex semi-automatic 12-bore shotgun, one Manufrance 12-bore pump-action shotgun, 1 Remington pump-action shotgun and 1 Savage 12-bore shotgun. Benefield and his associates had driven a stolen Cortina through the shop's front window and then dashed in and grabbed the weapons.

The gang also had a number of 'bent' security guards on side, including Brian McIntosh, who was employed by Security Express as a driver/custodian. One day he drove his car, in his uniform, into a repairs garage in the East End run by a man who knew Chopper Knight. The man told McIntosh he knew a bloke – Chopper – who could earn him some extra cash. McIntosh eventually had several meetings with both Chopper and Jimmy Moody. They slipped him £50 at every meeting 'for a drink' and to pay his phone bill so they could always be sure of contacting him. Then Moody and Chopper started pressing McIntosh for information about security van runs.

Initially, McIntosh fed the two villains false information. Then Chopper paid McIntosh's family a visit and the van driver changed his mind and started giving the gang valuable tips. McIntosh gave Moody and Knight details of security van movements which would eventually help the gang net at least £500,000.

Another 'friendly' security guard was Brian Upton, employed by Group 4. He was introduced to Chopper by an associate called Kenny Clark who shared his love of fishing – the two men had met when both were hooking up on a riverbank. In addition Clark knew that Upton was short of cash because he was funding an addiction to alcohol. Chopper and Jimmy Moody were soon putting the proverbial thumbscrews on Upton to supply routes, times and places involving his employer's vehicles. Upton was promised a percentage of the takings from any blaggings. When the team scooped £96,000 from one robbery, Upton was handed £3,000 by Chopper.

Jimmy Moody and eight members of the gang of robbers needed all their criminal skills and nerve for one of their first jobs together, which took place in the West Midlands in the winter of 1976.

The robbers – all wearing balaclavas – packed into three Land-Rovers and swept into the British Steel Corporation works on the outskirts of Bilston. The team then leapt out of their khaki-green ex-Army vehicles and, brandishing sawn-off shotguns, climbed the steps to the wages office two at a time.

Once inside the office, Moody and two gang members angled their weapons at the ceiling and peppered the office lights before two robbers demanded the wages. The two wages clerks didn't argue. The gang grabbed three big bags – containing a total of £70,000 – and headed back down the steps to the ground floor where the three drivers were revving up their getaway vehicles.

The nine-man team crashed into gear and headed towards the exit gates, having pulled off what they thought was the dream job. Just then, at least 50 angry workers appeared in front of the gates having decided no one had the right to deprive them of their hard-earned wages. They were armed with iron bars and were shutting the gates as the vehicles approached. Others stood, arms crossed defiantly, aggressively slapping their palms with those iron bars.

'Fuckin' mad Brummie bastards,' muttered one of the blaggers.

The team screeched to a halt and Jimmy Moody angrily got out of the first Land-Rover.

'Get the fuck outta here unless you want some of this!' yelled Moody, waving his sawn-off in their direction.

'We want our fuckin' wages back!' screamed one steel worker, smashing a pipe on the exit gate to make his point.

'I said open the fuckin' gate now!' bellowed Moody, whose voice was by now shaking with rage.

'Bugger off! We'll fuckin' 'ave the lot o' you!' Another two workers smashed steel pipes onto the gates.

This last act of defiance was too much for Jimmy Moody to tolerate. He swung his sawn-off up with both hands and the butt pressed into his shoulder. 'You really want some of this?' he asked, taking aim.

'You ain't got the bottle!' sneered the foreman.

Moody took a deep breath as his finger stroked the trigger.

Two other gang members moved alongside him and also aimed their weapons at the steelworkers.

'This is yer last fuckin' warning,' screamed Moody.

There was still no response. The two other hooded robbers looked at Moody for a split second, waiting for him to lead the way. In Moody's view they had to stand their ground or else they'd get massacred – and lose the money. He said later there was no choice in the matter.

Moody closed his left eye and took aim with his Remington pump action. Right in his line of fire was the man who'd first challenged them. Moody squeezed tight and let go with one almighty shot that thundered across the forecourt. His target crumpled to the floor. Just then the two other armed blaggers let off two shots each. At least three more steel workers fell to the ground as others ran for cover.

Moody turned towards the man and said calmly, 'That enough for you?'

Moody stared into the eyes of the crowd of steel workers in front of him.

'Now open the gates, you bunch of fuckin' wankers.'

As the gates were opened. Moody and the team jumped back in their Land-Rovers.

The robbers drove through the gates and noticed at least four of the steel workers clutching their stomachs. Moody later admitted that two of the injured looked 'as if they might kop it'.

'Fuckin' stupid bastards. They'd have got their fuckin' wages in the end. Didn't have to hurt no one,' Moody later told one associate.

Jimmy Moody always regretted being involved in the steel works robbery because he knew he'd have got a very heavy sentence if the police ever pinned that job on him. One old associate recalled: 'He knew that the law would have come down really hard on him. That job was a bloodbath.'

Less than a mile down the road from the steel works, the team dumped one of the Land-Rovers after it broke down. Later at a safe house in the same area, the team leader split the money and insisted someone would have to go back the following day and pick up the Land-Rover in case it provided police with forensic evidence. Moody later said going back was 'really hairy' because by then a helicopter was up searching the area for the robbers. Moody and another gang member eventually fixed the Land-Rover and drove it back to the safe house 30 miles away.

The steel works robbery proved that Moody and his team of bandits were prepared to travel far and wide to commit crimes if the quality of their information was good. It was to be the key to the gang's success. Moody told one old associate: 'It's fuckin' incredible. We're gettin' info from these bent security van drivers about deliveries all over the country.' The whole of Britain was a potential target. If one security driver told them that on a Thursday there was a particular pick-up with a certain amount of cash, they'd travel to the location, check it out carefully and then pull off the robbery.

Moody and Chopper Knight always warned the gang before every job not to get over confident because that could spell disaster. They insisted the success of every robbery was in the planning: 'How you prepare for a robbery is as important as anythin'. Have a plan. Rehearse it,' Chopper always told his team before they struck. 'Think through every detail.'

But it was a robbery in the Blackwall Tunnel on 29 September 1977 that made Scotland Yard really sit up and take notice of the gang. This job was a huge boost to Jimmy Moody's underworld reputation because he dressed up as a policeman to hold back the traffic. Moody's bravado brought the following reaction from a lawyer who later defended him in court: 'Those were the days when an awful lot of policemen came from the same background as the villains they were chasing. It was hard to tell the Flying Squad guy and the armed robber apart, and Jim made a very plausible copper!'

In the Blackwall Tunnel raid 'PC' Moody created a gap in the traffic and forced a security van to stop just past the bend, about two-thirds of the way into the tunnel. At the same time, two of the robbers staged a crash behind them to block the tunnel just before the bend. The gang used three stolen cars and a stolen van to surround the security wagon. The team had done their homework because once inside the tunnel, the security van's radio was useless.

'PC' Moody then leapt out of his car and 'confiscated', at gunpoint, the keys of several motorists behind them in the tunnel so they couldn't drive off and raise the alarm. The underworld loved such subtle touches; Jimmy Moody seemed unstoppable. There were even rumours a detective had provided the police uniforms for the job. Other officers were later rumoured to have been given 'payoffs' from the takings of the Blackwall Tunnel job to ensure the robbers weren't apprehended.

Three of the gang – including Moody – were armed with sawn-offs, one with a pistol and another with an axe, which was used to smash the security van window to force the crew to cooperate. But what few villains mentioned was that Jimmy Moody attacked the custodian of the money and felled him with a shotgun butt during the job. The man was so badly injured that he ended up drawing a disability pension.

The Blackwall Tunnel job provided Jimmy Moody and his teammates with a new four-letter word, which summed it all up – the *buzz*. As one of the robbers later explained: 'The buzz on that job was better than any drugs. All that adrenalin pumping through you was fuckin' incredible and the feelin' of elation once you'd snatched that cash was out of this world.'

The transfer of the money into the getaway vehicle had to be done with precision timing because the longer it took, the more likely the police would arrive and nobody wanted a shootout. One robber described the Blackwall Tunnel job: 'As we got into the back of the security van I asked myself why was I putting myself through all this shit? Nerves, fear, excitement, all combined. Earlier, the worst period had been waitin' for the van that you're gonna rob to turn up. You think everyone's lookin' at you because you're standin' around on a warm day with gloves on. One fingerprint and you've had it. But once the job started it was fuckin' beautiful. It was a feelin' I can't put into words. First my eyes went watery and supersensitive to light. Then I got that little "ping" and that's when it really all kicked in; that feelin' of complete and utter invincibility. Then the security vehicle – the target – finally turned up. All of a sudden we're in for the kill. The minute you go for it your body relaxes. It's happenin'. At that moment I felt so strong I could have picked up that van and run along the road with it. Next thing you're lookin inside that bag at the cash and that's fuckin' beautiful.'

The gang escaped from the Blackwall Tunnel that day with almost £100,000 in wage packets that had been destined for the Greenwich group of hospitals. Only a small fraction of the cash was ever recovered. Once the money was divided up at a flophouse within hours of the crime being committed, the team made a point of going their separate ways. Gang member Bernie Khan explained: 'That was how it happened. I knew I wouldn't see any of them for another month. We weren't big mates or anythin' like that. It was better that way. They didn't know where I went and I didn't know where they went. There was no conversation about it. Greed was the only thing that came into it. Get yer money and fuck off.'

But the line between Moody's home and criminal lives was blurring. Just after Moody pulled off the Blackwall Tunnel job, daughter Janine, aged ten, was walking along an East End High Street with her mother when they saw the headlines at a newstand.

'Good luck to 'em,' muttered Janine.

She later recalled: 'I didn't even know it was my dad who'd carried out that job, but I had a hunch. In any case, our attitude in the East End was to wish good luck to any team that had pulled off a big job.'

That was the way it was.

TEN

Secret Weapon

Around this time Jimmy Moody completely dropped any pretense about what he did in front of his wife and children. A classic example was when Moody walked into the bedroom at their flat in Hackney and asked Val, straight faced, if she had any tights he could use. 'He took two pairs but never said what he needed them for,' explained Val. 'But when a man takes your tights and he's a robber it's pretty obvious.' The following day, Val and the children saw a television news report about a robbery and immediately knew Moody was involved.

Jimmy Moody even started asking his 13-year-old son Jason to clean his guns for him. Explained Jason: 'Obviously I knew what he needed them for, but like Mum I didn't think it was my right to ask too many questions, although I felt as if he was giving me his stamp of approval by allowing me to clean his guns.'

Naturally, Moody's wife Val saw it in a different way. She explained: 'You know how a normal man would come home from work and his wife would go "How has your day been, darlin'?" Well Jimmy would come in and answer, "We just robbed a bank today, darlin'. It was fuckin' brilliant! I copped loadsa money."'

Jimmy Moody might have been ducking and diving between safe houses in south and east London and his family home, but that didn't stop him keeping up his fanatical keep-fit campaign. In the mid-'70s, Moody even took up the ancient art of ju-jitsu. Jason recalled: 'A bunch of them used to go to the hall in the Old Kent Road and train together when everyone else had gone home. He also did unarmed combat.'

'Rambo' Moody also bought a caravan on the south coast and equipped it with a makeshift mini-gym. He then took up scuba-diving. Moody was also careful to keep to his pledge not to touch spirits again: his alcohol intake had dropped significantly from those far-off days with the Richardsons.

But not every job the gang touched turned to instant gold. Their next robbery was at a mill on the Lea Bridge Road, in east London, where they planned to hold up a security van delivering at least £100,000 in wages. Chopper, Moody and the rest of the team, armed with shotguns, sat tight in two vehicles and waited for the van to show up one grey afternoon in the early winter of 1977. When the vehicle finally appeared, it stopped nearly 300 yards away from the delivery point they'd been told about. The gang looked at each other for a moment before driving their cars in for a hijack, but by the time they got to the van the guards had driven off without even realising how close they'd come to being robbed.

When the gang attempted to hold up a security van at the Car Park Auto Stop Café, at 113 Cambridge Road, near Wimpole, in Cambridgeshire, a quick-thinking van custodian spotted the team swooping from a parked furniture van and saved the cash by throwing the keys into some bushes. Chopper Knight immediately realised it was a waste of time trying to break into the van and abandoned the operation.

Meanwhile, the Flying Squad were growing deeply frustrated by their apparent inability to even identify members of the Thursday Gang, as they'd been dubbed in the tabloids. Sweeney detective Charlie Snape later explained: 'They were takin' the fuckin' mickey and gettin' away with it. Something had to be done.'

On 6 December 1977, Sussex detectives visited Canterbury Prison in Kent to interview a man known only as 'MB' about a series of burglaries committed in Brighton. The prisoner immediately asked to speak to Flying Squad officer Charlie Snape. The following day, the man told Snape he'd heard two other prisoners, Terry Read and David Bale, boasting about several big 'jobs' they'd pulled off.

Both men bragged about a post-office robbery in Rochester, Kent, and the Blackwall Tunnel job. MB also named senior gang members as Knight, Benefield, Moody, Sears and Woodruff. It was a major breakthrough for the Flying Squad. Informant MB later made a full statement and gave evidence on oath at three subsequent trials. Later that same month – December 1977 – MB pleaded guilty to numerous burglary offences at Maidstone Crown Court and was jailed for five years.

Charlie Snape quickly established that many of the suspects were enjoying a high standard of living, with large expensive cars, caravans, speedboats and even luxury yachts. Yet two were still drawing social-security benefit. Others spent thousands of pounds on holidays abroad staying in five-star hotels. But detectives knew they needed more substantial evidence and that would probably only come from a grass.

The Yard's biggest initial problem was that many of the gang's names had already been linked to robberies they hadn't actually committed. A vindictive wife of one of the team had claimed to police that virtually every job committed in the south-east at that time was by the gang. This including a blagging in Kingston, Surrey, an attack on a Group 4 security van in Mitcham, Surrey – where a guard was killed – and another robbery when three men armed with shotguns and a pistol shot and killed a security guard in a £90,000 raid on the London headquarters of building contractor J. Murphy's.

Detective Charlie Snape explained: 'Some officers from a county force insisted these jobs were done by Chopper Knight's team. That really cocked our investigation up because we were just getting started and now other forces were trying to turn over our team – which was the last thing we wanted at that stage. Eventually they nicked another gang which I'd originally given them for those jobs.'

Charlie Snape and his Flying Squad colleagues also stepped up their unofficial surveillance work on gang members. One detective later explained: 'We intercepted all their movements. We tapped their phones. We got an intercept on an address for Moody but he'd gone by the time we got there. I'd never met Moody by this time, but he was so well known to all of us that his picture didn't even have to be up on a board because we all knew what he looked like.'

The Flying Squad travelled hundreds of miles to different parts of Britain to discuss past raids with detectives and speak to witnesses. They also noticed that several members of the gang disappeared to Spain a day or two after every robbery. Other members of the gang led respectable middle-class lives playing golf, drinking at their local and tipping their cap at their suburban neighbours. One of the gang even boasted he had a Scotland Yard detective as his golfing partner. A later investigation by police cleared the officer of any improper conduct.

Towards the end of 1977, Jimmy Moody and Chopper Knight held an 'emergency meeting' with most of the team in The Paxton Arms pub in Crystal Palace, south London. It was a risky undertaking to bring the team together in one place, but Knight and Moody felt it was imperative to discuss certain issues well away from their usual haunts.

After those two disasters at Lea Bridge Road and in Cambridgeshire, Knight and Moody knew they needed to devise a method of robbing that would mean there would be no need for the custodian's keys to even be used. Knight, Moody and the rest of the team compared security vans to sardine cans – both difficult to open without a key. So they came up with the ideal solution: a chainsaw. Thus was born the Chainsaw Gang. 'It was the same principal as a tin opener,' explained team member Bernie Khan. 'Just as long as we knew exactly what part of the van had the money, then we'd just fire the chainsaw up and start cutting. Fuck the keys. We wouldn't even need them.' Chopper and the gang also knew that pulling out a chainsaw would scare security van staff and make them instantly more cooperative.

Pint-sized Khan and Moody's closest pal Tony Knightly would handle the chainsaw itself. 'But we had to have hardmen like Jimmy Moody covering our backs,' recalled Khan. 'They were our eyes and our ears.' It was ten years since Bernie Khan had first met Jimmy Moody through Charlie Richardson, but by the time they both joined the same team of robbers they were mixing in different circles. 'That was good for security,' explained Khan. 'If the Old Bill saw us comin' out the pub together all the time then they'd soon be on to us.' Bernie Khan was so low-key he was the only member of the gang whom the police knew nothing about.

Meanwhile, Chopper and Moody told the team in The Paxton Arms they would 'persuade' security-van source Brian McIntosh to draw the exact interior of a Security Express vehicle, highlighting where the safe was located. Once the new method of robbing had been devised, Chopper Knight told the team that he was prepared to wait it out until the perfect job came along – Knight only wanted to target vans carrying more than £200,000.

At the Paxton Arms meeting, Jimmy Moody was increasingly irritated with the way fellow gang member Sammy Benefield was staring at him as they discussed the chainsaw. Moody later told a detective: 'It was really gettin' on my nerves. I knew the moment I looked in his eyes somethin' was happenin'.'

Moody was so disturbed by Benefield's behaviour that he insisted on speaking to Chopper Knight in a different part of the bar.

'That Benefield's fuckin' gonna grass us up,' spat Moody.

'Don't be fuckin' silly, Jim,' responded Knight, unsure how seriously to take Moody's outburst.

'I know it, Chopper. I fuckin' know it.'

They went back to the rest of the gang, but Moody didn't utter another word throughout the meeting, which lasted another half an hour.

Moody's instincts were correct. Shortly after that meeting, two of the gang – Benefield and Segars – confided in their families that if they were ever arrested they'd make a deal and grass up their comrades. The two were embittered about being deprived of what they saw as legitimate expenses and distrusted other members of the gang. They also feared they'd be looking at 20-year sentences if they did get caught. Chopper Knight had already dropped another gang member because of fears his common-law wife was a police informant.

The relationship between the gang members also wasn't helped when Chopper decided to hit another security van going through his favourite Blackwall Tunnel on Saturday, 4 March 1978. One gang member explained: 'It seemed crazy to pull another blaggin' in the tunnel, but Chopper was adamant that he had good info so off we went.'

The job was a disaster when the chainsaw failed to fire up because no one had remembered to charge it properly before the job. The gang gave up after five minutes and left the scene in a stolen Sherpa van. Ironically, they later discovered the security van had already dropped off its load of cash so there was nothing on board to steal.

The botched Blackwall Tunnel raid deeply frustrated Flying Squad detective Charlie Snape – who'd been divisional detective superintendent at Greenwich Police Station when the original Blackwall Tunnel job was carried out on his patch in September 1977. The job had been committed on his doorstep yet no one had even got a whisper that it was in the pipeline. It was clear to Snape that the vast scale of the Flying Squad investigation into the gang meant that it was coming up against inter-police force problems. *Too many cooks really were spoiling the broth*. Charlie Snape believed the only way to catch the gang was to create one special unit targeted at the robbers.

On 1 June 1978, the police held a conference at Hatfield Police Station, Hertfordshire, where it was unanimously agreed that a joint force should be formed. Senior officers present that day included police from forces in Cleveland, Berkhampstead, Birmingham and the Met.

Codenamed Operation Ohio, 73 crime squad officers – helped by Scotland Yard's Central Robbery Squad – would work around the clock to bring Chopper Knight and his team to justice.

Snape was to head up Operation Ohio with Detective Chief Inspector Peter Humphrey as his deputy. Snape knew all about Jimmy Moody from when he was a detective constable at Deptford Police Station and the investigation into the Mr Smith's shootout. Snape was also aware of Jimmy Moody's other reputation – as a contract killer.

The Operation Ohio squad set up headquarters at Westcombe Park Police Station on the south side of the Blackwall Tunnel, allowing easy access to east London, where many of the gang were based. One of the other senior officers involved was Detective Chief Inspector Bill Forman, an operational command leader from the Met. He explained: 'We were deadly serious about catching this team. I'd come across a few of them down the years but they had to be stopped – permanently.' Soon logs, photographs, messages, statements and other info began coming in to Operation Ohio. Detectives collated information, manned static observation posts and watched properties round-the-clock.

Without such intelligence they didn't stand a realistic chance of ever bringing Moody and the rest of the gang to justice. Photographs of most criminals were at this time well out of date. As Forman recalled: 'Clothing was changing constantly. Hairstyles were changing. A lot of blokes started wearing moustaches. And we were often working with descriptions of robbers which were 15 years out of date. The key was observation. Get a photo. Something that would identify the bad guys. It was our lifeblood. Without it we didn't stand a chance.'

Forman was a classic copper's copper. A brittle Scotsman from Peterhead, married with two daughters, he'd started his working life as a fisherman and then – just like Jimmy Moody and Charlie Snape – joined the merchant navy before signing up with the Metropolitan Police in 1956. He went on to serve at various stations including Bow Street, King's Cross, Paddington, Southwark, Old Street, Battersea and in the Flying Squad's Regional Crime Squad.

Bill Forman had first heard of Jimmy Moody at the end of 1976 when the gang struck on Forman's patch in central London and his name was put up by one of Forman's best informants. But Forman had other, even more sinister, elements to contend with. He explained: 'There were leakages galore coming out of the Flying Squad at the time, which meant we couldn't even trust our own colleagues.'

Operation Ohio's first big observation point was a transport yard just beyond the north approach to the Blackwall Tunnel, run by a local man called Vic Huckle. Detectives knew that suspected gang member Alex Sears had invested much of his robbery money in the business and it was also believed that the team sometimes held meetings at the yard.

Another police observation point was at 146 Hedge Lane, Tottenham, north London, home of Vivien Minchington, common-law wife of Alex Sears and ex-wife of John Minchington, aka Johnny the Bosh, who'd recently been sentenced to 23 years for the Bank of America robbery in London's West End. There were also surveillance teams at addresses linked to Moody, Knight and Benefield.

However, Forman's fears about 'leakages' from within the police were soon realised when some of the gang made it clear they knew about Operation Ohio's undercover activities. At one stage, Alex Sears got out a pair of binoculars and spied back at his police shadows watching him from 400 yards away near the yard at the Blackwall Tunnel. Sears later told detectives their squad was 'leaking like a fuckin' sieve'.

Yet despite this, police photographed numerous criminals visiting Huckle's yard, including characters with such illuminating nicknames as Beer Belly, Ski Nose, Strawberry Nose, Gimpy, 'issing Pete, and Bone Head. But Sears was the only member of the Chainsaw gang pictured at the yard.

The most difficult subject of all to follow was Jimmy Moody. Operation Ohio chief Charlie Snape explained: 'We knew who he associated with, but what made Moody difficult to deal with was the fact that he was a bit of a loner and very difficult to pin down to any particular address. He was also ultra cautious whenever he visited any friends, family or associates. He never took a straight line to anywhere and would deviate just to confuse us. Then he'd call associates using false voices. He seemed to get off on giving those sort of performances and you couldn't help admiring the way he did it.'

Jimmy Moody seriously considered buying a house near his beloved Solent, in Hampshire, in the mid-'70s. He already had two mobile homes down in the same area. 'One of them was his spare home which nobody, not even his family, knew about,' explained one old friend. 'But that was typical Jim, always covering himself, always with a plan in case everything went pear shaped.'

Moody also kept an inflatable boat with a high-powered outboard engine and many hundreds of pounds worth of deep-sea diving gear at the two caravans. Moody adored diving because it was a form of escape for him. He liked the way that sensations we all take for granted on land were suddenly meaningless when you slipped below the surface for a dive. Divers cannot rely on fundamentals like the ground and the horizon to judge posture and balance. That feeling of disorientation under water sometimes left him not knowing what direction was up or down. But he liked that sense of loss of control because most of his life had been spent controlling every movement in order to survive.

Moody would sit, facing inwards, on the edge of his inflatable dinghy, fully equipped and dressed for a serious dive. One last check on his air would be made. Then he would place one hand over his mask to keep it from being dislodged and with his other hand grab the harness to prevent the cylinder riding up and striking him on the back of the head. Then, he'd take one last glance to make sure the water was unobstructed, tuck his head forward on his chest and roll backwards into the water.

Once in the water, Moody would start a gradual descent using the initial few metres to equalise, adjusting his body's pressure to that of the water around him. Once on the bottom he was careful not to over-swim. Diving in open-water conditions demanded a rigid code of personal discipline and managing by touch alone was a real challenge to Jimmy Moody in the dark depths of the Solent. His imaginative mind thrived in such an environment. He'd also learned to be aware of and use 'kinaesthesia' – the sensations that were stimulated by movement, body posture and the perception of weight. Even in the pitch dark, Moody managed to perform complicated movements and delight in weightlessness. Diving into hostile environments was nothing new for him.

Moody and his close friend and Chainsaw Gang member Tony Knightly often loaded up a crate of beers and headed off on his boat to the Isle of Wight for a break. They'd stop at quiet little spots, have a meal at a local pub and then move on to do some diving off the deepest points. The two men had both served in prisons on the island and particularly enjoyed their freedom so close to the very places where they were once locked up.

During one of these trips across the Solent, Moody and Knightly encountered the *QE2* cruise liner. 'The minute they saw that ship they thought about blagging it,' explained son Jason Moody. 'It was like the old man just spotted it and thought, "Hello, we're gonna have that."'

Moody pulled up his inflatable as the huge ship came into view, turned to Knightly and winked. 'Now that's what I call a real job.' Knightly laughed, but he knew Jimmy Moody was serious.

Jason later explained: 'As they circled the ship a few times they couldn't stop thinking about how to rob it. The old man said it was really great to feel he had the power and confidence to consider such an outrageous blagging.'

Over the following few days, Moody and Knightly did their homework on the *QE2*, determined to turn their dream into a reality. Moody discovered there was a £1 million float of cash taken on board before every cruise. And that didn't count the cash needed for the ship's casino. As Moody told Knightly at the time: 'It's a fuckin' goldmine, son. We gotta have a pop at it.'

Moody's brother Dickie recalled that he made a point of mentioning the *QE2* to him as well. 'He had it earmarked as the perfect job, the one that would give him enough money to retire.'

Moody reported back to Chopper Knight about the ship's 'potential'. Knight reckoned it would take 15 highly trained pro's to pull off the job. They'd be armed to the teeth with Knight himself even packing a Sten gun. Moody, Knight and Knightly visited the docks and watched security vans delivering money in British and foreign currency to the liner before she sailed on a cruise. Chopper Knight decided that robbing the van crew just before they boarded the ship would 'be a piece of cake'. He believed that they'd scoop a minimum of one million pounds.

It wasn't just the *QE2* that Jimmy Moody had his sights set on, however. In the more familiar territory of Loughton, Essex, lay another potentially massive haul. Jason remembered: 'One Sunday the old man took me and Janine for a day out. First we went to a pub so he could down a couple of pints while we had the usual Coke and a packet of crisps. Then we headed to a nearby country field which backed onto this big industrial estate. The old man described it as a prime job and we both knew what that meant. Anyway, he parked the car – I think it was a Granada – at the end of this deserted country lane, which backed onto the industrial estate. I had this huge pair of binoculars around my neck and he was holding me and my sister's hands so we looked like a happy family out in the countryside, bird spotting.

'Anyway as we got closer I noticed all this razor-sharp barbed wire wrapped around the perimeter of one particular warehouse. Suddenly the old man leans down and looks through those heavy binoculars while they're still around my neck. That was what Janine would call "Daddy going to work". After a couple of minutes studying his target the old man let them drop back round my neck and said, "That's where they burn loads and loads of money and Daddy's goin' to get it all one day."

Turned out it was the place where they burned all the old Bank of England notes.'

Moody and Knight discussed a number of other 'retirement jobs' they hoped would bring in enough money for them to give up their lives of crime altogether. One was dubbed 'The Great Plane Robbery'. Moody heard how a private plane was hired once a month to fly all over Britain picking up Scottish banknotes, which were then taken back to Edinburgh. 'The idea was to hijack the plane after it had picked up what was always at least £1.5 million,' explained one of Moody's oldest associates. It later emerged that the gang intended to recruit the pilot of the Scottish currency airplane. The plan was to take it over after it left a small London airfield and then collect all the other money before stealing the cash. Chopper realised that the Scottish notes would be more difficult to spend in England so he even arranged for the Scottish cash to be kept hidden for about a year before being 'sold' to a Scottish money launderer.

Around this time, Jason Moody noticed his father was being extra careful about where he travelled and avoided being spotted in certain places. Jason recalled: 'He was obsessed with always sitting with his back to the wall in any restaurant and liked to be near enough to the window to always see who was comin' in. His eyes would dart all over the place, examinin' people's faces, checkin' them out in case they were cozzers.'

Jimmy Moody's attitude was: 'You can never be too careful.'

ELEVEN

Taking the Mickey

In mid-July 1978, the gang's Security Express informant Brian McIntosh told Chopper Knight that each week a company van picked up cash from a bank in the leafy town of Banstead, Surrey, and headed back to London via a main road called Sutton Lane. McIntosh reckoned the van always carried at least £250,000 in cash. This was just the type of big-money job Knight and Moody were after, especially since they now used chainsaws, which could cut open any armoured van 'like butter'.

In early August, Moody's children Jason and Janine found themselves sitting with their father in his Ford Granada watching the home of the Banstead Security Express van driver. Jason recalled: 'The driver had parked his wagon outside his house to have lunch. The old man whipped out his favourite binoculars and waited for him to come out.' Moody noted down the relevant times and locations as he and his two children followed the security van driver as he picked up his colleague, collected money from a bank in Banstead and finally drove down Sutton Lane towards London. When the children asked a couple of awkward questions, they got a stern warning from their father: 'Don't you tell a fuckin' soul about this, specially not the law. You understand?' Then Moody chuckled. The kids smiled nervously.

The following day, Jimmy Moody met with Chopper Knight and the rest of the gang and told them about the van driver's precise movements. Then, a week before the scheduled robbery, the gang bought a van at an auction and practised their chainsaw cutting techniques in an abandoned garage in east London. Team member Bernie Khan recalled:

'It wasn't exactly the same kind of van, but it had similar metal sides. We knew how big the bags of money were so we cut the holes just the right size. We'd thought about all this very carefully. We knew the van had an outside skin and once you got past that you got to the safe.'

Chopper Knight and Jimmy Moody then organised the theft of seven 'nicked to order' vehicles, which they moved around various locations in east and south London to make sure no one tracked them down before the day of the robbery. All the cars had been stolen using a special screwdriver with a barrel – known as a 'donka'. Bernie Khan recalled: 'Chopper loved nickin' cars. It was all like a big chess game to him. Movin' them around from place to place, having his plan and sticking to it.'

Two days later the team arrived in Banstead – just as the Security Express van driver was leaving the bank an hour earlier than scheduled. The robbery was put on ice. Chopper Knight assured his gang this was nothing more than a temporary setback and immediately drew up a new set of plans to accommodate the time changes. 'We'll still do it inside the next week,' he told his men. Bernie Khan explained: 'Chopper knew exactly what he was doing and we trusted him implicitly. He was the perfect pro and this was nothing more than a temporary setback.'

On the evening of 14 August 1978, Jimmy Moody called in at Val's parents' home in Poplar to see his family as he always tried to do before a job. 'He did it because he wasn't sure if he'd ever see us again. It was a sort of good-luck thing,' explained son Jason. Moody's ten-year-old daughter Janine even made her daddy a packed lunch to take with him to work the next morning. 'It was his favourite: cabbage sandwiches,' Janine later recalled. 'I made them really carefully for him. Then next morning I waved him off when he left early.'

That morning – 15 August 1978 – Jimmy Moody, Chopper Knight, Bernie Khan and the rest of the nine-man team met at Moody's flat in Hackney, which was the gang's 'out' (safe house) for the job. Chopper gave his men a final briefing before they all left the flat separately – at one-minute intervals – to head for the stolen vehicles, parked in pre-designated spots within a few hundred yards of the flat.

Bernie Khan found himself driving a Ford Escort in a six-vehicle convoy as it headed across the river and into the south London suburbs en route to Banstead. Khan explained: 'I was drivin' alone and wearing a boiler suit. I could see the boys in their motors in front of and behind me. It was quite a turn-out, but we kept our distance from each other so no one realised we were in convoy.'

Then Khan was caught at a red traffic light. 'Suddenly there's a siren and I see the police in my rear view mirror. I thought, fuck it, my time's up. I'm gonna get a pull.' Khan pulled his car over, got out and waited for the police.

Khan's teammates watched what happened from a safe distance. 'I had enough equipment on me to get convicted for goin' to rob,' explained Khan. 'I was a gonner.' The police car floated right past Bernie Khan without giving him a second glance. 'I couldn't fuckin' believe it,' recalled Khan. 'They didn't even look at me.' It was all a false alarm. Khan got back in the Escort and the robber's convoy continued.

Eventually the gang stopped next to a small forest on the outskirts of Banstead, on the Sutton Road, right in the heart of the Surrey countryside. Khan recalled: 'We was early so we set the motors up in their right positions.'

Over in Banstead, two of the robbers' vehicles were shadowing the Security Express van from the moment it left the bank in the High Street. Khan explained: 'We picked it up at the bank at around 11. We had a car in front and a car behind the van.'

Less than a mile out of Banstead the car in front of the security van put on its right blinker so that the van had to slow down. Bernie Khan explained: 'Now the van's caught in the middle and having to slow down. Then another of our cars being driven by Jimmy Moody pulls out of a side turning to stop all the traffic behind the security van.'

Just then the robbers' own Sherpa van – covered in dents to make it look as if it had been in an accident – pulled out of another nearby lane and screeched to a halt alongside the Security Express vehicle. Three robbers with sawn-offs emerged, surrounded the van and blew its tyres out with their weapons. Khan recalled: 'Then I jumped out with all our tools. We'd already warmed the chainsaw up earlier that morning because sometimes they didn't start easily.' All the men were wearing flesh-coloured latex gloves and a variety of masks and helmets. Chopper Knight got out of a Ford Granada and stood to attention with a stopwatch in his hand. Pressing the button he said: 'Three minutes, gentlemen.'

Chopper knew only too well they had to get the cash and move *very* quickly. Perhaps surprisingly, at least three of the robbers – Khan, Knight and Knightly – were not even armed. Khan later explained: 'That wasn't our job. Jim and the others were the hired guns, not us.'

On the other side of the Security Express van, gang member Sammy Benefield waved a sawn-off at the driver and his mate as he dragged them onto the grass verge. Benefield then stood over them with his weapon.

Team leader Chopper Knight stood, arms folded, watching the entire proceedings and keeping an eye out for any unforeseen problems. 'That clock of his was fuckin' tickin' away inside all our heads,' recalled Bernie Khan.

Jimmy Moody was holding up traffic and covering the back of the security van at the same time. He was wearing his favourite policeman's uniform, complete with a white helmet. Khan explained: 'Jimmy could see behind us and in all directions. He was crucial.'

By this time Khan had pulled his cutting goggles over his balaclava and he and Tony Knightly got down to work. 'We've got all the gear on,' recalled Khan. 'We look well professional and that fuckin' grinder is makin' a hell of a racket.' The security van staff looked terrified when Khan fired up his chainsaw. 'As we're cuttin' away there's lots of smoke 'n' noise.'

Bernie Khan recalled the Banstead job in almost reverential terms. 'We had the whole road blocked off. It was masterful, a piece of art in a way. Everythin' went like clockwork.' And the star of the show wasn't Jimmy Moody, Chopper Knight or any of the rest of the team, it was that chainsaw ripping open the side of the security van like it was a can of sardines.

Bernie Khan never forgot the image of Jimmy Moody dressed as a policeman ordering traffic to stop while he and Knightly got to work. 'Jim was standing there in his Old Bill uniform lookin' just the part. Only difference was he had a pump [shotgun] under his arm. Wearin' that uniform was a brilliant idea 'cause it definitely impressed a lot of people. All them motorists just sat quietly. No one questioned us. Jim looked big and was holding that shooter [gun] like it was official.'

'Two minutes, thirty seconds,' bellowed Chopper to his men.

Khan was still cutting away at the outer skin of the van. He explained: 'The hole had to be big enough to get those money bags out. It was a precision cut.'

Gang member John Segars remained on lookout in the driver's seat of another back-up car parked alongside the security van. Just then one of the security van guards tried to get up from the grass verge where they'd been ordered to lie. Segars jumped from his vehicle and panned his sawn-off into the air. 'Don't fuckin' move!'

The van driver ignored the order.

Segars let off a warning shot and the driver dived back onto the ground.

Two minutes!' screamed Chopper Knight, consulting his stopwatch and completely ignoring the incident.

Khan explained: 'That's when I got through the outer skin and was trying to bend it open so we could get into the cash. I remember turning to see if everything else was all right. I saw Jim waving at the traffic jam behind us. What a fuckin' impressive sight he was.'

'One and a half!' shouted Chopper.

Khan and Knightly then started pulling the money bags out of the van and transferring them straight to the robber's van. They later discovered there was £25,000 in each bag.

As the last minute started counting down, the team upped the pace and formed a chain to get the bags out more quickly. Khan recalled: 'It just went on and on. We didn't realise there was so much fuckin' money in that van.' Forty bags in total were thrown in the back of the robber's van.

Behind them, Jimmy Moody continued waving his sawn-off in the direction of an increasingly irate group of motorists.

'Go! Go! Go!' screamed Chopper before blowing his football ref's whistle at full pelt just in case anyone hadn't heard him. The nine robbers piled into three vehicles, leaving three other cars behind.

The gang were careful not to exceed the 30 mph speed limit as they drove away from the scene of the robbery. Bernie Khan explained: 'We were keeping a low profile. Everyone was lookin' for motors screeching up the road like they'd seen on films. But we didn't do that. No one noticed us and we never even heard a siren.'

The gang had earmarked a barn near the local hospital where they were going to swap vehicles. Chopper had even insisted on them putting their own padlock on the barn so no one else could get into it. Khan explained: 'The motor was bumping around on a narrow lane. I'm sitting there opposite Segars and Benefield with Jim right at the back of the van. There were two others up front. Then we went over these sleepin' policemen and it got really bumpy.'

Suddenly there was an almighty explosion. Khan recalled: 'This sawn-off in Segars' hand went off and the shot skimmed my ear leaving a huge fuckin' hole in the side of the van.'

There was stunned silence in the back of the van as Khan and Segars looked at each other.

'What the fuckin' hell you doin?' asked Khan.

Segars looked embarrassed and clambered into the front of the van without uttering a word.

Bernie Khan insisted: 'I was nearly killed by John Segars. No two ways about it. If I'd been further away the shot would have spread and finished me off.'

The robbers' first vehicle then nudged open the gates to a field just ahead of their drop point. Segars jumped out and shut the gate behind them before they headed down a dirt track. At the barn, they transferred their loot into three stolen Fords before heading back into London.

Jimmy Moody, with John Segars sitting alongside him, drove a metallic green Granada through the suburbs of south London. In the boot were sack loads of money, guns and the chainsaw. Moody ducked down when a police car with its siren going and blue light flashing passed in the opposite direction. Segars later recalled: 'My fuckin' bottle went when I saw that cop car and I told Jim.' Moody was appalled by what he saw as Segars' cowardly behaviour and ordered him out of the car to cool down. He told Segars to meet the gang at the 'out' later that afternoon.

Segars went into the nearest pub, bought a large brandy and a pint of bitter. When he put his hand into his pocket to pay for the drinks he felt a spent cartridge case which he'd earlier put in his pocket after discharging it during the robbery. He later hid it behind the pub toilet.

At 6 p.m. on the evening of the Banstead robbery, nearly 40 bags of cash containing a total of almost £700,000 were carried up to Jimmy Moody's flat at 38 Lexfield Court, Pownall Road, in Hackney, in a plastic body bag with a zipper down the front. Bernie Khan recalled: 'We arrived in the three motors and lugged the cash up the stairs over our shoulders. We were all fuckin' knackered. The old buzz had long since gone.'

When Khan walked into Moody's flat he was astonished to see that Moody's 13-year-old son Jason was already there. Khan explained: 'Jason just sat there watchin' us, which was really out of order because there shouldn't have been anyone else in that 'out'. But no one dared have a go at Jim because we was all shit scared of him.'

Then John Segars turned up with his Saluki dog to claim his share. Instead he was immediately told by dog-hater Moody to 'fuck off and come back without yer mutt'. Jimmy Moody hated Segars more by the minute and had no doubt he was a potential grass.

Chopper Knight then discovered the team had left at least five bags in the van, which was still parked outside. Two gang members were sent out to bring them in. After they returned Chopper ordered the team to strip to their underpants to avoid leaving any forensic clues on their clothing, but the gang were allowed to put their clothes back on before leaving. Not even Chopper Knight or Jimmy Moody realised the gang had just pulled in close to a million pounds. Ten minutes later, Chopper had counted up so much cash, organising it into piles on the floor, that Benefield and Khan were sent out to a shop up the road to buy holdalls – the gang's kitbags weren't big enough to take each robber's share of the bank notes.

Bernie Khan later described the scene in the flat that day: 'Each room had been cleared of furniture and Chopper had made piles of the money and packed them into plastic parcels, each with £25,000.'

When 'dodgy' John Segars returned he was also ordered to also take off his clothes. He later explained: 'The whole team were in their vests, sweating like bullocks, counting the bundles of notes into separate piles.'

Each share came to exactly £96,000.

Jason Moody never forgot what he saw that day. 'There were just thousands upon thousands of notes stacked up in neat little piles on the bare floor. I sat there with me mouth hangin' wide open. I couldn't believe what was happenin'. The money was everywhere, inches deep on the floor.' It wasn't until some time later that Jason fully appreciated the significance of his presence that day. 'That's when I realised that any one of them could have lost his rag with me being in that flat and who knows what they might have done to me.'

Bernie Khan had other memories of that afternoon: 'You know those films where they're thowin' the money up into the air? You know what? That's so fuckin' unreal. This was the opposite. Really low key. None of that movie nonsense. All Chopper kept saying was, "There's still a lot more to do yet."'

As John Segars was leaving the flat carrying his holdall full of cash, Chopper Knight asked him for £300 he'd loaned him some months earlier when Segars was broke.

'Fuck off, Chopper,' replied Segars.

'I want that fuckin' £300 or you don't leave here,' said Knight, rising to his feet.

Jimmy Moody also stood up with a gun clutched in the palm of his hand.

'D'you want some of this?' he said to Segars, not even bothering to look down at the gun. Another member of the gang who was in the flat recalled: 'So John had to pay up before he was allowed to leave. It was a heavy moment and I've no doubt Moody would have done him if

Chopper had given him the go ahead. Moody fuckin' hated John anyway.'

The entire transaction at Jimmy Moody's flat – including handing the money to each gang member – took just 20 minutes. Bernie Khan recalled: 'We all got it into our zip-ups and got out one at a time. I put my money in the boot of my motor and away I went to my flop in north London where I put the money in a safe and sat tight watching telly and didn't go out for days.'

That afternoon of 15 August 1978, Operation Ohio detective Bill Forman got a call from Surrey Police to say a gang had just used a chainsaw to prize open a Security Express van. He believed the gang were throwing down the gauntlet. 'It was their way of saying: "Come and get us – if you can,"' Forman explained.

Forman telephoned the Operation Ohio observation post at Huckle's Yard, near the Blackwall Tunnel, where detectives insisted Alex Sears had been on site at the scrapyard by the entrance to the Blackwall Tunnel the entire day. Forman was puzzled. It was only later he discovered Sears had been dropped by the gang's 'A-team' because of security concerns about his common-law wife.

The first senior police investigator on the scene was Detective Chief Superintendent Jim Sewell of the Robbery Squad. He was full of admiration for the robbers' skills. 'It was very unusual and well planned; really an old-fashioned Dick Turpin, Robin Hood-type robbery using motor cars and sophisticated equipment,' he told one reporter.

That evening a very weary Bill Forman left Banstead Police Station after examining the attack vehicles and hearing descriptions of the robbers. He had no doubt the Chainsaw Gang had been at work again. The Banstead robbery also sent shockwaves through the security industry. It forced banks to find better ways of protecting their cash. The robbery was such an audacious crime that it also drew admiring comments from many in the London underworld.

Within 30 minutes of leaving the Hackney flat, Jimmy Moody was driving Jason and Janine down to spend a couple of days with him at his caravan close to the Solent. Following his near-£100,000 payoff from the Banstead job, Jimmy Moody was in an extremely generous frame of mind. Moody's Range Rover was passing a toyshop in Hackney, next to one of his favourite pie-and-mash shops, when he screeched to a halt. Jason takes up the story: 'Me and my sister walked in that toyshop with him and he stuck his chest out proudly and said, "Pick anythin' you want."'

Jason ended up with a Subbuteo football set complete with a full-sized plastic stadium and numerous model cars. Janine got Barbie dolls galore. 'It took two runs to the car to get all the stuff in the boot. It was magic, like the old man was Father Christmas for the day. I'll never forget it. Never,' recalled Jason.

On the way to the south coast that same evening, Moody almost fell asleep while driving so he immediately stopped on the motorway's hard shoulder. The children knew from previous experience they had to remain totally quiet while he had some shut eye. Jason explained: 'Looking back on it, I s'ppose he was actually being a very responsible parent because he didn't want to risk crashing the car.' Thirty minutes later, Moody fired up the car's engine and they continued their journey.

The moment they arrived at the caravan, Jason rushed in to switch on the TV. The Banstead robbery was all over the news and Jason had no doubt his father was involved.

Later that evening, Janine noticed an unopened package on the kitchen counter. It was those cabbage sandwiches she'd made with such loving care and attention the previous day. Janine explained: 'By this time Dad had spread all his cash across the caravan floor to count it, but all I cared about was that he hadn't eaten my packed lunch. I was heartbroken.'

As a tiny tear rolled down her cheek, her father patted her on the head and said, 'Wot's up, love? You all right?' Janine bravely nodded her head and wiped away her tears. She wasn't scared of her father. She just felt so disappointed. Janine saw things from a different perspective than her brother. She explained: 'We never questioned what Dad did. That might sound bad, but that was the way it was with him. In the end the bad things just became normal.'

But all the old Moody obsessions were never far away. Jason explained: 'He still had us cleaning our teeth at least three times a day. He'd shout at us, "Must do yer railings" – that's what he called teeth.'

The family was suffering in other ways, as Jason recalled: 'We were not a proper family unit. Dad would go away and then come back. Then he'd be off a few days later. Him and Mum were undoubtedly good together, but it was not a normal set up. He was always looking over his shoulder, always. And we all worried so much about him. I remember as a kid wondering why. Why didn't I have anyone to ask to find out what was normal?' As a result, Jason and Janine relied heavily on Val's parents

– their grandparents. Jason explained: 'They were so good to us. I'd be lying if I didn't say they were our parents in a way. Without them we would never have survived.'

Back at that caravan near the sea, Jimmy Moody made open references to Operation Ohio detectives Bill Forman and Charlie Snape. 'The old man had a lot of respect for them and said openly to us that they were after him. Forman and Snape this, Forman and Snape that. He was always goin' on about them.'

The day after the Banstead job, Operation Ohio detectives got a tip about Jimmy Moody's movements. Bill Forman explained: 'We headed down to the south coast where Moody was said to be hiding in a chalet with his wife and kids. We had armed officers in support and smashed the door down, grabbed the man we thought was Moody and almost shot him only to find out he was a rather pleasant second-hand car dealer. Luckily he didn't lodge a complaint. He turned out to be having a quiet weekend with his family on the Isle of Sheppey. It was very disappointing.'

Bill Forman and his Operation Ohio colleagues knocked on Val Moody's parents' front door in Poplar at least three times in the days following the Banstead robbery. Val recalled: 'One time I was there making some lunch and they burst in and searched the house from head to toe. It was nothing short of police harassment.'

Operation Ohio officers were determined to crank up the pressure on the Chainsaw Gang. Dozens of informants were briefed about the rewards on offer for information. As Charlie Snape pointed out: 'Remember, it was one of my informants who'd initiated the operation in the first place. I knew they were the key to cracking this team wide open.'

The police heard rumours that Jimmy Moody was abroad, but they didn't believe the stories. 'He just wasn't the type of person to leave the country,' explained Charlie Snape. 'We heard he might have a caravan on the south coast, but that was like looking for a needle in a haystack; so for the moment we concentrated on all Moody's usual London haunts.'

Jimmy Moody had paid £2,000 for a fake passport from a contact in south-east London so that he could travel abroad if the Operation Ohio detectives got too close for comfort. The photo featured Moody with dyed blonde hair and thick glasses. But, as another one-time associate explained: 'The problem was that Jimmy was very reluctant to step outside England. It just wasn't his style. He only had the passport so he knew it was there if he really needed it.'

In the middle of this so-called police dragnet, Moody showed up at his cousin Christine's wedding in south-east London. Dickie Moody explained: 'He also met a girl at the wedding. This one was from Jersey and was very rich. I think Denise was her name.' Dickie Moody says his brother persuaded Denise to invest some of her cash in the gang's next job.

That afternoon at the wedding, Moody nearly had a punch-up with another guest who tried to take his photograph. He was worried it might fall into the wrong hands.

TWELVE

Ear to the Ground

Within less than a week of the Banstead robbery, a notorious London villain called Mickey Calvey (now deceased) told detectives that John Segars was one of the eight robbers at Banstead and that he'd gone to Scotland to escape the heat. But a few days later, Segars and most of his family were traced to a guesthouse in Minehead, Somerset, after a Range Rover he owned was spotted in the area. When Segars was arrested he was in possession of 14 pounds of cannabis resin and over £2,000 in cash, plus the Range Rover, purchased with £4,500 cash from the Banstead job. Initial interviews with Segars' wife Theresa also confirmed he'd been involved in the robbery, but Segars refused to talk after his arrest. As Operation Ohio detective Bill Forman later commented in his report: 'Segars sat in his cell with his legs crossed like a Buddha.'

When Segars' mother and father were interviewed in Scotland they told police that Segars' share of the robbery loot was in two large brown suitcases at the home of another relative in Notting Hill, west London. A team of five armed officers including Bill Forman and his boss Charlie Snape crashed into the house at 26 Droop Street W10 and demanded to be told the whereabouts of Segars' relative, known as 'Aunt Sally'. As Forman later admitted: 'To our amazement the occupiers had never heard of her. It was the wrong house.'

The red-faced police officers then dispersed to make further street inquiries, with the exception of Bill Forman and Detective Constable Roy Clark who sat on a low wall feeling thoroughly despondent about the mix-up. Clark began moaning to Forman about the robbery squad trying to muscle in on Operation Ohio and a detailed discussion of inter-force politics followed. Just then, a young girl walked up to them and asked who they were looking for.

'Aunt Sally,' replied Forman. 'D'you know where she might live?'

The girl nodded her head and promised to find her for the detectives. She returned a few minutes later and said Aunt Sally lived at 10 Droop Street. A drunken woman answered the door, asked them in and then tried to light a cigarette from an unlit gas fire. Forman got straight to the point.

'Where are those two big brown suitcases of John's, love?' he asked.

'Up in the spare room under the bed,' came the deadpan reply. 'Iris [Segars' mum] asked me to keep them for her. I don't know what's in them.'

Bill Forman took the stairs three steps at a time, pulled two suitcases out from under the bed and took them downstairs into the living-room where he forced them open. As he later recalled: 'To Aunt Sally's surprise, I found they were full of bundles of twenty-, ten- and five-pound notes to which she said, "Fuckin' hell, I never seen so much money in my life." Then she fainted.'

Minutes later, Operation Ohio chief Charlie Snape and a colleague arrived at the scene and took the suitcases straight to Segars at Banstead Police Station. Segars threw up his hands and said, 'Fuck it – I've had enough.' He eventually made 39 statements about other major robberies throughout Britain.

By ten that night, he'd told Snape and Forman all the names of the Banstead team, plus the role each man played and how they'd shared out the Banstead loot at Moody's flat. Segars even disclosed how the gang escaped and what vehicles they had used. Segars insisted he had no idea where the rest of the team were, but he did admit Jimmy Moody and Tony Knightly had caravans on the south coast and Sammy Benefield had a caravan in Surrey. The police eventually counted out £84,500 from Segars' two suitcases.

The Saturday morning after Segars arrest and written confession, Bill Forman and his colleagues drove the getaway route from Banstead all the way to the exact address of Jimmy Moody's Hackney flat. They even found a new witness in Wallington High Street – not far from the crime scene.

Operation Ohio detectives Charlie Snape and Bill Forman then decided to try and protect John Segars. Forman wrote out a false police

statement of admission in which Segars put his hands up to the
Banstead robbery, but only his own involvement – no names were
provided. This was then inserted into the Met system because Forman
knew that a crooked officer would eventually leak the information to the
gang.

A couple of days after Segars' arrest, Val Moody went from her parents'
home to the Hackney flat to pick up some clothes. 'The front door was
boarded up. I went and found a bobby on the beat and asked him to
come up to my flat because I thought it had been broken into. He forced
the door open and everywhere was covered in white powder. Then he
goes to me: "This looks like fingerprint powder." Then he turned to me
and says, "Reckon the heavy mob have been in here. Is your husband a
criminal of any sort?" I said no, naturally.'

The following day, Val stormed into City Row Police Station and
demanded an explanation. She recalled: 'They said there'd been a serious
robbery and the detectives had a warrant and were lookin' for the
robbers.' Operation Ohio detectives had found Moody's fingerprints in
the flat, as well as those of Benefield and Knightly. But, more
importantly, police also recovered cash bags originally containing the
Banstead money, plus a crash helmet worn by Moody on the same
robbery as later described by witnesses.

On 29 August 1978 – just two weeks after the Banstead job – Sammy
Benefield and his wife Edith were arrested at his caravan on the Roof of
the World Caravan site, in Box Hill, Surrey, on the outskirts of London;
£82,994 was found in his caravan. To cover up John Segars' help, police
let it be known the Benefield's were tracked down after his wife used a
credit card at an Indian restaurant in Chelsea, West London.

Detective Bill Forman explained: 'Sammy Benefield was easy meat.
He couldn't stand the thought of going back to prison for another 20
years so he spoke to us about a possible deal.' Benefield was warned he'd
still get a 10 to 15-year sentence but he decided to spill the beans
anyway. Benefield eventually confessed to a total of 45 offences but
detectives were careful not to tell him John Segars had also turned grass.
That bit of news wasn't passed on to Benefield until four days later. He
was gutted when he heard it.

At their respective hideaways, Chopper Knight and Jimmy Moody
had no idea Benefield and Segars were spilling their guts to the
Operation Ohio squad so they didn't make any attempt to come after
them. As Moody's son Jason explained: 'If the old man had known they

were turning the team over he'd have gone after them and God knows what would have happened.'

On 30 August 1978, two of the Operation Ohio team – Detective Sergeant Bill Brown from the Met and Detective Sergeant Jim Wallis from Cleveland — tracked Tony Knightly and Jimmy Moody to the Riverside Caravan Park in the Hamble area of Hampshire, where both men were spotted working on a Range Rover. Knightly even wandered off to make several phone calls from a nearby phone box. Brown and Wallis then requested a full-strength team of detectives to meet at nearby Eastleigh Police Station at 3.45 a.m. the next morning for a briefing before 'hitting' both caravans at 5.30 a.m.

Then at midnight Jimmy Moody drove off in his Range Rover. At 2 a.m., detectives watched Tony Knightly put a heavy holdall bag in the boot of his Vauxhall before also driving off. Police containment units had already been alerted to set up a roadblock a mile away on the only route out of the site.

Knightly drove through the police road block at 60 mph, badly damaging his vehicle but somehow managing to keep going. He was then chased by detectives for nine miles through the Hampshire countryside, having to lean out of the window in order to see because his windscreen was shattered. Somehow Knightly managed to dodge trees and road signs along the way. He finally came to a halt at the bottom of a slope into the waters of the Solent. But Tony Knightly wasn't finished yet.

As he fled the scene, he was challenged by armed detectives who later claimed he pulled out a weapon. The Ohio officers immediately opened fire on Knightly as he dived into the dark and murky waters of the Solent, one of the most dangerous stretches of water in the world. The four officers presumed they'd hit their target and he was sinking to the bottom of the sea. Back at Knightly's Vauxhall, detectives found a holdall containing £78,000 in the boot.

In fact, Tony Knightly wasn't even grazed by the police bullets and was swimming out into the middle of the Solent, despite the strong tides and currents. At one stage he was nearly hit by the *QE2*, one of the gang's next targets. Then he got to the middle of the five-mile-wide stretch of water and found a boat anchored, so he clambered on board.

Jimmy Moody had no idea what had happened to his friend. The following morning he picked Jason and Janine up in the East End and took them back down to the south coast in his new Range Rover. When they stopped at a café in the Hampshire countryside, Moody spotted the front page of a tabloid featuring a story about the dramatic Tony Knightly chase. Jason recalled: 'Dad dragged us back into the Range Rover and sold it half a mile away to a local car dealer before buying a Morris Minor for £500 cash.' Moody then drove straight back to the East End.

The following day, an old lady noticed a soaking-wet man matching Tony Knightly's description behaving suspiciously as he waited at a roadside to be picked up by a car from London. She immediately phoned the police and Knightly was arrested. Bill Forman headed straight down to see Knightly at Fleet Police Station in Hampshire. 'He still had his shoes on, although they were a little damp,' Forman recalled. 'Tony quipped that he wouldn't have got very far without shoes.'

Forman had a sneaking admiration for Knightly's efforts to avoid arrest. He later explained: 'He was quite a character, as they all were in different ways. He was pleased I was taking him back to London and pleased to be alive. He said he didn't like the bullets flying about, and, having had time to think, he naturally said he never had a weapon.' Officers never did find a gun.

Knightly confessed his part in the Banstead robbery to Forman during the two-hour drive back to London, but he denied all knowledge of the money in the boot of his Vauxhall. Back in Hampshire, police surveillance continued at the caravan site because detectives believed Jimmy Moody might still return.

Bill Forman and his Operation Ohio team then tried to arrest pint-sized driver Brian Sims. On 4 September 1978, Ohio officers approached Sims in his Jaguar when he arrived to visit his wife at a block of flats in Stamford Hill, north London. But Sims sussed out they were police and slammed his foot on the accelerator pedal. One officer – Detective Constable Graham Welch – tried to hang onto the driver's door before Sims swerved away and roared off into the traffic.

On 9 September 1978, it was Chainsaw Gang member Big Bad John Woodruff's turn to have his collar felt. He was arrested at Manchester Airport as he stepped off a plane from Malta, having been warned by another gang member not to return. Woodruff's wife Ellen told detectives their holiday in the Med had been financed by money he'd stolen from earlier robberies that he'd already served time for. Police were convinced she also knew where all her husband's share of the

Banstead cash was hidden. Woodruff eventually admitted taking part in seven major armed robberies with Chopper Knight, including the first Blackwall Tunnel job in September 1977. Police noted that although Woodruff said he never got his share of the money, his wife seemed to be living a very luxurious lifestyle.

On Friday, 15 September 1978, gang member Bernie Khan had just left his girlfriend's home in Bacon Street, Bethnal Green, in the East End and was getting in an S-reg Volkswagen Passat when he noticed a motorcyclist drive past him. 'He seemed to be studying me very closely,' Khan later recalled. 'I knew somethin' was up.'

As he drove off, Khan recognised two Kent detectives in the street and a car chase began. Other police vehicles were soon called in and Khan was eventually 'bottled' down a dead end in Delta Street, Bow. As two armed detectives approached Khan, he drove off. Swerving towards them, three police shots rang out, shattering Khan's windscreen and causing him to crash into a lamp-post. Khan then hotfooted it into a huge council estate at the end of the street. Detectives spent hours searching for the pint-sized half-Indian robber. He'd disappeared into thin air. Khan believes to this day he was the intended victim of a police shoot-to-kill policy. Within hours, Khan was heading up the M1 to start a new life in Manchester. As he later explained: 'When the balloon went up I thought, I just gotta get the fuck outta here. Everyone goes south but I went north.'

On 17 September – two days after Bernie Khan's miraculous escape – Bill Forman got a call from an informant who told him that team driver Brian Sims would be at his girlfriend's address in Sycamore Court, Chingford, Essex. Bill Forman and a team of armed officers surrounded the block before breaking down the front door and finding Sims outside on a balcony, dressed in pyjamas with his clothes over one arm, about to jump from the second floor. Sims put his hands up when he saw six Webley .38s pointed in his direction.

Forman explained: 'Of course, Sims said he didn't know what all the fuss was about and he knew nothing about the Banstead robbery – or driving his car at those two officers earlier.' Sims was taken to Greenwich Police Station while Bill Forman accompanied his girlfriend to a lock-up garage where £86,000 of Banstead cash was found in a holdall. She insisted he'd made the money from car deals. Later, at Greenwich Police Station, Sims remained tight lipped until he saw the bag of money. Forman explained: 'He virtually fainted with shock and after we revived him he confessed. Poor little Brian.'

On 6 October 1978, an informant told Bill Forman that gang leader Chopper Knight was due to meet a contact that afternoon in Solebay Street, off the Mile End Road, right in the heart of the East End. More than 40 Operation Ohio and robbery squad officers, many armed, swamped the area. Chopper was eventually spotted crossing a nearby canal bridge into Solebay Street where he got into a mustard-coloured Fiat occupied by grass John Segars' wife, Theresa.

Detectives – convinced that Chopper would come out shooting if cornered – gave the order to move in. All hell broke lose. Chopper spotted a brigade of detectives in his rear-view mirror and decided to drive his way out of trouble. Two officers tried to rip open the Fiat's doors as a robbery squad vehicle blocked Chopper's exit. But the man they called 'The General' was having none of it. His Fiat mounted the pavement and bounced off several parked cars. More officers jumped on the bonnet and started smashing the windscreen with truncheons.

Chopper was still fishtailing down the street when Operation Ohio detective Dave Bassett wrenched open the driver's door and yanked Chopper out with his bare hands. Seconds later the car slammed into a brick wall. Chopper immediately found himself staring down the barrels of at least four Webleys. He was led away in handcuffs. Theresa Segars suffered shock and cuts from flying glass. And Chopper turned out *not* to be armed. He had £500 cash on him that he said was 'for a drink' for Theresa, whom detectives alleged was one of his many girlfriends.

None of Chopper's robbery proceeds, apart from the £500 in his possession on the day of his arrest, were ever recovered. His personal share came to at least a quarter of a million pounds.

When Bill Forman interrogated Chopper, he asked the gang leader how he felt about Benefield giving evidence against him. 'I feel fuckin' numb about it, but Jimmy Moody will no doubt have made an effigy of Sammy by now and he won't be stickin' fuckin pins in it, if I know Jim – it'll be fuckin' great big swords. I'll bet you a packet that Jimmy's the last one you nick, if you ever find him.'

Detectives next arrested Alex 'Bone Head' Sears after an informant told them he'd be with his common-law wife Vivien Minchington at The Telegraph pub, in Stratford, east London. Chopper Knight had dropped Alex Sears from his team a year earlier because he suspected

Minchington of being a police grass. Her disappearance shortly after Sears' arrest seemed to confirm these allegations.

As Sears was taken into the charge room at Greenwich Police Station, he came face to face with grass Sammy Benefield and immediately laid into him, accusing him of betraying the whole gang. Six police officers were needed to drag the two men apart.

Sears refused to sign any confessions. Then Detective Inspector Ernie Brown, of Tayside Police, visited Sears in his cell at Greenwich Police Station and formally charged him with an armed robbery committed in Dundee. As Forman explained: 'Alex pleaded to be dealt with down here as he did not want to go across the border where he could disappear for ever, as he put it.'

Jimmy Moody – who never stayed at his family home for more than a few hours during this period – was incensed when he finally heard a whisper about grasses Benefield and Segars and swore to have his revenge on them. Detectives went to great lengths to protect their two Chainsaw Gang informants. They had round-the-clock guards and paid the men's families hundreds of pounds a week to lay low. Newspapers were even requested not to publish photographs or make any references to their movements.

In February 1979 – just before Chopper Knight and some of the other gang members were due to make an appearance at Maidstone Crown Court – police got wind of an audacious £100,000 plot to kill four supergrasses, including Segars and Benefield. There were strong rumours Jimmy Moody was orchestrating the operation. Police eventually assigned 79 officers to protect the court proceedings for the trials: marksmen were positioned inside the court buildings, on the roof and even in the basement. Other armed detectives escorted witnesses and took prisoners from Maidstone Jail each day. Everyone entering court was searched and anyone with criminal records was turned away.

At Maidstone Crown Court, squealer Sammy Benefield was given a verbal roasting by his co-defendants within seconds of appearing in the dock: 'For God's sake, tell the truth,' shouted one gang member, who grabbed the dock rail and glared across the courtroom at Benefield. Grass Benefield received a relatively light five-year sentence after admitting taking part in the Banstead robbery, the Blackwall Tunnel job and the Rochester post-office raid as well as asking for 41 other offences to be taken into consideration. Fellow grass John Segars, also got five years. Not surprisingly, Segars' family had to move away from their home in the East End for fear of reprisals.

In November 1979, the Chainsaw Gang members on trial were jailed for a total of 218 years at Maidstone Crown Court. Before sentencing Chopper Knight to 18 years, Judge Justice Stocker told him: 'I have not the slightest doubt that you were the leader – and a very good one, too. You would have been the leader in any field you chose to follow. You chose this one. You are a very dangerous man. These robberies of which you have been convicted showed a high degree of organisation and extremely careful planning and execution.' Later the judge told the team as a whole: 'You all possess qualities which would have fitted you as leaders among your fellow men. You are all extremely intelligent with abilities of organisation and planning and you all possess courage. It's tragic that you used these qualities to make war on us.'

Jimmy Moody was outraged by the sentences and particularly the roles played by those 'fuckin' grasses'. His son Jason explained: 'The old man taught us to hate them. We didn't even hate the coppers as much as Segars and Benefield. He'd describe in vivid details what he'd do to them and these were like our bedtime stories. He'd lecture us on being loyal to our friends and then start ranting about how "those fuckin' dogs Benefied and Segars sold us down the river". He always swore blind he'd get 'em both in the end.' Moody told one associate, 'I'd fuckin' do 'em for nothin'. Free of charge!'

Segars and Benefield believed they could save their own skins by serving short sentences in solitary confinement and then living abroad under assumed names. But Benefield admitted Moody was a real threat. He told detectives: 'Jim's a mad bastard, mad enough to take us out if he felt like it.'

Moody's obsession with grasses led to an incident in the East End which sent a shiver down the spine of people like Benefield and Segars. Moody was out in his car when he spotted a well-known police informant alongside him at a set of traffic lights. Moody overtook the man when the lights went green. Then he forced him to stop, jumped out of his car in broad daylight, grabbed a bottle off the pavement, smashed the head off it and started waving it at the man in the car. When the man got out of his car, Moody spat on him. 'Fuckin' grass.' Moody then walked back to his car and drove off.

By the autumn of 1979, Jimmy Moody stopped staying with Val and the children because he knew the Operation Ohio squad were closing in. Then Moody's brother Dickie found him a proper, full-time hideout at a former slaughterhouse on Coldharbour Lane, in Brixton, south London. A man called John Kennedy had rented it for many years, but then announced he was emigrating to America. Or as Dickie put it: 'Kennedy was given a lot of cash in key money [rent on the flat] by Jim and went over to the States to work.'

Despite being a wanted man, Moody still kept in touch with one 'straight' friend from his school days. One evening Moody took his children Jason and Janine and this friend out for a meal. It proved an eye-opener for the teenaged Jason. He explained: 'This geezer told us how he and my dad had grown up and been involved in all sorts of mischief together.' Then the man looked towards his old friend Jimmy Moody and said: 'But then there comes a time when you have to decide which way to turn. I went one way and your dad went the other. Thank God I chose my way.'

At that moment, Jason turned towards his father and noticed a look of awkwardness on his face. 'The old man knew he'd taken the wrong turning, but it was way too late by then to turn around,' recalled Jason.

In mid-December 1979, Jimmy Moody's much beloved mother Rosina, 62, was knocked down and killed in a hit-and-run accident near the family home in Rosendale Road, Dulwich. Moody was devastated. His brother Dickie explained: 'Jim felt really guilty because he was on the run and couldn't risk coming home in case the police spotted him.' Dickie was still living at home with his mother at nearly 40 years of age.

Moody was despondent about his mother's death but there were even bigger problems lying just around the corner.

THIRTEEN

Game's Up

On Friday, 21 December 1979, Jimmy Moody's son Jason stayed with his father at his new hideout at Coldharbour Lane. It was the night before Jason's 15th birthday and as a birthday treat Moody had promised that the following day he would take him and the rest of the family down to his caravan on the south coast to learn scuba diving.

Within minutes of arriving at the house that evening, Jason noticed his father seemed tense. 'He kept pacing up and down the main room,' Jason recalled. 'But he wouldn't say what was wrong.' Moody was awaiting the arrival back in London of John Kennedy, the man whose house he was staying in. Kennedy was flying into Gatwick Airport from Texas and had promised to bring a couple of guns for Moody. Kennedy's flight had touched down three hours earlier but Moody hadn't heard a word from him. Moody knew Kennedy had a big drink problem and he'd probably got legless on the plane, but he hoped nothing more serious had happened.

Later that night father and son shared a Chinese takeaway which included Moody's favourite dish – beef chow mein. Then they played a video game together, followed by a game of chess in which Jason noticed his father cheating as usual. 'I didn't say anythin'. I was just happy to get him to forget his problems for a while,' explained Jason.

Jason never liked the crumbling Victorian house his father now called home. He explained: 'It was a huge place with a massive cellar that I never wanted to go anywhere near. And the abandoned abattoir in the yard featured lines of rusting meat hooks and old fridges. I kept

119

imaginin' all sorts of horrible things comin' out of those fridges.'

At about 11 p.m., Moody popped out 'to see a man about a dog', leaving his son desperately trying to make himself go to sleep, but with little success.

What neither father nor son realised was that at Gatwick Airport that afternoon a very drunk John Kennedy had been stopped by customs officers following his arrival from Dallas. They discovered Kennedy had packed two snub-nosed .38 revolvers and 100 rounds of ammunition inside a box of chocolates he said were for Jimmy Moody. With an Irish background, Kennedy was immediately suspected of being an IRA terrorist. He was so insistent this was not the case that he asked to be interviewed by Operation Ohio detectives. John Kennedy wanted to strike a deal.

Kennedy informed officers Bill Forman and Jim Davies that Jimmy Moody was at his house at 186 Coldharbour Lane, Brixton, and repeated that the guns and ammunition were for him. Forman was astonished to hear Moody had been living right under their noses for months. Kennedy also claimed he'd left the country earlier that year because he was so scared of Moody. Bill Forman insisted that no deal was made with Kennedy, but he was later acquitted of harbouring Moody and given only 21 months.

In Coldharbour Lane, Jimmy Moody arrived back that night to find Jason still wide awake. With no sign of Kennedy, his instincts told him something bad had happened. To take his mind off his problems, Moody sat down on the edge of Jason's makeshift bed and started running through all the scuba-diving equipment they'd need for the following day's adventure. Ten minutes later he looked down at Jason to see he'd finally nodded off. Moody then did a dozen bench presses in the makeshift gym he'd set up in one of the back rooms before trying to get some sleep. He had a feeling tomorrow was going to be a very long day.

At 5.30 a.m. the following morning – Saturday, 22 December 1979 – an Operation Ohio team led by Charlie Snape finally got the all clear from their command superiors to brief the D.11 squad (the Yard's specialist armed-response unit) to lay siege to 186 Coldharbour Lane, where they now knew Moody was in hiding.

At approximately 6 a.m., detective Bill Forman asked his sergeant to call the phone number of the property in Coldharbour Lane provided by John Kennedy. However, it turned out to be a Lady Beaverbrook in Mayfair. Forman later recalled: 'It was 6 a.m. and she was furious I'd just woken up her cat. Turned out we'd dialled the wrong number!'

This time Forman dialled the number himself and Moody answered. 'Hello.'

'It's me.'

'I know it's you, Guv. I see all your pop guns.'

'Don't try anythin' stupid, Jim. You haven't a chance in hell.'

'Gimme ten minutes.'

'Why should we give you ten minutes?'

'I need to get dressed.'

'All right.'

'And Jim . . .'

'Yes, Guv?'

'There's no chance of doin' a runner, you understand?' added Forman in his clipped Scottish accent, brisk and to the point as ever.

'But wot about my boy?'

Forman stopped in his tracks. He had no idea Jason was in the house and he certainly didn't want the death or injury of a child on his conscience. As Forman later explained: 'The goal posts changed in that split-second.'

'Your kid?' asked Forman.

'Yeah.'

'Just let him out first and he'll come to no harm . . .' Forman paused for a moment. '. . . And Jim . . .'

'Yes, Guv?'

'I don't want any fuckin' around from you. This is serious.'

In the next room, Jason Moody woke up and heard his father talking quietly on the phone. 'I hadn't slept much that night so it didn't take a lot to wake me,' he later recalled.

Jason shouted through to his father. Moody didn't reply.

Jason then heard Moody tell someone on the phone, 'Gimme ten minutes, all right?'

A few seconds later Jason walked into the next room. 'What's happened, Dad?'

Moody was already putting a suit on. He looked up as his son walked in and said: 'Look out the window, boy.'

Jason recalled: 'There were police marksmen everywhere. The whole flamin' world seemed to be lookin' in our direction.'

Jason glanced at his father for a few moments. Neither uttered a word.

'Game's up, ain't it?' Moody shrugged. Jason later said his father sounded almost relieved.

Then it was back to business.

'Now get yer skates on, son. We got work to do.'

Jason followed his father into the bathroom, where Moody ripped open a big zip-up bag. Jason was transfixed by the bank notes virtually spilling out. Then Moody began grabbing handfuls of money and trying to flush them down the toilet. 'So I joined in and started ripping them up and mixing them with torn-up magazine pages,' Jason recalled.

The toilet cistern soon got blocked up.

When the ten minutes was up, Detective Bill Forman put another call into Moody, who promised his son would be out 'in a minute or two'.

'And Jim . . .' began Forman.

'Yes, Guv'nor?'

'Make sure your kid comes out first, all right?'

'Abso-fuckin'-lootly.'

Jimmy Moody then moved swiftly back to the toilet and continued tearing up £20, £10 and £5 notes and stuffing them down the toilet even though it wasn't flushing properly. He also tore up a US arms magazine which Kennedy had sent him from Dallas and tried to flush it away at the same time.

Then Moody told Jason it was time to go. At first the youngster was reluctant to leave.

'Don't worry about me, son.'

'But Dad . . .'

'You gotta go in case all the fireworks go up.'

Jason nodded his head slowly and bit his lip to try and hold back the tears. It was hard to reconcile himself with the fact that this gentle giant of a father was also public enemy number one.

Moments later, Jason opened the door and walked out into the freezing cold December sunrise.

'Jason?' shouted Bill Forman, 20 yards in front of the door.

'Yes.'

'Keep your hands up in case you get shot and walk to your left.'

He did exactly as he was told.

As Jason later explained: 'They made me lie on the pavement and all they was worried about was whether the house was booby-trapped. They kept askin' me over and over again about it.'

Then Bill Forman hit the megaphone. 'Jim, you comin' out? What you doin'? You've had your ten minutes. Come out now.'

'All right, all right,' came a voice from behind the front door.

As Moody came out, Forman clearly saw it was him.

'Now, Jim, turn round, hands up. Hands to me. Up against the wall.'

Moody glanced up at four rooftop police marksman training their rifles at him before deciding to do what he was told for the first time in his life.

Bill Forman walked forward and cuffed him. As Forman later recalled: 'I could see he was shaking and so was I. I held him tightly. He didn't struggle.'

Father and son were put in separate police cars. Both asked where they were going, but neither Forman or his colleagues would say a word at this stage. Jason recalled: 'Then, shortly after the car moved off, it came over the police radio that my dad had said the house was not booby-trapped and one of the officers in the car said: "If Jimmy says its not, then it's not." At least they showed a bit of respect for him.'

At Brixton Police Station, Jason was thoroughly searched by a uniformed sergeant who found one of his father's £50 notes in his back pocket. 'I bet you get loads of these on your birthday, son,' said the officer as he carefully unfolded the note. The £50 and Jason's impending birthday became a running joke at the police station: 'All they kept saying was how much I must have wished they'd let me keep the note because it was my birthday.'

Over in the East End, Moody's wife Val had been hard at work all day on her clothes stall in the Roman Road market, unaware of the drama unfolding in Brixton. As Val later explained: 'Jim was going to pick us up that afternoon to go down to the coast for the weekend. It was Jason's birthday treat.'

At Brixton Police Station, Moody and his son were kept in separate cells. Jason explained: 'The worst thing was that I kept askin' to see my dad and they wouldn't let me near him.'

Back at the house in Coldharbour Lane, detectives found files of evidence statements from the previous Chainsaw gang court cases – which meant Moody had an inside informant and knew all the evidence that would be thrown at him in court.

Later that morning Jimmy Moody found himself facing his two great police pursuers, Charlie Snape and Bill Forman, across a table. After a general chit-chat about various aspects of his criminal activities, DCI Snape tried to wrong-foot Moody by asking him about an Australian girl he'd been dating. The tape-recorded interview provided a fascinating insight into the police/criminal relationship and how Moody dealt with severe, but fair, pressure from the two officers. Moody happily chatted about certain subjects, just so long as they didn't incriminate himself or others in acts of crime. Bill Forman later said he was flattered when Moody said he'd heard of him and his boss Charlie Snape. He called the two officers 'Mister Snape' and 'Mister Forman' from the very first moment they met.

Moody: What chance have I got? The only thing I can do is plead and hope they'll treat me a bit more leniently. But if I thought I'd get a 20 whether I pleaded or not then I'd have to fight it, Mr Snape.

Snape: Tony Knightly only got 16 years and he fought it and then he got found guilty in the Hemel Hempstead one. Doesn't that influence you?

Moody: How many charges are you going to hit me with?

Snape: I should imagine the DPP will go for the same three main charges: the Blackwall Tunnel southbound, the one you had off the Rochester Post Office and of course the one at Banstead. There's not much point in going through the book.

Moody: That don't sound too bad.

Snape: I said you can have the rest. There's a few there, Jim.

Moody: I'd have to think about it. I knew Segars and Sammy would grass me up and I told the rest of the firm. I feel sorry for Tony [Knightly]. He's a right good 'un, Mr Snape.

Snape: Knightly thinks a lot of you too, Jim.

Moody: What about my son?

Snape: You can see him before he goes. Would it be in order to let him go home to his mother?

Moody: Yeah, but I would like to see him.

Snape: You have my word on that. Now what about a cup of coffee and a bacon sandwich?

Moody: I'd love one.

[Moody requests a change of clothing and his toothpaste from the flat and Snape agrees to this.]

Moody: I s'ppose it was John Kennedy who set me up? In fact, I've no doubt it was him, that shit.

Forman: That's right, Jim.

Moody: I don't know why I didn't listen to all the advice I'd been given. He's an alcoholic. I'd been told he was an alcoholic. I guess I knew it would come and it's no real surprise.

Snape: Did you hear about [Bernie] Khan getting shot at in east London?

Moody: Yeah, I thought that was the way I was going to go.

Snape: I think those bullets hit his car boot and he still got away.

Moody: So I heard. If it hadn't been for my son I was going to go to the window and fire, try to pull a gun in the hope you fellows would shoot me. It would be better than all this.

Forman: Charlie [Chopper] Knight rates you. What did he think of the situation?

Moody: Charlie would make a great soldier. He is a born leader and loves a challenge. He doesn't do a robbery for the money. It's all a game with Charlie.

Forman: Your brother Dick will take your son home to Mum?

Moody: Yeah, she's got a stall down the Roman Road. You can take him yourself if you want.

Forman: No, your brother can do that. I understand you are a keep-fit fanatic and a bit of a karate expert. Is that right?

Moody: I don't abuse my body, if that's what you mean. I have never smoked and I try to keep in trim, although I am carrying a bit of extra weight at the moment.

[Moody then taps his waist]

Forman: Have you been living in that flat very long, Jim?

Moody: Yeah, several months. Now I know I shouldn't have trusted that grass Kennedy.

Forman: He got caught coming in with a couple of guns which he said were for you. He didn't have much option, Jim.

Moody: He didn't have to grass me up. I kept a low profile and I was paying him well. I was hoping to hang it out for another year or so then try and get out of the country. I knew you would have all the ports and that covered.

Forman: Sorry to hear about your mother's death, Jim. That must have cut you up.

Moody: Yeah it did. I s'ppose there's no chance of visiting her grave before I go inside, is there?

Snape: I can't promise but I will try my best for you. But don't look on it as a favour.

Moody: Enough, Guv'nor!

Snape: What about all the money you have had.

Moody: It's all gone, apart from what I was flushing down the toilet.

Snape: Jim, Sammy and John put you on plenty more. If you like I will go through them.

Moody: I ain't gonna tell you all about those big ones no more.

Snape: But there were other big ones, Jim.

Moody: I'll have the ones Charlie had. That's fair enough, surely?

Forman: What about guns though, Jim? I find it hard to believe you haven't got any hidden away somewhere. Our information was that you are supposed to carry a couple of shotguns with you all the time!

Moody: That's a load of bollocks. You people think I am a psychopath. Do you know what that really means? It means like an accountant who has a load of money off from his firm and gets caught. He doesn't know he has done wrong. I know what I have done and I'll plead guilty unless those cunts Benefield and Segars drop dead, then I'll fight it.

Snape: What about your fingerprints, Jim?

Moody: Yeah, that's tricky, I'll admit. I knew that Benefield would grass us up. I told Chopper as he was staring at me in the pub. I think there was a few of us there at the time. I felt his eyes on me. Didn't seem right.

[A cup of tea is provided and there is a general conversation.]

Forman: What about Segars' firm? You haven't said much about him?

Moody: I didn't trust that grass either.

Forman: You don't seem to trust many people, Jim.

Snape: What about bent police officers, Jim?

Moody: I won't grass my mates. So I wouldn't grass them. I know how you feel though. You must think of this like I do of Benefield and Segars.

Snape: I am positive you have had a bent policeman on your payroll.

Moody: Leave it out.

Snape: It's one thing giving information, but this was working both ends against the middle for cash.

Moody: Can't get involved in that, Guv'nor!

Snape: You know we intercepted some of your mail to your Aussie girl. We thought you'd try to get out there.

Moody: I am disappointed in her. I really thought a lot of her. Did you have a phone tapped where she worked?

Snape: We can't do things like that, Jim.

Moody: I'd like to know what you fellows can't do!

Forman: Didn't you think of going out to Saudia Arabia with your brother?

Moody: Not really. Too hot for me.

Forman: Even hotter than here, Jim?

Moody: You were lucky, be fair. Even though I knew it had to come. What do you reckon I'll get if I put my hands up to the three?

Snape: Well, Jim, we didn't get much money back from you, did we?

Moody: That's right. But Knightly only got 16 didn't he. But you got their money back.

Snape: It's up to you, Jim. We have ample evidence. All right, Jim we will break off now but we will interview you again tomorrow before we charge you with the Blackwall Tunnel, Rochester and Banstead robberies.

Moody: Thanks for being straight with me.

[Moody's interview terminates at 3.05 p.m.]

Operation Ohio chief Charlie Snape – himself at least 6 ft 2 in. tall and with an athletic build – was surprised to see that legendary Moody was not as tall as he'd heard, but commented: 'Moody was well proportioned and clearly very fit.' Snape continued, 'He wasn't really a problem. We had him bang to rights and he knew there was no point in denying all this and fighting it. But on the other hand he would never have grassed anyone up. Never.'

At around 5 p.m. the same day, Jason Moody was taken out of his cell at Brixton Police Station and led down the corridor. He had no idea where he was going. It turned out to be one of the most disturbing experiences of his life. 'Without sayin' anything, they unlocked my father's cell and when I walked in I noticed he had bandages on both wrists. Then I realised he must have tried to kill himself. He'd always told me they'd never take him alive, but it was such a disturbing thing for a kid to see.'

Moody asked Jason if he was all right and he nodded, transfixed by the injuries. 'He didn't mention it. But he looked down,' recalled Jason. An awkward silence fell between father and son before two uniformed officers escorted Jason out of the cell. When he got back to his own cell, he found two policemen carefully removing all sharp objects. 'They musta thought I might try and do the same thing,' recalled Jason.

After the officers had locked the cell behind them the teenager sat down on the bunk bed and started sobbing. It was the day of his 15th birthday.

Jimmy Moody, teenage tearaway, in the early '60s when he linked up with the notorious Richardsons in south London. (Dickie Moody)

Jimmy Moody and Val on their wedding day, 23 May 1964, in the End End, where Val was born and bred. (Moody family)

Jimmy Moody (right), with his loyal brother Dickie, at his marriage to Val. (Dickie Moody)

Happy families. A wedding-day pose that looks like any other, although Jimmy Moody was already heavily involved with the south London underworld at this time. (Moody family)

Jimmy Moody in typical hardman pose. (Moody family)

Moody proudly shows off baby granddaughter Chayce in his rundown East End flat, as the net closes following his 13 years on the run. (Moody family)

Moody was over the moon after the birth of Jason in 1964, even though the family were then living in a tiny flat near the Blackwall Tunnel in the East End. (Moody family)

Jimmy Moody enjoying lighter moments with wife Val, son Jason and baby daughter Janine in 1968, just before he was convicted of manslaughter at the Old Bailey. (Moody family)

Moody greatly valued his time with baby granddaughter Chayce – as this pose in the bath of his East End flat shows. (Moody family)

Despite being on the run from the Operation Ohio police team over his involvement with the Chainsaw and Thursday gangs, Moody still managed to take his children Jason and Janine on outings to the countryside. This shot was taken near one of Moody's favourite spots on the Solent, where he kept a speedboat and a caravan. Other outings often turned out to be reconnaissance trips for future robberies. (Moody family)

A Christmas card sent to Moody in Brixton Prison by his children Jason and Janine after his arrest by the Operation Ohio team. (Moody family)

Operation Ohio's Detective Inspector Bill Forman (second left in dark suit) and Detective Superintendent Charlie Snape (far right in dark suit) were familiar names – even to Moody's young son, Jason. (Bill Forman)

A recent photograph of Chainsaw Gang member Bernie Khan outside The Blind Beggar pub where Ronnie Kray shot dead Jimmy Moody's criminal associate George Cornell a few days after the infamous gun battle at Mr Smith's club, Catford, in 1966. (Wensley Clarkson)

Fleet Street reported the escape of Moody, Gerard Tuite and Stan Thompson from Brixton Prison, although most coverage was given to the IRA man – much to Moody and Thompson's advantage. (Associated Newspapers)

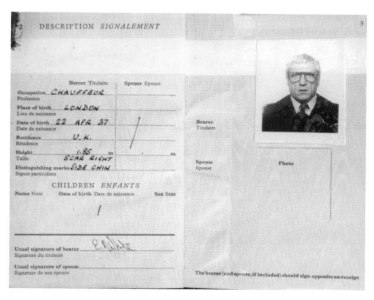

Moody's fake passport, in the name of 'Eddie White', with his blonde-hair-and-glasses disguise, was always kept in a secret hiding place wherever he was staying while on the run for 13 years. (Dickie Moody)

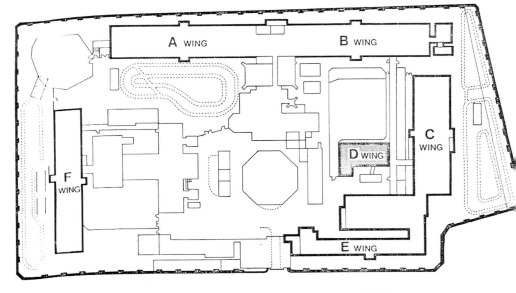

A plan of Brixton Prison, with D-wing shaded. (HM Prisons)

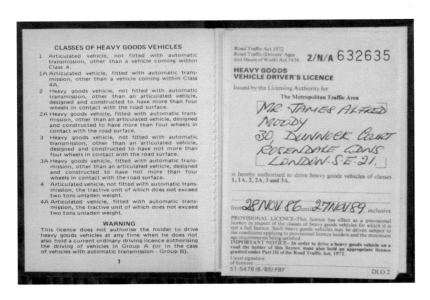

Moody even dusted down his old heavy goods vehicle licence (which he'd passed the test for in the mid-'60s) and tried to get some work as a lorry driver to help make ends meet during his final couple of years on the run.

Former IRA man Gerard Tuite as he is today at his home in Ireland. His loyalty to Moody has never faded. (Wensley Clarkson)

Dickie Moody, who still lives in the same flat in south-east London that he and his brother were brought up in by their hard-working mother Rosina. (Wensley Clarkson)

Moody in Victoria Park, Hackney, with his beloved granddaughter Chayce, just days before his death at a nearby pub. Typically, he refused to reveal his face in case the photo – taken by Janine – 'fell into the wrong hands'. (Moody family)

The Royal Hotel, next to Victoria Park, where Moody was finally awarded his own O.B.E. (Wensley Clarkson)

How the London *Evening Standard* revealed the full details of Moody's death across the capital. Moody's contract killing set off a spiral of underworld retribution that is still talked about to this day. (Associated Newspapers)

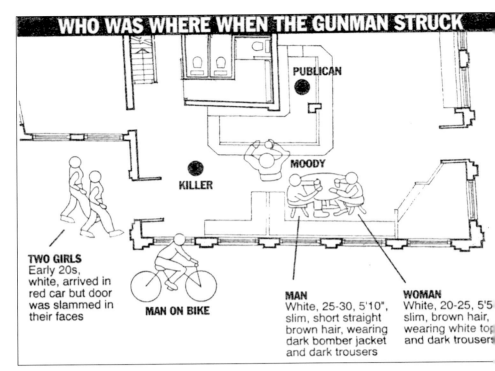

WHO WAS WHERE WHEN THE GUNMAN STRUCK

PUBLICAN

MOODY

KILLER

TWO GIRLS
Early 20s, white, arrived in red car but door was slammed in their faces

MAN ON BIKE

MAN
White, 25-30, 5'10", slim, short straight brown hair, wearing dark bomber jacket and dark trousers

WOMAN
White, 20-25, 5'5 slim, brown hair, wearing white top and dark trousers

How the London *Evening Standard* (11 June 1993) reconstructed the death of Jimmy Moody in a graphic. (Associated Newspapers)

The London *Evening Standard* billboard that Jason Moody has kept as a reminder of those dark days following his father's brutal murder. (Associated Newspapers)

Moody's final resting place at a cemetery in east London. (Wensley Clarkson)

Jimmy Moody's son Jason, now 38, who made a huge personal contribution to this book. He spent long periods of time with his father while he was on the run. (Moody family)

FOURTEEN

Across Enemy Lines

An hour after seeing his father, Jason Moody was picked up in Brixton Police Station's reception area by his uncle Dickie. It was 6 p.m. on the Saturday night before Christmas. Jason recalled: 'I knew we had to get out of there quick before the coppers got to my mum and sister in the East End.'

Dickie Moody put Jason in a black cab, which got to his mother's flat in the nick of time. Jason recalled: 'I remember being excited because there were Christmas lights everywhere but scared at the same time.'

Val was shocked when Jason showed up alone. 'But he did well to get here and warn us the police were on their way,' she recalled.

Moody's daughter Janine was deeply disturbed by what was happening. She'd sent one Christmas card to her mother and father *together* for the first time in her life that year. 'It was the first and only time I got my mum and dad a joint Christmas card. Turned out to be a bad omen. I started to think all this mess was my fault.'

Back at Brixton, Jimmy Moody wasn't saying much, which hardly surprised Bill Forman and his team. Forman explained: 'Jimmy Moody was the type of old-fashioned villain who never gave the game away. It just wasn't his style. We knew he'd be a tough egg to crack.' Jimmy Moody never relied on solicitors much because he prided himself on not telling the police anything incriminating in the first place.

It is clear that Forman respected Jimmy Moody even though he was officially 'the enemy'. He recalled: 'That raid on Coldharbour Lane was my first meeting with Big Jim and he was every bit as impressive as I thought he'd be. The man definitely had certain principles. He was very fastidious. No doubt he would have preferred to lead a normal family life but that just wasn't possible.'

Bill Forman and his colleagues felt a lot of sympathy for Jason. Forman explained: 'It must have been tough on the lad. He was just a kid and yet in many ways he was his father's minder.'

Jimmy Moody was still fuming about that 'fuckin' grass' John Kennedy. Now he was banged up and well aware a long sentence awaited him, something he'd sworn he'd never go through again as long as he lived. That was undoubtedly why he'd tried to take his own life. Moody looked on suicide as honourable and a good way of putting two fingers up at the law. But now he'd tried the easy way out he wanted to see if he could still beat the system and stay alive at the same time.

Many detectives believed Moody's arrest showed the balance of power was tilting back in favour of the police. A number of highly publicised shootings by the Flying Squad following Moody's arrest seemed to prove the point. 'It was as if the cozzers were saying to us that they'd wipe us off the streets unless we stopped blaggings,' recalled robber Bernie Khan. 'It was a right hairy time for villains.'

The Operation Ohio team swooped on Moody's family twice in the days following the dramatic arrest. Yet again, Moody's family were finding their lives divided between the outside world and the crime-fuelled, crazy existence led by their wayward father and husband. Explained Jason: 'Dad being nicked wasn't such a big surprise, but I knew it hurt him deeply. Problem was that there was overwhelming evidence against him. Guess that's why he tried to top himself.'

The arrest of Jimmy Moody itself got little coverage in the newspapers because the police didn't release details of his identity, and Christmas was fast approaching so little real news was appearing in print.

The *Daily Telegraph* dated 24 December 1979 ran a small piece headlined: 'KEY MAN HELD AFTER BRIXTON POLICE SWOOP'. The story stated: 'A man, believed to be a key figure in a major police investigation into serious crimes over the past ten years, was being questioned at Brixton Police Station last night.'

That same day – Christmas Eve 1979 – at Brixton Police Station, Bill Forman visited Moody in the cells once again and confirmed he'd be charged with the Blackwall Tunnel, Rochester and Banstead robberies.

Moody's only response was to nod his head, shrug his shoulders and say: 'I understand.'

Moody remained in Brixton Police Station for more than a week. He also once again asked Bill Forman if he'd allow him to visit his mother's grave. Rosina Moody had been buried a few days earlier at the West Norwood Cemetery, in south London, after Moody made sure Dickie was given an envelope with £2,000 to cover all the funeral expenses. Moody wanted to go to his mother's grave before he got the expected long sentence for his part in those robberies. Moody's brother Dickie explained: 'He was so cut up about Mum's death. It shook him to the core. Jim really did want to see her grave. It wasn't some ploy to hoof it.'

Although Bill Forman seriously considered allowing Moody to visit the cemetery – it was en route to the magistrate's court – he changed his mind on the basis that if Moody did make a run for it then they would certainly all lose their jobs. However, officers at Brixton Police Station did a whip round and collected enough money to send some flowers to Rosina Moody's grave.

A few weeks later Moody did persuade his police guards to stop near the cemetery on the way to another court appearance. As one of the policemen present later explained: 'I cuffed him, which he didn't like, and looked around carefully to see if anyone was there because we knew Moody was capable of anything. But we didn't want to deprive a bloke of seeing his mother's grave, especially since it might have been the last time he'd see that grave for 20 or 30 years.'

But neither Moody or his police guards could find the grave and officers began to suspect Moody was using his mother's good name as an excuse to 'hoof it'. Eventually they gave up looking for the grave and returned to the police van. Moody didn't argue, which seemed to suggest he'd been tumbled. The police guard later explained: 'He was very polite, no trouble, but I had that feeling about him and that's why he was cuffed. He'd have made a break for it if ever he got the opportunity.'

At 10 a.m., on Saturday, 28 December, Operation Ohio detective Bill Forman held another interview with Jimmy Moody. This time it was in a single interview room at Brixton Police Station.

Moody said he was prepared to put his hands up to the Banstead, Rochester and Blackwall Tunnel jobs, but refused to make a written statement, although he did agree to sign a copy of the notes taken during the interview. When asked what he'd done with his share of the money from the robberies – estimated at £200,000 – Moody said he'd spent most of it on the run and also flushed the rest down the toilet. 'Rest of it went on the leeches who hang around you once they know you've pulled a job,' he told Forman.

'What about those two sawn-offs, Jim,' asked Forman. 'You'd use them at a drop of a hat. Have you got any more secreted away?'

'That's a load of bollocks,' said Moody. 'I have never used guns, nor have I hurt anyone in any of my robberies and that I can be proud of. A gun on my robberies is only for show – past robberies that is.'

When Forman once again mentioned the arrest of Irishman Kennedy at Gatwick Airport, Moody was still infuriated: 'This man Kennedy lent me his pad for £15,000 cash and also asked me for £500 about a month ago for his fare to come over to see his brother, who was badly burnt. I knew he was coming but I never had any knowledge that he had any guns whatsoever.' Moody described Kennedy as an alcoholic and he claimed he could get a gun anytime he wanted in the UK. Moody continued to insist there were no firearms in the Brixton flat and that he'd never carried a gun. He then mentioned the £25,000 he said was still owed to him by Kennedy. Moody reckoned that Kennedy set him up to avoid paying off those debts.

Then Forman asked: 'Did any of your family know you were involved in robberies, Jim?'

'Not one of them. I respect all my family and I wouldn't involve one of them. My boy was in the flat, as you know, and no way would I have had him there if any of my family had known.'

Forman confirmed that police had found the Range Rover Moody had bought in the name of Collins and then sold in such a hurry when he heard about the Tony Knightly car chase. Moody insisted the man who bought it from him had no idea about its background. Moody also claimed he was 'skint' when he carried out the Banstead job. 'All my money had gone on caravans, boats, mobile homes, gambling and good living.'

When the subject of other robberies came up, Moody got angry and snapped at Forman: 'I don't want to be asked about other robberies. I've been very fair with you and put my hands up to the three but I refuse to answer questions about any others.'

'Then all this is a waste of time, Jim?'

'Yes, it is. Why not throw in the Jack the Ripper murders, IRA bombings and anything else you want?'

'Any idea where Bernie Khan is? He is the last robber we want for the Banstead job,' asked Forman.

'Haven't got a clue.'

Moody was then asked about money found on Jason. He insisted Jason didn't know that it came from a robbery. Moody said he was admitting the three jobs because he didn't want to waste money on legal representation.

When the interview was terminated, Moody wrote in his own scrawling handwriting at the bottom of the final page of the statement: 'Never at any time have I been threatened, induced or offered any deals. All my answers have been verbal. I would like to thank the officers Mr Snape and Mr Forman for being straight with the proceedings.'

A few minutes later, the interview was reconvened at Moody's request. Forman told Moody that gun carrier John Kennedy stated Moody's brother Dickie had visited his hideaway in Brixton. 'Definitely no. Not true,' responded Moody.

Forman laid in with another question about so-called airport grass John Kennedy. 'He claims you paid him to get a fake passport and driving licence. Is this true?'

Moody then described Kennedy as 'a filthy IRA sympathiser and maybe he was doing it for his own ends. He comes from Limerick.' Moody claimed Kennedy had blackmailed him out of £10,000 by threatening to inform the police of his whereabouts.

When asked once again about other robberies, Moody replied: 'I swear on my mother's grave I have not been in any other robberies.'

Moody even insisted on signing the bottom of the last page of the statement and drawing lines across it to ensure nothing was added later. He obviously sensed that the police were growing increasingly frustrated with his refusal to help them with 'other matters', including claims that detectives investigating the Chainsaw Gang had given robbers routes of security vans, helped plan raids and even warned the Chainsaw mob when they were about to be arrested. Moody dismissed all Forman's questions. 'It's totally against my principles to help the cozzers.'

Bill Forman tried to do a deal with Moody that if he offered information and pleaded guilty he'd get 16 years, but Moody wanted it reduced to 10 years.

He told Forman: 'I'll only hold me hands up for ten.'

'No way, Jim. No one's gonna agree that deal.'

'Then bollocks. I don't wanna know.'

By refusing to fully cooperate, Moody was effectively putting off his actual trial for at least a year while prosecutors gathered enough evidence to secure a prosecution against him for every single robbery he'd committed with the gang.

But the Operation Ohio team were pleased to just have Moody off the streets. Bill Forman summed up the police investigation in this report to his Scotland Yard superiors: 'As far as I am concerned this operation has no equal and it is one I feel proud to have been associated with, together with all its loads of grief.'

FIFTEEN

The Thinkin' Factory

Jimmy Moody's new home was to be inside Brixton Prison, which had been used for trial and remand prisoners in London since 1896. Much of its construction dated back even further to 1819, when some of the buildings were used as a factory. The average population of Brixton Prison was around 1,000, but by the time Moody arrived it was down to around the 600 mark. As one-time inmate and Chainsaw Gang member Bernie Khan put it: 'We call Brixton the thinkin' factory because it's where the inmates lie on their bunks, hands behind their head, thinkin' about who put them away, who they want revenge on and how the fuck they'll get out without serving loadsa bird.' Jimmy Moody preferred the single cells – measuring 12 feet by 6 feet – in Brixton because, as he told one inmate, 'I'd rather not have to talk to any other cunt.'

Inside Brixton's notorious D wing, Moody found himself incarcerated with a range of alleged criminals from hitmen and IRA bombers to domestic murderers. By this time prison authorities had segregated paedophiles for their own protection – which helped avoid any of the scenes from Moody's earlier prison terms when he'd targeted child molesters for some special 'Moody treatment'.

Shortly after Moody arrived at Brixton, Val filed for divorce. They'd somehow survived 16 years of marriage, but Val believed that now her husband was going to be locked up for a long time she had to get on with her life and start afresh. 'The kids were getting older and Val needed to find some stability from somewhere. Jimmy couldn't provide that,' one old family friend later explained. But Val still promised to continue visiting Moody and bring the kids along.

Moody was philosophical about the end of his marriage. He'd always enjoyed Val's company and they had undoubtedly loved each other very much indeed, but he'd lead a life completely independently of marital ties for a long time. Son Jason explained: 'It wasn't much of a marriage in most people's eyes, but it still had a sparkle when they were together and that made it sad when it ended, but Dad being banged up yet again left Mum with little choice.'

Once again, Moody's family had to cope with prison visits and the knowledge that Moody was probably going to spend most of the rest of his life in jail. In some ways, it was less stressful to know exactly where he was instead of worrying about whether he was going to be shot and killed during an armed robbery out on the highways and byways of Britain.

Whenever Val visited Brixton with Jason and Janine she was allowed to bring in food, such as Moody's favourite, sirloin steak, because he was a remand prisoner and not yet found guilty in a court of law. On their first visit, Moody even mentioned to Janine that the first time he'd ever seen her as a baby was inside Brixton's D-wing when he was locked up during the torture trials in 1967. This time Moody was inside Brixton knowing there was no chance he'd be acquitted.

In January 1980, Moody sent Janine – 'Janina' as he called her – a birthday card. It read:

> To my darling daughter
> Janina xxxxxx
> Happy birthday on your 13th one
> Now a teenager xxxx
> Amazing pooh, how time flies. I first saw you when you was 2
> weeks old in this cell block 'd' (the youngest ever to be in here),
> now 12 years and 11 months 2 weeks later in the same lousy visit.
> But my darling daughter is strong and understands why now xxx
> Love Daddy Jim
> Love always XXXXXX

Moody's fearsome reputation ensured that most Brixton inmates and staff steered clear of him, apart from the bigger-name criminals intrigued by the prisoner many said was the hardest man in London, if not the entire country. Moody slipped into tough-guy-in-prison mode with ease. Eyes down, shoulders rounded, chewing gum. He played the game and knew only too well that inside a place like Brixton only the strongest survived.

Also awaiting trial in Brixton's D-wing was notorious alleged hitman Big H Henry MacKenny, who along with fellow professional killer John Childs, were labelled 'Murder Incorporated' at their later Old Bailey trial. The pair were said to have touted for 'business' among the wealthy friends of Lord Lucan as well as asking the National Front if they wanted 'troublesome Pakistanis' killed. The two men and their general 'dogsbody' Terence Pinfold used guns, axes, knives and a sword-stick to kill at discount prices – dismembering bodies, often burning the pieces like logs on an open fire and leaving no remains.

Big H was eventually found guilty of the killing of ten-year-old Terence Brett and his haulage contractor father George, a double murder which Jimmy Moody had once been linked to. MacKenny's other alleged victims included toy manufacturer Terence Eve and restaurant proprietor Frederick Sherwood.

Security in Brixton Prison was supposed to have been beefed up after a number of prisoners broke out for 'pub crawls' and returned to their cells in the early morning. One inmate, Alan Rutty, 21, got so drunk he couldn't climb the wall to get back inside the prison. He even told an inquiry that Brixton was 'ridiculous and relaxed'.

Inside Brixton in January 1980, yells of delight went up when news of a £4 million silver bullion robbery reached the prison. A team of south-east London robbers had hijacked a truck carrying bullion near the old docks behind Tooley Street, in Bermondsey, south London.

One inmate at Brixton not cheering was Gerard Tuite, alleged to be one of the most deadly Provisional IRA terrorists of the late 1970s – a master of disguise and a man whose beliefs were so strong he'd happily die for the republican cause.

By this time, Provo attacks on the mainland were a sad fact of life. When four people were injured a few months earlier by a bomb in a crowded Woolworths store in Yoevil, Somerset, and another device went off in a nearby car park, the police linked the attacks to a terrorist known as 'the limping man'. That man was said to often use the name 'Gerrard Fossett', leader of a Provisional IRA active service unit in Britain. He'd already been linked to a London car bombing and two other explosions in January 1979 in the south-east of England. His real name was Gerard Anthony Tuite and one day he was going to play a vital role in Jimmy Moody's future.

In the autumn of 1979 – just before Moody's arrest in Coldharbour Lane – Scotland Yard got wind of a plan by the Provos to spring one of their incarcerated leaders Brian Keenan, from Brixton using a helicopter and a big bribe to one crooked prison officer. The plot was uncovered when police swooped on properties in London, Liverpool, Manchester, the West Midlands and Hampshire in the early hours of Wednesday, 12 December 1979. One of those arrested was Gerard Tuite.

After Tuite's arrest, police raided a flat where the Irishman had lived with a young English nurse in Trafalgar Road, Greenwich – just a stone's throw from Jimmy Moody's home territory. Detectives found traces of nitro-glycerine and a taped hit-list of leading politicians and royalty including then foreign secretary Lord Carrington, Roy Jenkins and the Duke of Gloucester. The tape also went on to detail military targets and the movement of nuclear waste trains. It was also alleged Tuite had hired a car that was then involved in an explosion in London. Gerard Tuite's family were steeped in violent Republican history. Death stalked his own parents' marriage in 1942 when their wedding party ended in a gun battle between guests and police. Two men died in the shootout – a police officer and Tuite's uncle, Patrick Dermody, an IRA gunman on the run after an armed bank robbery. Tuite was born 13 years later at the same house in Mountnugent, Co. Cavan.

Tuite – the fourth of seven children – went to a local school run by monks and then worked as a caretaker before joining the merchant navy in his teens. It's alleged that those long absences from home were cover for his training as a Provo bomber. Tuite also developed the skill to disguise his appearance, an art he put to good use when he moved to London as a Provisional IRA 'sleeper' in the late '70s.

By the time Tuite arrived in Brixton Prison at the end of 1979, he already had his mind set on one thing. 'First day I walked into Brixton reception I said to my mate, I gotta get out of here,' Tuite later explained. He knew that staff at Brixton would keep a closer watch on him because of his alleged activities as an IRA terrorist.

Tuite shared A-wing with three other Provos arrested with him for their part in bombings and the plot to free Brian Keenan, who was over with Jimmy Moody in D-wing. Tuite immediately began defiantly digging a hole in his A-wing cell wall after being provided with some tools by a friendly English prisoner. Tuite also had a radio brought in to him and listened avidly to the constant flow of publicity surrounding his case. He even befriended guards. Gerard Tuite's first escape scheme involved two vans and would require the skill he had acquired through

IRA training to take off handcuffs. He later explained: 'I was going to run up over the van and across and over the wall. Everyone on the wing was helping. One chap's girlfriend even taped blades inside a newspaper and brought them in for us.'

But staff heard rumours about Tuite's scheme and he was transferred to D-wing. Tuite was put in the ground-floor cell next to an armed-robber called Kenny Baker, while above them on the first floor was the alleged contract killer Big H. Next to him was master prison escapee and bank robber Stan Thompson. Thompson – quite short, stocky, square faced, with a small mouth and his hair combed forward – had escaped from Chelmsford and earlier Brixton (through a window in 1966) in addition to his headline-hitting breakout from Dartmoor in 1971. Next to Thompson was Jimmy Moody with Provos chief Brian Keenan at the end of that row on the first floor. Tuite recalled: 'Obviously Brian was the only one I knew on the wing. We had a heart-to-heart chat one night and he told me there was a way to escape. He said he'd already discussed it with Jimmy Moody.' Tuite laughed out loud as he later explained: 'It was a joke. I was in D-wing – they called it the Submarine – because the prison considered it more secure, yet here we were discussing how we'd get out.'

Tuite was already intrigued by Jimmy Moody after he overheard three inmates talking on the prison landing about Moody being the most dangerous man in the prison. 'That got me thinkin': now that's a man I need to get to know,' Tuite explained. When Brian Keenan was suddenly transferred out of Brixton that left the way open for Tuite to start planning his own audacious breakout so he approached Jimmy Moody and was surprised how easy Moody was to deal with. 'I was expecting this big tough animal but Jim wasn't a problem.' Moody insisted on calling Tuite 'Pat' or 'Paddy' from the first moment they met but that didn't bother Tuite in the slightest. He recalled: 'The London police had called me a lot worse and they meant it.'

Jimmy Moody had already decided he had to escape from Brixton and had spent a few days walking around the wing looking for the prison's weak spots. But the odds were obviously stacked against Moody and Tuite. Most inmates in D-wing were serious alleged offenders, which meant it was supposed to be more secure than other areas of the prison. However Moody concluded the best plan was to go through the end cell on the first floor. The current resident of that cell was Big H. No one liked him or even talked to him and he rarely came out of his cell. Even the prison officers hated him.

A number of modifications had been made to D-wing over the previous few years to avoid the embarrassing escapes which occurred in the '60s and early '70s. Closed-circuit TV was in place, as was an electronically operated locking system on certain internal doors. The official description of category A prisoners like Moody and Tuite was: 'Those whose escape would be highly dangerous to the public or police or to the security of the State.' Moody noticed that cells and prisoners were rarely personally searched and visitors were searched even less thoroughly and frequently. Moody also noted the dog patrols were ineffective because they only included small areas of the wing.

Moody told Tuite that if he wanted to join his escape team he'd have to change cells with Big H. Tuite immediately turned to Moody and said: 'No problem, Jim. I'll get him to move out of his cell.'

Moody rolled his eyes. 'You'll be fuckin' lucky. He's a right miserable git.'

'If necessary we'll get rid of him – kill him,' said Tuite. Even Moody was surprised by Tuite's cold-blooded response.

Tuite later explained: 'It was that important. The inmates said he'd never move. I said he's got to move, end of story.'

So Gerard Tuite went to work on Big H. 'I just went in and introduced myself and he just said, "I've heard about you," and I said "I've heard a little about you, too. You are not exactly a popular being around here." So he explained to me his case, which I found fascinating, and I definitely believed the man was innocent.' More importantly, Big H made it clear he had no interest in escaping himself.

Tuite persuaded Big H to ask for a move on the grounds that no one would talk to him on the first floor. When he was told there were no vacant cells on the ground floor, MacKenny suggested Tuite could swap with him. It looked as if he was doing Big H a favour. By the end of June 1980 Gerard Tuite had replaced Big H in that first-floor cell alongside robber Stan Thompson and Jimmy Moody. Tuite already had in his possession three hacksaw blades he'd hidden in the lid of his art-box before he left A-wing. Tuite also continued his getting-to-know-you sessions with inmates and staff. 'It was tricky at first because the police and newspapers had made me out to be some kind of sick monster. But once they realised I was a human being they started to listen to my point of view.' Tuite made a point of listening to his fellow inmates' complaints about prison beatings, torture by certain staff members and gave advice on how to handle those guards – Tuite even advised other inmates on how to get longer visits from friends and family. It was all part of his crafty plan to get everyone 'on side'.

Stanley Thompson – the man in the middle cell between Tuite and Moody – was a quietly spoken character with a previous record as long as his arm and a penchant for escaping from whatever prison he happened to be in at the time. Thompson was not to be underestimated and Moody made a point of telling his new friend 'Paddy' Tuite this. Moody also encouraged Tuite to get fit and bulk up despite his leg injury, which worsened during his stay in Brixton. Tuite explained: 'There was a pipe up in the corner of my cell and I used to go up it many times every night to try and keep fit. Up, down, up, down – climbing it until I was sweating buckets.'

Tuite needed Moody because he had all the contacts outside prison to bring in the required equipment. Enter Moody's now ex-wife, children and brother Dickie. They would all eventually smuggle in masonry drills, hacksaws, screwdrivers and tubes of glue, all hidden in their socks under trousers.

Operation Ohio chief Charlie Snape obviously had no idea what Jimmy Moody and his pals were up to inside Brixton Prison, but he 'had a feeling' Moody might try and escape. In the summer of 1980, Snape telephoned the head of D-wing to voice his concerns. He later explained: 'I warned them about Moody because I knew he didn't want to serve any more time. I had a feeling he might try and hoof it.' The Brixton officer who spoke to Snape responded: 'Oh he won't get out of here, this is a secure unit. No one escapes from D-wing.'

Other inmates soon heard about the escape plan but none of them dared risk upsetting hardman Jimmy Moody by telling the authorities. In any case, most presumed the plan wouldn't succeed. As one prison official later admitted: 'Twenty-three inmates knew what was happening but not one thought it was possible. Many considered it not even worth talking about. And of course many of them were shit scared of Jimmy Moody!'

The inmates were also given other 'incentives' not to talk. Gerard Tuite explained: 'We got to know where the families of some inmates lived and I said that if anyone informed on us I'd visit those families – which put an element of fear into them. It made sure there was no danger they'd split on us.'

Jim Moody had a problem with his cell cupboard because it was on wheels, which made it easier to move and therefore expose the hole he intended to dig. So he screwed it to the wall to stop it being moved during cell-inspection times. Prison officers making regular security checks of cells on the wing never questioned why it was no longer free standing.

Moody would have the hardest time working because his cell was just above the prison's visiting area. Stan Thompson explained: 'There was a screw who sat at the table all day long supervising visits, so all Jim's digging had to be done at night.' When Moody worked on his hole he used a radio/cassette player to drown out some of the noise and particularly adored listening to Stevie Wonder's 'Masterblaster'. Moody was eventually nicknamed 'Masterblaster' by other inmates who'd hear him singing along to the track most evenings.

Moody covered the hole in his wall by screwing his locker back into place at the end of each session. Thompson did the same in his middle cell, while Tuite dug his hole mostly at weekends. Two of the escape team always ensured that the other member could dig without interruption by playing cards together in the rec. room. Thompson explained: 'That way the screws could always see us and if they came near our cells we'd call out "Liverpool!" as a code and then whoever was digging would know the screws were about to come in their cell.' Stan Thompson was surprised how well he got on with Gerard Tuite. 'Gerry was a very reasonable person. A good guy. That's why we all worked well together.'

There were problems between Moody and Thompson, however. They had two serious fights while working on the holes in their cells, although Thompson later put this down to the stress of trying to get the job done. Thompson recalled: 'Jim was a "Moody" bastard, no doubt about that, but he was also a solid, reliable fella who was as good as his word and no one in D-wing ever had the bottle to take him on except me. We had this stupid argument about what we'd do if our kids were grasses. Naturally, Jim would have killed anyone who was a grass, including his kids. I told him he was being over the top. We started shoving each other and then I whacked him out of sheer frustration. He didn't flinch and it was my hardest punch. He was about to crush me into little pieces when the screws saved me.'

Another time Stan Thompson saw Jimmy Moody throwing a 'Moody' on the wing. 'It was an awesome sight. First Jim breaks a door down, then he takes on four screws and then hoofs up to the next floor and tries to knock down a cell door, all because some bloke was making a racket with his radio. You could say Jimmy had a bit of a short fuse.' Thompson believes to this day that the prison staff were so terrified of

Moody they gave him a wide berth and didn't bother him. That attitude certainly helped Moody get away with digging the hole through to Thompson's cell without too many interruptions.

Meanwhile, Val, the children and Dickie started smuggling in parts of tools in their socks – at that time all body searches involved scans by metal detectors which never covered anything below the knees. Once in the visitors' room it was easy to slip across the tools under the table. Inside, the three men even cobbled together a drill 'powered' by an old pencil-sharpener Tuite had borrowed from an unsuspecting staff member. With a coat-hanger for a handle and the bit forced into the sharpener, Moody, Tuite and Thompson took it in turns to drill their way through the first layer of granite in each wall. This was followed by half a brick a day, which took an average three hours of work. Moody had already estimated the entire job would take at least three months.

The width of the entire hole in each room had to be a minimum of 15 inches by 10.5 inches. It was 11 inches off the ground. When one inmate on the wing was allowed to repaint his cell he gave some of the paint to all three men to use to cover the wall where they'd been digging.

Moody then decided to speed up the process by making use of a tubular bar – an integral part of all prison tables – the only problem was that type of table wasn't allowed in the cells. Tuite solved this by developing a craze for large jigsaw puzzles. When his puzzle outgrew his cell table, he persuaded the warders to let him have the bigger type of table in his cell. They cut the tube they wanted from the table in such a way that, with the help of tape, paint and a dab of superglue, it could be replaced rapidly.

A broom head was then added to the end of the table leg to enable pressure from the body or shoulder to be applied to it. It was then used to smash away at the masonry and brickwork to speed up the digging process.

In all, Moody's wife, children and brother Dickie smuggled in two screwdriver bits in four-inch-long hardened steel; about six hacksaw blades; two flexi hacksaws; two tubes of superglue and three drill bits for quarter-inch tungsten masonry. These were then concealed in the holes attached to the cell walls behind their lockers.

But prison visits by the Moody family could also be highly emotional. One day Jason went with his mother and sister to Brixton and announced he wanted to join the merchant navy. Instead of being proud that his son had chosen to follow in his footsteps, Moody went ballistic. Jason recalled: 'He said there was no way I could sign up. I'd taken all the paperwork and brochures to show him. He just grabbed the merchant navy magazine off me and prodded the photo on the cover of this blonde-haired man. 'You're not fuckin' joinin'. Only poofs join the merchant navy these days. It was different when I was a kid.' Moody tore the magazine into little pieces in front of his heartbroken, teenage son.

Back inside D-wing, the escape work continued. Tuite was covering up all his digging with a piece of cardboard and tape. In front of the painted cardboard patch, he stood his paintings and his cabinet. None of the guards suspected anything. Gerard Tuite recalled: 'The screws left it to the people with the cameras to keep an eye on us, and the people on the cameras left it up to the screws on the wing.'

Moody, Tuite and Thompson all relished getting one over on the prison authorities. Tuite explained: 'Being in the know was brilliant. One time the prison guv'nor came in to my cell and he didn't even realise what was happening. We knew we were up against it but all three of us were fuckin' determined.' Tuite then added: 'I have never been as close to anyone in my life as I was to those two boys [Moody and Thompson].'

Other problems appeared on the horizon in the run-up to the escape. When a new prisoner moved onto the wing, Moody became suspicious when he spotted that the man lit his cigarette with a lighter (forbidden in prison) as opposed to a match. When Moody told Tuite about his suspicions they watched the inmate very carefully. Was he a plant? Moody and Tuite put it around that there was a spy on the wing. Within hours, the man had been beaten up so badly he was sent to hospital. He was never seen again.

Work on the holes stopped and started continuously, depending on the activity on the wing. But none of the three men once considered giving up. Then, in late November 1980, Moody, Tuite and Thompson had an extraordinary stroke of good luck when roof tilers began work on an extension right alongside Tuite's cell. They were using a wooden frame on wheels to get across the roof and it was left there each night.

Jimmy Moody then calculated the breakthrough point from Tuite's cell over the sloping, tiled roof of the small extension. He'd worked this out by first measuring the single brick in the wall during an exercise period and then counting the bricks. Within another week all the bricks on the outside wall – in Tuite's cell – had been removed. Tuite left about an inch of plaster on the outside so all he had to do was punch a hole through it on the night of their escape.

On Sunday night, 14 December 1980, Jimmy Moody broke through the final, thin layer of plaster into Thompson's cell between him and Tuite. But the hole wasn't big enough for him to get his body through. Tuite explained: 'Jim was like two filing cabinets stacked on top of two more filing cabinets.' He was stuck.

Moody immediately told Thompson, who'd already punched through his hole into Tuite's cell, to go ahead without him. But neither of the men felt they could abandon Moody. Tuite explained: 'It was a fuckin' disaster. We couldn't leave him behind after all we'd been through together.'

Moody managed to squeeze himself back into his cell and the escape was abandoned for the night. A car and driver waiting in a side street close to the prison gave up and disappeared into the darkness. Thompson's hole into Tuite's cell was covered by a pillow made to look as though it had fallen off the bed, while Moody's hole into Thompson's cell was disguised by a bedspread hanging down from a table.

Luckily for them, Tuite hadn't completed his opening, wanting to wait until all three inmates were in his cell, so no one could see the hole from the outside of D-wing. Now they were going to have to wait until the next night and hope no one would uncover the holes between their cells.

SIXTEEN

On the Hoof

Jimmy Moody and his two partners knew they had to escape the following night – Monday, 15 December – before the holes in their cells were uncovered and all those months of hard work gone to waste. During the morning a phone call was made to arrange for the pick-up car to return that night. That afternoon, Stan Thompson arrived back at Brixton after a court appearance. By mid-evening, Jimmy Moody was trying to make his hole big enough to get through. The duty officer locked in D-wing that night did hear noises, but thought they were prisoners using the cell toilets.

In his cell that evening, Gerard Tuite wrote a letter to a contact in Southampton – to make it sound as if that was where he would be heading. Tuite provided this clever red herring after a policeman had once told him that everything he wrote down on any piece of paper found in his cell would be looked at by the authorities. Tuite later explained: 'So I ripped up the letter and left an indentation for them to examine on the pad of paper in my cell. I knew they watched a ship from New York and it all made sense to them. I'm headin' down your way, blah, blah, blah. I tore the letter up. Burned it. It was all a con and I knew they'd fall for it hook, line and sinker.'

At 2.45 a.m., all three men carefully put dummy figures made of clothing stuffed with newspapers under the covers of their beds. Moody and Thompson then squeezed through both internal holes into Tuite's cell. Now the escape team were ready to punch out Tuite's outside hole completely. They'd scheduled a further 30 minutes to ensure it was big enough.

At just before 3.15 a.m. on the morning of Tuesday, 16 December 1980, Stan Thompson went face down into the hole through Tuite's outside wall. Tuite followed seconds later. Then it was Jimmy Moody's turn. He looked down at the hole and shook his head.

'It's too small, I can't do it,' said Moody.

Tuite looked at Moody and wondered if he'd developed extra muscles through his work that day.

'Just get on with it, Jim,' whispered Tuite back through the hole to Moody.

Moody took a deep breath and crouched down. He got his head through the hole and struggled to put his arms under his stomach.

'I'm stuck, I can't do it,' mumbled a breathless Moody.

Tuite leaned down and started trying to pull him through by the shoulders.

'It's no good. I can't get through, I'm stuck,' whispered Moody.

He couldn't go back or forward.

'Listen, I'll give you an hour,' said Moody. 'As long as I can stick it. Just get the fuck outta here."

'No fuckin' way, Jim. We're a team. You're comin' with us,' whispered Tuite, motioning to Thompson to help. Both men then leaned down, and grabbed Moody under his arms.

Tuite later recalled: 'So we literally tore him through the hole. I could hear the muscles tearing right off his back. He left a lot of flesh behind but we got him through.'

Now Moody, Tuite and Thompson were on the roof of the next-door B-wing. An outside CCTV camera failed to spot them thanks to another inmate shining a light in his cell at the moment they got on the roof. That diverted the camera from its regular route.

Moody, Tuite and Thompson moved quietly along the flat roof, going southwards alongside the ground adjacent to B-wing. Then they each took turns to ride the wooden 'crawlerboard' left by the construction workers round the razor-sharp barbed wire along the edge of the roof. After jumping down to the ground, Moody and his team moved along the end of Brixton's C-wing in a westerly direction, before turning towards the far corner of the prison perimeter wall where a 12-foot-high steel mesh fence surrounded the 17-foot-high perimeter wall. They got over the fence to the top of the wall, which they crawled along until they reached a blank spot not covered by security TV cameras. Jimmy Moody had earlier carefully selected the time when a prison officer with an Alsatian was at the other side of the prison grounds.

Moody then threw a blanket over the barbed wire on the top of the perimeter wall. The mesh fence provided a firm standing next to the brick wall. A rope and grapnel was then dropped onto the ground outside the prison before the three inmates slid down from the wall. They left their bag of tools at the base of the wall as a calling card.

They headed for the dimly lit side street that bordered the prison. 'But there was no fuckin' car waitin' for us,' recalled Stan Thompson. 'I think they just thought, "Well, it's hard luck, we're not comin' back a second time."' Stan Thompson continued: 'So we walked down the hill towards the centre of Brixton. The original plan was for the car to take us our separate ways, but now we had to stick together because that bastard vehicle hadn't turned up. We was waiting for a car to hijack when Jim saw this cab . . .'

Mini-cab driver Jim McDonald, 29 at the time, was answering a call to pick up a fare from a house close to Brixton Prison. McDonald knocked on the door of the house but got no reply. He was just getting back into his car when three men came running round the corner from the direction of the jail.

McDonald heard one of them say loudly: 'That was a crackin' party'.

'Nice party? Yeah, it was good,' said another of the men.

McDonald had just fired up his orange Marina when Moody tapped hard on his window. 'You a mini-cab?' he said, breathing clouds of steam on the glass.

McDonald looked at the man for a moment, considering his options. Three hard-looking characters after a fare in the early hours. As he later explained: 'I didn't want any trouble so I said I'd take them.'

Two of the men wore T-shirts, which seemed a bit strange to McDonald considering it was a chilly winter's night. The other man was wearing a boiler suit.

As Jimmy Moody climbed in the car he told McDonald: 'It's OK, we've got money,' and waved a fiver at him.

Moody asked McDonald to take them to the south London suburb of Herne Hill. The three men all sat in the back seat whispering to each other while Moody occasionally chipped in with directions. McDonald explained: 'When we got to the Herne Hill area they didn't seem to know exactly where they wanted to go.'

As the car drove along a main road, Moody shouted: 'There it is.' He was pointing at a chocolate-brown J-registration Austin Maxi parked at the side of the road.

'This'll do, mate,' said Moody.

Little did McDonald realise that the Maxi had nothing to do with the three escaped prisoners. They were simply laying a false trail on the assumption that McDonald would eventually talk to the police.

As they piled out of the mini-cab, McDonald heard one of them say: 'I hope there's petrol in it.'

The fare for the ten-minute trip was £1.50. Moody gratefully flung his fiver at the driver and didn't bother asking for any change.

As McDonald drove off, he saw the men standing round the car talking to each other.

It was 3.40 a.m. Moody, Tuite and Thompson waited for the mini-cab to disappear round the corner. Then Moody told the others: 'Follow me, gents.'

They walked half a mile to a quiet residential street where Moody stopped outside a three-storey house. He then picked up a handful of gravel and threw it at a first-floor window.

Eventually a head poked out of the window.

'Who's there?'

'Jimmy.'

'Jimmy who?'

'Jimmy fuckin' Moody.'

'Can't be, he's in the nick.'

'Just fuckin' let us in, will ya?'

Thompson recalled: 'When we finally got up to his mate's flat, his wife was eight months pregnant so we knew we weren't going to be there for long.'

As Tuite and Thompson stood around awkwardly, Moody made a series of phone calls. Within an hour the three men were being driven through the suburbs of south London by a balding, middle-aged man in a Ford Cortina. Two hours later they pulled up outside an isolated cottage next to a vast field near the ancient city of Canterbury in Kent.

Back inside Brixton Prison, the officers of D-wing had just discovered that the figures in each of the men's beds were crude dummies. A home-made drill was lying on the foot of Moody's cell. In Tuite's cell, hacksaw blades used to cut away metal security strips implanted in the outside brickwork were lying on a table. It was 5 a.m. The night-duty officer hadn't made an earlier check on D-wing, as was his duty.

'Home sweet home,' said Jimmy Moody, as he let himself into the small, whitewashed cottage.

Jimmy Moody and his two pals immediately took special precautions to ensure they weren't seen inside the cottage by keeping all the lights turned off and watching TV in virtual darkness. There was blanket coverage of the escape and all the emphasis was on Tuite. Moody and Thompson needed to quickly split from Tuite because, as Thompson later commented, 'He was hotter than a fuckin' chicken vindaloo.' Thompson explained: 'The good thing was no one gave a toss about us two. It was the big bad IRA man the entire nation was after. We might as well not have existed, but we needed to get away from him quickly.'

But for the moment all three knew they had to sit tight. Thompson explained: 'Jim wasn't happy in that cottage. He thought it was too cut off but we stayed put because we had to let the dust settle. It would have been madness to show our faces anywhere for at least a couple of days.'

All three were glued to the TV set when Stan Thompson's attractive 45-year-old girlfriend Pat Read came on screen. 'Give yourself up, Stan – and let's get married,' she told an ITN reporter.

'Awwww. Ain't that sweet, Stan. Your bird looks like a real good 'un,' said Moody.

Just then the reporter revealed that Thompson had earlier that day been acquitted in his absence at his robbery trial at St Albans Crown Court. There was stunned silence in the little white cottage in the Kent countryside.

Then Stan Thompson leapt up from his armchair. 'YES! YES! YES!' he screamed, punching the air with delight. 'I'm goin' home! I'm goin' home!'

But then Stan Thompson looked at the two other mens' faces.

That's when Moody muttered, 'Maybe not yet, old son.'

It was a chilling moment. Moody and Tuite were seriously thinking about killing Thompson because they didn't want to risk him talking to the police.

Thompson went stoney silent, his eyes snapping between both men.

Moody then turned to Thompson and said: 'Stan, you know what's gonna happen here?'

Thompson took a long gulp. 'Whatever you decide, lads.'

Moody looked at Tuite and then they both turned to Thompson and Tuite asked, 'What'd you wanna do, Stan?'

Thompson hesitated for a moment then took another deep breath. 'Hand myself in.'

'Mmmm,' said Tuite.

'Might not be as easy as that,' chipped in Moody.

Thompson knew what was going on in Moody and Tuite's minds.

He had to say something. 'I'll take my time, lads. The cozzers won't get nothin' outta me.'

Moody and Tuite looked at each other again.

Thompson held on tightly to the arms of his chair and looked back at the TV.

Tuite sucked a mouthful of air in through his gappy teeth before letting it out and smiling over at Moody. He nodded.

'We trust you, Stan,' said Moody, slapping Thompson hard on the knee. 'You're a free man. You lucky bastard!'

Tuite chipped in: 'And make sure you send them off on a few wild goose chases, all right?'

Thompson later admitted: 'I felt like I'd just won the fuckin' pools. I knew Jim and Tuite could have topped me there and then. They were certainly capable of it.'

That same night minicab driver Jim McDonald got his first chance to look at the newspaper headlines about the Brixton escape. He immediately called the police, who failed to call him back, so he shrugged his shoulders and went on shift for his minicab company.

Back in their Kent hideaway, Stan Thompson was happily preparing for an early start the next morning. All three had agreed he should get a bus and take his time going into London. They were staying on at the cottage. 'And,' Thompson explained, 'I didn't want to know where they were going after that.'

Early the following morning, Moody and Tuite strolled with Stan Thompson to the end of a narrow farm lane that reached the main road before leaving him to walk two miles to the nearest bus stop. He waited another two hours before hopping on a bus. The woman sitting next to Thompson was reading *The Sun*, which featured a photo of him alongside Jimmy Moody and Gerard Tuite on the front page. 'And you know what? That woman didn't once look at my face to compare it to the photo,' Thompson recalled.

Later that afternoon, Stan Thompson telephoned his girlfriend at the house they shared in Rainham, Essex, to say he was about to give himself up. Then he walked into the south London offices of his solicitor James Saunders and two hours later the two men entered Brixton Police Station.

'I believe you're lookin for me,' Thompson told a young woman police constable on desk duty.

'What?'

'My name's Stanley Thompson.'

Thompson later explained: 'Then this WPC at the desk disappears and suddenly eight cozzers burst out of the back office and grapple me to the ground. It was completely over the top.'

Within an hour, Thompson was being interrogated by Scotland Yard's Special Branch. Thompson recalled: 'They tried to make me talk but I wouldn't have any of it. There was no way I'd stitch up Jim and Tuite. That's not the way I operate.'

Thompson appeared at Brixton Magistrates Court the following morning and was remanded in custody on charges of conspiring to escape and escape. Scotland Yard announced to the media they were satisfied Thompson had no contact with Moody and Tuite after the men had broken free. Thompson's solicitor James Saunders told newsmen outside the court: 'He's very relieved it's all over. He was particularly moved by his girlfriend's plea. He certainly didn't have to be talked into it. It would be foolish to pretend that the fact he was acquitted was not a factor in him giving himself up. He found himself in a bizarre position and he has done the direct and sensible thing.'

In Kent, Moody and Tuite were confident Thompson wouldn't grass them up. Tuite later explained: 'When we waved goodbye to dear old Stan that morning we both agreed that we trusted him. He could have made a fortune out of telling the cops and the papers where we were, but he never said a word.'

Tuite and Moody watched TV, played cards and talked about their respective lives over the following 24 hours. 'We started to form a real bond of friendship,' recalled Tuite. 'I didn't hammer him over the head with all my beliefs, but I wanted him to understand that we [the Provos] weren't the animals the police and the press made us out to be. It was important to me that Jim respected me.'

Moody asked Tuite if the Provos would publicly announce he was dead so he could stay on the lam more easily. But Tuite refused because he believed the 'movement' would be discredited if Moody was later found alive. Moody respected Tuite's argument, but remained convinced for many years that if the IRA had put out the statement it would have made his life a lot easier.

The day after Stan Thompson's departure, one of Moody's associates picked up the two men in a white Rover 2000 and drove them back up to London. Tuite explained: 'The easy bit was over. Now we had to survive in an environment where every person on the streets was a potential enemy and my photo was on the front page of every newspaper.'

A perfect example of the paranoia felt by both men occurred before they'd got to their new hideout. Tuite explained: 'Me and Jim were in the back seat chatting away when this fellow appears on the pavement next to us with what looks like a gun sticking out of his rucksack. I grabbed Jim and pulled him down. It was only as the man walked past we realised it was just a fishing rod. Jim and I laughed about that one afterwards, but it just about summed up the state we were in.'

A few minutes later the two men arrived at a top-floor flat in a quiet south London street. Tuite was worried because the safe house had been organised through Moody's criminal contacts. As he nervously entered the flat, Tuite noticed a cardboard box on a table in the sitting room. Moody went straight to the box and opened it. Tuite recalled: 'It was full of banknotes – tens of thousands of pounds worth – and Jim started counting the lot.'

Moody turned towards Tuite and pushed a pile of money in his direction.

'There you go, Pat, that's for you.'

'What?' asked Tuite.

'It's money for you. You'll need somethin' to keep yer goin'.'

'Oh, I dunno about that, Jim. I don't need it. I'm all right.'

'But you gotta survive, Pat.'

Tuite shook his head and smiled.

'I don't need yer money, Jim. But thanks for the offer.'

Moody looked puzzled. 'You sure?'

'One hundred per cent.'

It was only later that Tuite found out from Moody he'd been trying to give him £20,000. 'I still can't believe it now. It was an incredible gesture and says it all about Jim,' explained Tuite, who still refuses to reveal the flat's location 'out of respect for the people who put us up'.

Jimmy Moody even put his own hatred of smokers on ice to allow

Tuite to puff on cigars in the flat. Tuite recalled: 'Jim and I talked a lot about our families and everything. He was so proud of Jason and Janine and still loved Val very much despite all their separations. Jim was so frustrated because he couldn't get in contact with them. But he was such a pro he knew there was no question of him risking everything by calling them.' Then Tuite coolly added: 'In any case, he knew that might have jeopardised our relationship.'

Jimmy Moody revealed a lot of self angst about his criminal life during that conversation with Tuite, who later recalled: 'Jim said he wanted to know how he was going to end up. It bothered him a lot. He couldn't do anything about it, but was questioning it all the time. He was determined his son Jason shouldn't end up like him, almost obsessed about that. As a result I feel strongly about Jason and what happens in his life to this day.'

Tuite told Moody he couldn't risk more than another day in the south London safe house. 'I needed to get out of London. The place was crawlin' with people looking for me,' he explained.

Tuite was then told by his Provo taskmasters to go to a known safe house in east London. Jimmy Moody insisted on accompanying him. 'He said it was as back-up. Shows how close we'd become even in that short period of time,' explained Tuite.

On arrival outside the flat in east London, Tuite was immediately suspicious when no one answered the door. Moody remained in a car in the street. 'So, I let myself in with a key I had. I looked around the place and found a woman in there, even though she hadn't answered the door. She said our contact "Marty" had left a message for me to stay there until he came back. I said to her, "No problem, got a few little things to do first. Tell Marty I'll be back later."'

Tuite returned to the waiting car and jumped in besides Moody.

'Something's up. Let's go.'

Tuite's instincts subsequently proved correct because his contact had just been arrested by Special Branch and the woman he met had been instructed to keep Tuite in the flat until the police came back.

Moody and Tuite returned to the south London flat where Moody cooked up a huge fry-up of eggs, bacon and sausages. For the next few days they lived on a diet of Chinese and Indian takeaways and continued to exchange views and opinions on everything from the state of the Tory party to Bloody Sunday. Although the two men were miles apart politically speaking, they allowed each other to express opinions and reasoned through healthy arguments. Tuite explained:

'Jim was a right-wing sort of fellow, but he was fair. And I've never told anyone the sort of things I told Jim during that time we were together.'

The following day Tuite got in touch with his 'friends' across the water and told them to get something arranged; a message was circulated that Tuite was in need of a ride back to Ireland. Those 'friends' included a London criminal with strong Provo links called 'Danny'. Tuite explained: 'He always organised the transport for us if we needed to get back across the water in a hurry. I can't name him now, but long after all this he even got involved with MI5. He was into all sorts. But basically he was a hood from south London.'

Jimmy Moody was surprised to hear that some of the same London faces he'd known down the years were helping the Provos. It got him thinking. If there was the chance of a bit of work then what did it matter if terrorists were paying the bills?

Tuite was eventually picked up in south London by a fruit-and-vegetable lorry. Tuite recalled: 'Jim walked me to the back door of the lorry as one of the other fellows swung it open so I could get a foot up.'

Just before he got in, Tuite turned to Moody and said: 'Why don't you come with me, Jim?'

Moody smiled and shook his head. 'Nah. I prefer it here. But you never know, I might pop over for some work.'

As Tuite later explained: 'I figured if we could get him over there he'd be much better off. I really wanted him to come with me. A man like Jimmy Moody was always worth having on your side.'

The two men hugged. Then the back door of the lorry closed. Moody stood and watched from the pavement as the fruit-and-vegetable lorry slipped off into the heavy south London traffic. One associate who knew Moody well at this time said: 'Jim definitely became more of a thinker after that escape with Tuite. Don't get me wrong – he was still the same hardnosed London villain, but he started to question certain aspects of his life. Tuite taught him that your beliefs can get you through life whatever the outcome.'

Tuite arrived home in Eire less than 24 hours later and was soon singing Jimmy Moody's praises to his Provo taskmasters. Moody's brother Dickie has no doubts his brother stayed in touch with the Provisional IRA after Tuite's departure. He says: 'Yeah, Jimmy had meets with the IRA. It was heavy stuff. But he never told me what really happened.' Moody's name and that of the two criminals who'd helped provide their safe houses were now known to the Provos as potential freelance operatives. Jimmy Moody was always extremely careful not to tell anyone about those terrorist connections.

Gerard Tuite had undoubtedly taken the heat off Jimmy Moody by attracting all the headlines. Throughout the days following the Brixton jailbreak, Jimmy Moody's name continued to get only the briefest mention, and all of Moody's friends and family approached by newspapers insisted it just wasn't in Moody's nature to hand himself in.

Val talked to her local newspaper, *The East London Advertiser*, a few days after his escape. The article headlined: 'GOOD LUCK TO MY JIM − Jail Break Wife's Message' was just the sort of morale booster Moody needed as he ducked and dived his way around the capital.

The article stated:

> The wife of a prisoner on the run after an amazing escape from Brixton jail's top security wing has wished him well with a 'good luck' message.
>
> Valerie Moody, wife of 39-year-old James Moody − who got away with an IRA man on the 'most wanted' list and another prisoner − said from her Poplar home: 'I'm pleased for my husband. Good luck to him!'
>
> Valerie revealed how she'd first heard the news of Moody's escape on Tuesday morning by a friend living near her then home in Teviot Street. Valerie explained: 'She said a radio broadcast had named her husband and two other men in a story about the escape from Brixton.'
>
> Valerie added: 'Life's terrible inside Brixton. I have been told the men are shut up for up to 23 hours a day. What else can they do other than find a way to escape? James had been inside for a year without being called for trial. He is innocent. I'm certain of that.'
>
> Val was furious at national newspaper reports which had branded Moody as violent and a danger to the general public. 'That's simply not true,' she said. She also admitted she was certain Moody would survive the police hunt. 'I've no idea at all where he is. But now it's the children I'm concerned for most. Their Christmas was spoiled last year when their father was arrested at his home in south London. The kids have to go through a lot at school.'

Elsewhere in the national press, well-known villain turned pundit John McVicar – once Britain's public enemy number one and now a media expert on criminals – wrote about what it would be like for Moody and Tuite while they were on the lam. He'd spent two years on the run from Durham top security prison in 1968. Once over the wall, said McVicar, there might not be many problems for the escapees. 'They could go to friends who have no criminal record and then get their own place. Actual expenses will probably be no more than £100 a week.' Jimmy Moody was paying out a lot more than that to stay on the run.

Six days after the escape, minicab driver Jim McDonald contacted the police a second time and was finally interviewed by detectives. But by that time Moody and Tuite were already on their toes and far away.

SEVENTEEN

Deep Cover

The name 'Gerard Tuite', with its IRA associations, sent shockwaves throughout the British mainland in the winter of 1980–81 following the Brixton escape. Commander Peter Duffy, head of the Yard's anti-terrorist branch, initially told journalists he believed Tuite was still in the London area and urged crowds at the after-Christmas sales to be extra vigilant in case Tuite and his bomb-planting comrades decided to break cover. Duffy warned that Tuite was adept at disguising himself and he believed the terrorist suspect was waiting for a chance to make a break for Ireland or to reach IRA sympathisers in England. Special watches were being kept at all sea and airports.

The police's wanted poster described Tuite as a 'master of disguise'. Scotland Yard admitted that one photograph, showing Tuite wearing a T-shirt, was hopelessly out of date. The other photo was an even older picture in which he was sporting a beard. The Yard also issued nine startlingly abstract versions of the wanted man in specially generated photofit images. A video film version of the images was even shown at a hundred locations in London, as was a list of Tuite's known aliases. The Yard also made loudspeaker appeals for information about Tuite at Christmas carol concerts in Trafalgar Square. Tuite was described as 5 ft 11 in. tall, of slim build, fresh complexion, with a thin face and a soft Irish accent. There were said to be extensive burn scars down the left side of his body.

Tuite was also linked to a car bomb which exploded outside the Oasis swimming pool in High Holborn, in December 1978, as well as bombs at Canvey Island, Essex, and at Greenwich where a gasholder with seven million cubic feet of gas exploded. Detective Chief Superintendent Peter Phelan, deputy head of the Yard's Anti-Terrorism Branch, issued warnings to the public to be extra vigilant following a spate of letter bombs sent to leaders of British industry and other VIPs. The anti-terrorist squad were 'very disappointed' over Tuite's breakout. Many presumed the escape was linked to the IRA campaign in support of the prisoners on hunger strike in Northern Ireland at the time and with persistent threats of a Christmas bombing campaign on the mainland.

Tuite's escape from Brixton provoked many Fleet Street headlines, including claims that if he got to Ireland it would be a major coup for the Provos. Duffy admitted: 'Tuite is very important to the philosophy of the IRA, and it is in everybody's interest that he is put back into police custody as quickly as possible.'

There was media speculation that much of Jimmy Moody's supposed fortune from the Chainsaw and Thursday Gang robberies had gone towards financing his escape with Thompson and Tuite. Operation Ohio boss Charlie Snape told the *Daily Telegraph*: 'You only have to put two and two together to see that Moody was the man behind the escape plot. There is still a lot of money which has never been recovered from a number of armed robberies, some of which Moody was awaiting trial on.'

Privately, Charlie Snape was 'sickened' when he got the call about Moody's escape since he'd predicted it months earlier. 'We'd done all that work to get him and now he'd gone again. It was typical of Jimmy Moody. He was a hell of a determined character.' Snape called all his Moody contacts, but sensed his old adversary had long gone. 'We heard he was in Ireland and God help them once he started inflicting some damage over there,' added Snape.

Jimmy Moody was happy for the police to believe he'd moved to Ireland. 'And the cops were happy because they could just shrug their shoulders and say he was out of their jurisdiction. It was a perfect scenario for Jim,' explained his brother Dickie. With Gerard Tuite now really back in Ireland, Jimmy Moody believed the search for him would be quickly wound down, meaning he was better off on home turf. As one old associate explained: 'Many in south and east London knew Jim was around, but the man was a walking timebomb. No one would dare grass him up. His fearsome reputation was his biggest guarantee of freedom.'

The escape of Moody, Tuite and Thompson had certainly caused maximum embarrassment to the British government and Home Secretary Willie Whitelaw immediately appointed Gordon Fowler, deputy director of prison services, to conduct an inquiry into the escape. The *Daily Mail*'s huge front page headline a couple of days after the escape proclaimed: 'HOW COULD HE GET AWAY?' And the paper demanded a 'massive inquest' into Tuite's escape, virtually ignoring Moody's and Thompson's roles in the getaway.

Over at Brixton Prison there was further embarrassment just a week after the Moody and Tuite escape when it was revealed that the staff officers' club had been burgled for the fifth time in a year. The thieves had boldly scaled the perimeter wall and forced their way into the building where the warders' canteen and bar were housed. Meanwhile Scotland Yard still insisted they had a plausible trail leading to Ireland. There was talk that the IRA had rewarded Moody handsomely for helping Tuite escape. One report claimed Moody was given specialist weapons training in Ulster so that he could become a one-man killing machine for the Provos.

Back in south-east London there were occasional sightings of Moody, but the police dismissed these claims as a smokescreen, believing the tip-offs to police had been orchestrated by Moody's friends in order to 'muddy the water' of the hunt for the London villain, which continued to take second place to the search for Tuite.

Throughout this period, Jimmy Moody remained a very canny individual, staying on the move and never leaving anything around that might link him to a particular address. He often used a bicycle rather than a car because he knew he'd never be stopped on a bike and also wouldn't be required to produce a driver's licence. It also helped keep him fit. At various hideaways in south and east London he kept up his strict bodybuilding routine and even set himself special targets to develop specific new muscles each week.

But it wasn't long before Moody's loyal brother Dickie had his collar felt by the Yard. When detectives discovered Dickie had an Irish girlfriend who worked in the immigration department at Heathrow Airport, they brought her in for questioning and threatened to arrest her on charges connected with terrorism unless Dickie admitted bringing in the tools that were used for his brother's escape. Dickie recalled: 'So I said to them, if you lay off the girl, then I'll take the rap. She had to go to the Home Office to explain it all. She was completely innocent.'

Dickie admitted responsibility for supplying the tools used for the escape, but insisted he had no idea where his brother was. Typically, he covered for his niece, nephew and sister-in-law, who'd also taken tools in to Moody. Dickie Moody claimed detectives put him under even more pressure by threatening to frame one of his cousins for rape. 'You gotta remember this was the IRA they were after and they were prepared to do anythin' to find Tuite,' explained Dickie.

One detective told Dickie. 'We'll drop you at any phone box in the country and you get hold of your brother and get him to tell us where Tuite is. You can tell your brother to take a walk 'cause we're not after him. We want that evil Paddy.' As Dickie later recalled: 'They wanted Tuite real bad, but I knew I couldn't trust them. They'd probably stitch me up and nick Jimmy on the spot – and he wouldn't have been very pleased about that.'

Dickie and Moody's fellow escapee Stan Thompson were eventually committed for trial. Thompson was charged with conspiring with Tuite and Moody to escape; Dickie Moody was accused of conspiring with his brother to effect the escape and supplying his brother with tools, including hacksaw blades. Dickie was bailed on two sureties of £1,000 each and Thompson on one surety of £10,000.

In the weeks following his escape from Brixton, Jimmy Moody laid a careful trail so that none of his close family and friends knew how close his connection to the Provos was becoming – he didn't want to endanger the lives of anyone by telling them. Over in Ireland, many of the Provisional IRA's most difficult, unloveable, opinionated and dogmatic men were concerned at the heat being generated by Tuite and Moody's escape. Often small in stature but big in mouth, with huge egos and antagonistic personalities, they believed that the humiliation of the Brits might provoke a very nasty backlash. These were characters, however, who were prepared to kill for their cause.

In Belfast, the RUC heard rumours that Gerard Tuite was back on 'home territory' south of the border. He was wandering around his home town of Drogheda virtually untouched by security services, thanks to a variety of disguises and the help and admiration of the local population. Tuite and his advisors believed the Irish Government would never dare try a man for offences carried out on the British mainland.

Security services on both sides of the Irish border heard whispers that the hard-nosed Brit who'd gone on the run with Tuite was also around. Certainly, it does seem that having initially resisted the offer to go,

Jimmy Moody made an appearance in Ireland quite soon after his escape. Tuite knew he could trust his fellow escapee. But was there a paid-up role in the 'movement'– albeit freelance – for Moody.

Sources claim that Moody sat in on meetings of an IRA internal security unit, known as 'the nutting squad', who tortured suspected IRA informers into confessing their betrayal before shooting them in the back of the head. The nutting squad struck terror into IRA units across Ireland and went on to be held responsible for up to 50 killings during the Troubles. Moody must have been reminded of the 'good old days' of the Richardson torture sessions in the mid-1960s. As one Northern Ireland source explained: 'Moody looked on the Provos as nothing more than another gang of villains paying him some decent wedge.' Moody's victims in Ireland were claimed to be the type of grasses he'd always despised back in London. It was even said that on one occasion a suspected informant was summoned by the Provo leaders to hear his punishment and met Moody instead.

Details of Moody's crimes in Ireland are sketchy because his work was highly secretive and in the new climate of peace, many of those who committed appalling acts in the name of the movement are trying to distance themselves from what occurred back then. But three separate sources have told this author that Moody was one of the first killers in Ireland to adopt the phrase *O.B.E.*, which stands for One Behind the Ear. It was a chilling slogan adopted by the Provos as the ultimate anti-British statement.

Jimmy Moody was spotted by the security services in Ireland, although it was only later they officially confirmed his identity. Another close Moody associate told this author: 'The IRA saw Jimmy Moody as a perfect secret weapon. He was already trained in killing and torture and he knew how to rob a bank. Those were three very important skills as far as the Provos were concerned at the time.'

Gerard Tuite denied Jimmy Moody's involvement with the Provos, but he admitted staying in touch with Moody for many years following their escape together. At one stage, the Provos even teamed up with one of Moody's south London criminal associates to set up a cannabis ring to raise funds for the movement. They offered Moody a role running it, but he turned them down flat because it involved drugs and would have meant travelling to Spain and North Africa on a regular basis.

Tuite admitted: 'We did talk many times. I was always willing to help Jimmy in any way possible.' Moody later told one London associate that although he trusted Tuite implicitly he was not as happy about the Provisional IRA as a whole. 'Jimmy accepted money from them for certain jobs but he knew he had to watch his back.'

Moody never stopped looking over his shoulder.

EIGHTEEN

Shoot to Kill

In February 1981, Home Secretary Willie Whitelaw was presented with a special government report on the Brixton breakout. As a result of the report's findings, prison governor Michael Selby was moved to a desk job and Whitelaw was forced to admit in the House of Commons that there had been a catalogue of errors by staff inside Brixton. The government-run inquiry even revealed that the most important tool used by the escape team was Moody's makeshift brace made from that table leg, which was described as being of 'ingenious construction'.

The report conceded 'the frequency and effectiveness of prison searches left much to be desired'. Fixed furniture was rarely moved or checked. The amount of personal possessions in the cells was never questioned and only once in two years had a special search been undertaken in D-wing. The staff had allowed standards to slip. There was numerous evidence of carelessness, including poor monitoring of prison visits. The report highlighted the embarrassment felt by the prison staff and police and acknowleged that Jimmy Moody had pulled the entire operation together.

The *Daily Mail*'s editorial of 3 February 1981 put the knife into the prison service. Headlined 'OVER THE WALLS AND FAR AWAY', it read:

> We have no quarrel with Mr Whitelaw's verdict on those who allowed three men – one of them alleged to be a dangerous and desperate IRA terrorist – to tunnel their way out of Brixton prison.

To his credit, the Home Secretary has not dipped into the whitewash bucket. He admits that the escape was due to 'human error at all levels'.

So what is to happen to those responsible?

Are they to be sacked? Demoted? Forced to accept a drop in pay?

They are not.

In the Army, soldiers who allowed an important prisoner to get clean away would be court-martialled.

In business, an executive who lost a valuable account would expect to be given his cards.

Mr Michael Selby, who bears ultimate responsibility as he was the £18,250 governor of Brixton, is to 'take a well-earned rest' and then be shunted into another post.

Around this time the Met got a tip that Jimmy Moody was hiding out on the south coast and immediately distributed 10,000 posters in resorts from Kent to Cornwall. The police asked camp and caravan site owners to be on the alert and placed adverts in several camping and sub-aqua publications. Detectives knew that between 1977 and 1979 Moody had spent long periods at Hamble, near Southampton, and also that he took his inflatable to the Isle of Wight on several occasions. Detective Chief Superintendent Mike Taylor told *The Sun*: 'At this time of year people are going to caravan sites which have been shut for the winter. If anyone spots him they should call the police and not go near him.'

However, another detective later admitted: 'It was all really a matter of too little, too late. We'd put so much initial energy into finding Tuite that Jimmy Moody had melted into the background. As the months went by it became clearer and clearer that we might never capture him.'

Many villains in south and east London believed the Yard put out the alert on Moody because they'd been tipped off that he was in Ireland and were trying to catch him off guard. In the middle of all this, Moody heard that one of his old contemporaries, renowned robber King Billy Tobin, had been jailed for 16 years for his part in an attempted £800,000 armed robbery. It was a notable police victory over an old-school villain from south-east London. Tobin's arrest further reinforced Moody's determination not to be caught. If Billy Tobin – previously acquitted seven times over a seven-year period – could be brought to justice then Moody believed he wouldn't stand a chance. He told one friend at the time: 'I've had it if they get me now.

I'll never get out alive so I've gotta keep runnin' even though it's a shitty way to live.'

Moody's daring escape from Brixton also inspired other Chainsaw Gang members to try similar stunts. Up at Hull Prison, Alex Sears masterminded a plot for a mass breakout, but the plan failed when a prison workshop instructor grew suspicious of a group of prisoners always playing cards. A search of the workshop revealed cannabis and parts to make two pairs of bolt croppers. Two more pairs of cutters and maps were found in a further search after a message from one of the inmates was intercepted. Alex Sears was eventually sentenced to an extra two years after admitting conspiracy to aid prisoners' escape.

In July 1981, the Old Bailey was told how Jimmy Moody's escape succeeded through a combination of 'luck, ingenuity and outside assistance'. Before the Bailey were Stan Thompson, who admitted breaking out of prison and Jimmy Moody's brother Dickie, who admitted smuggling the tools in and handing them under the visiting-room table to his brother when the supervising officer's attention was elsewhere. Dickie – who insisted to the court he wouldn't have helped his brother if he had known IRA terrorist Tuite was involved – got 18 months for his troubles. Dickie later recalled: 'I ended up in Wandsworth. It wasn't easy but a lot of people respected Jim in there so I didn't have no bother.'

Stan Thompson walked free from the Old Bailey with a 12-month suspended sentence. He insisted to reporters it was Jimmy Moody who'd masterminded the breakout. 'Tuite was just the luck of the draw,' explained Thompson. 'He happened to be the only other man in the wing that was interested in escaping who would move into the end cell.'

Also in July 1981, the Chainsaw Gang's self appointed 'General', Chopper Knight – who'd closely followed Jimmy Moody's adventures on the run through the prison grapevine at Albany Prison on the Isle of Wight – attempted his own breakout along with two other inmates. Knight and his fellow prisoners sawed through bars on a cell window in the early hours and, using plastic skeleton keys made in a prison workshop, let themselves into the prison grounds. They then used a makeshift ladder to scale the inner perimeter, but were caught when the ladder broke while one of them was on it. Waiting on the other side of the prison wall was a Ford Transit van containing a rubber dinghy, a map of the Solent, details of safe houses in France and Spain and information about where to obtain cash and arms. There were rumours that Jimmy

Moody helped plan the caper because he felt he owed Chopper Knight for never grassing him up.

Back in London there were stories circulating that Jimmy Moody was living in a lock-up with a chemical toilet and using a bunsen burner to cook his food. Oh, and he only came out for air at about 3 a.m. every night. One of Moody's associates later explained: 'We made sure the cozzers were told lots of things about Jim that were a load of old cobblers.'

In late October 1981, Gerard Tuite was publicly paraded in Ireland by the IRA to taunt Britain's security services. Tuite believed he'd never be brought back to the UK to stand trial and the British authorities presumed the Irish Government would probably prefer not to arrest Tuite on their own territory. A spokesman for the Yard's anti-terrorist squad explained: 'It was as big a headache for the Irish Government as it was for us. We always feared he'd flee there.'

In an exclusive radio interview with a Belfast journalist, Tuite implied that some of the staff at Brixton had helped him smuggle tools into the prison. Tuite told the radio audience that one Brixton officer helped cover up previous escape attempts. Tuite's appearance was timed as a propaganda weapon by the IRA to take the spotlight off the end of the Maze hunger strike.

Gerard Tuite's radio interview provided fascinating details about the build up to the Brixton escape. Tuite admitted he befriended prisoners such as Henry 'Big H' MacKenny and Jimmy Moody was delighted when he heard about the interview because he knew that all Tuite's public claims took the heat off him even more.

Back in London in early 1982, one of Moody's associates, Richard Cocks, 41, was arrested and charged with harbouring Moody between the day of his escape – 16 December 1980 – and 1 September 1981 at his home in Walkford Way, Camberwell. All charges against Cocks were eventually dropped on the grounds of insufficient evidence and he walked free from Tower Bridge magistrates' court. Moody believed the arrest of Cocks was a desperate attempt by Scotland Yard to try and smoke Moody out. But it completely failed because Moody's friend Cocks would never grass on him.

Officers at the Yard were furious. As one detective explained: 'A lot of us wished that Moody would just go away and stop taunting us. We knew he was around cocking a snoot at us but we also knew we had no chance of getting to him. I remember one senior detective said he wished somebody would take Moody out and put us all out of our misery.'

Jimmy Moody was well aware of the damage he was inflicting on the Yard and loved every minute of it. Moving from safe house to safe house in London, he was on the lookout for a long-term base. Moody was spending money like water and at one stage even splashed out on five handmade mohair suits. 'He liked to have 'em made because he had very long arms and off-the-peg stuff didn't usually fit him,' explained son Jason many years later.

One day, Jimmy Moody had the audacity to turn up at Jason's school driving a Rolls Royce and sporting a thick beard which made him virtually unrecognisable. It was one of the few times following his Brixton escape that Jason saw his father driving a car. Jason recalled: 'I was gobsmacked when he turned up, watched me play a bit of footie and then disappeared again. I didn't even have time to have a chat with him after the game, but it was great that he even bothered to come.' Shortly after this, Jason left Langdon Park Secondary School in Poplar with O levels and the promise of a job with a large stockbroker in the City of London.

Gerard Tuite had made his 'home run' to Ireland confident of escaping justice. But he reckoned without the authorities' determination. At 11 a.m. on 4 March 1982, Tuite was recaptured by Irish Special Branch officers at a flat in the centre of Drogheda, just three doors from a pub called The Hideout. Eyewitnesses to the police raid said Tuite and two other men put up no resistance. Tuite's arrest came after a tip-off to the police, the latest in an increasing number of IRA leaks that were enabling authorities to capture huge hauls of arms and ammunition. Tuite expected he'd be the subject of extradiction proceedings to London and immediately produced an Irish passport to ensure he couldn't be sent to the UK. Then the Irish Government decided to deal with him themselves.

Four months after his dramatic arrest, Gerard Tuite was jailed for ten years at Dublin's special criminal court for possessing explosives and bomb-making equipment at a flat in Trafalgar Road, Greenwich, between June 1978 and March 1979. It was the first time an Irish citizen had received a conviction for terrorist offences committed on the mainland. Tuite appealed against his conviction, but the Court of Criminal Appeal in Dublin later dismissed the appeal.

Tuite's imprisonment didn't prevent him staying in touch with Jimmy Moody and regular messages continued to be sent between the two men. Moody was even warned to watch his back because the British secret services had heard about his earlier visit to Ireland. Moody – once again running short of cash – was seriously tempted to do some more work for the IRA.

In the middle of 1982, a 24-year-old man called Seamus Morgan was shot dead by an IRA hitman and his body dumped near the Irish border. Word in Republican circles was that he'd been murdered by British contract killer Jimmy Moody. If this was true it meant Moody was still working for the Provos – or was his name being used as a smokescreen to protect others?

Back in London, Moody's brother Dickie – when he was not in prison – was his unofficial banker. 'He'd send word and then we'd meet in pubs and I'd give him some money he'd left with me. I think I was one of the few people he trusted,' recalled Dickie, who then helped his brother find a permanent home in London.

Moody paid £10,000 in key money for a modest one-bedroomed flat at 38 Arnold House, Doddington Grove – a rundown council estate in Kennington, south London, not far from Coldharbour Lane, where the Operation Ohio team had come knocking only a couple of years earlier. Moody immediately started calling himself 'Tom the chauffeur' and set the wheels in motion to have a proper reunion with his family.

One day, Jason Moody was outside his grandparents' East End home when a ten-year-old boy handed him a note saying the whole family were to make their way to a specific phone box near The Oval cricket ground in Kennington. Five minutes after turning up at the phone box, they heard a voice shouting from a nearby block of flats. Jason recalled: 'We couldn't hear it clearly at first and then I turned in the direction of the shouting and there was the old man leaning over a balcony with a skinhead haircut and a long beard.'

When Jason, Janine and Val got to the flat they were shocked by the cramped conditions. As Jason explained: 'It was a bit of dump but he was just happy to be settled in one place.' In that flat a cold, hard realisation dawned on Jason and the rest of the family. He explained: 'This was going to be his prison. In some ways it was worse than being in a real prison. Dad felt all the pressure on his shoulders, but he was powerless to help us. It must have driven him crazy. He looked so manic that day. He was so pleased to see us, but I could see in his eyes that he was close to the edge and there was nothing any of us could do to really help ease his pain.'

And the family continued to suffer their own problems. 'Money was really tight and the cozzers were breathing down our necks,' recalled Jason. The family continued to survive Moody's long periods of imprisonment thanks to the generosity of Val's parents Charlotte and Ernest Burns. As Jason explained: 'They were fantastic. They brought us up. We wouldn't have survived without them. Yet they never once said a bad word about the old man.'

In Kennington, Moody set up a makeshift gym in the spare room of the flat where he trained for three to four hours a day. Jason recalled: 'When I called round he'd always have a scarf round his neck to soak up the sweat from training.' Moody, who at the age of 40 maintained he had the fitness level of a man in his 20s, would do 100 press-ups 3 times a day as well as numerous other exercises. He also ate vast quantities of protein to keep up his strength.

But, naturally, crime was never far from Moody's mind, as Jason explained: 'He'd get a pair of trousers and insist they had to be loose enough to kick out at anyone if he got in a fight. The old man was always thinking of trouble.'

Sometimes Jason and Janine spent the night at the flat in Kennington. And even though his children were now into their teens he still insisted on certain standards. Jason explained: 'He'd inspect our toothbrushes whenever we stayed at the flat and if they were dry he'd know we'd lied about brushing our teeth. He also chucked out our old toothbrushes once they got too ragged and insisted on buying new ones.'

One of Moody's favourite phrases was, 'You only got one set of teeth, son, so don't lose 'em.' Many of his habits undoubtedly came from having spent so much time in prison.

Moody was so worried about being recognised at his new flat in Kennington that he started borrowing a neighbour's dog and taking it out for regular walks. Jason explained: 'The cozzers knew he hated dogs so he'd take this dog out on a lead and suck on an empty pipe – because they also knew about him hating smoking.'

In June 1982, an underworld enforcer called Nicholas Gerard was shot dead by a contract killer in Mitre Row, Stratford, east London. Two men wearing red balaclavas and boiler suits approached Gerard, 32, as he walked towards his home. Gerard managed to scramble into his American Oldsmobile car, but was shot in the chest through the windscreen by a 12-bore. Gerard – who had just completed a 7-year sentence for assault – staggered 50 yards before the 2-man hit team caught up with him again. Then he was shot in the chest and clubbed to the ground. Gerard had such severe injuries he could only be identified through his fingerprints. One informant later told detectives the killers had IRA connections. Police were baffled because Gerard had no known terrorism links. They were certain this was a classic gangland killing. Gerard had earlier been acquitted of a Soho murder along with Barbara Windsor's one-time hubby Ronnie Knight. His own father had been acquitted of the Ginger Marks murder, linked for so many years to the Krays and Richardsons war. All this made him a 'soldier' so, as Jimmy Moody would say, he knew the risks.

A couple of months later builder Charlie Stimson was gunned down outside his south London flat. Five weeks later fifty-two-year-old Patrick O'Nione was brought down by a hail of bullets outside his family's wine bar in north London. One old face said many years later: 'Moody was a gun for hire and all those killings had his calling card stamped all over them.'

It was all just work to Jimmy Moody.

NINETEEN

The Living Dead

The aftershocks of Tuite's activities with an active service unit in London in the late '70s continued to be felt in the capital right up until 1983, when a cache of explosives hidden four years earlier by Tuite was found in a north London bedsit by the Yard's anti-terrorist squad. The flat, at 1 North Road, Highgate, had originally been searched 4 years earlier by police who'd somehow missed 20 lb worth of gelignite hidden under the floorboards.

Then an Armalite rifle, a sawn-off shotgun and a bandolier holding more than 100 bullets were found under floorboards in another flat where Tuite had once lived, in Trafalgar Road, Greenwich. Detectives also discovered a wooden box fitted with batteries and wires, four wigs and street plans of eight British towns and cities, and a watch modified so that it could be used as a 'delaying timing element in an electrical circuit'.

The police and UK media claimed these findings confirmed the so-called 'evil intentions' of Gerard Tuite, although Jimmy Moody remembered how Tuite used to tell him that both police and government regularly released such details to railroad any peace moves back in the province. But Moody wasn't comfortable being amongst the Provos after Tuite's imprisonment and genuinely feared his name might be given to the British government in exchange for certain consessions involving IRA negotiations with the then Tory Secretary of State for Northern Ireland, Tom King. An increasingly large number of people wanted to see Jimmy Moody wiped off the face of this earth.

The London Jimmy Moody settled back into in the mid-1980s was a very different place from the previous decade. Police intelligence-gathering had given the authorities the upper hand in the battle against the heavyweight criminals. Critics still questioned police methods, particularly the misuse of confessions, but new technology, such as video cameras, meant that if police waited long enough something was bound to happen. Eventually detectives began filming entire robberies before arresting suspects.

Naturally, police were now always armed to the teeth for such investigations. As one old-time south London criminal explained: 'We were on their target list. It was two-way traffic. If you're being chased and you know armed police are on their way then that is scary. It sorted the men out from the boys. We called them death squads and it was us or them. They were out to get us. It wasn't about getting sent down for ten or fifteen years no more, it was about being popped: killed – call it what you want. Getting dead.'

Although the new breed of detective believed that catching robbers red handed always risked a shootout, more robberies were allowed to run their course rather than being raided before they were carried out. That meant the chances of people losing their lives was high. In one classic example, a gang attacked a security van as it delivered wages to an abbatoir. Tipped-off cops were waiting and all hell broke loose when they took action. The robbers had handguns and sawn-offs, and as one blagger turned he was shot twice. A third bullet hit and killed another bandit, leaving the last one – seriously wounded – to surrender. This particular ambush sent an unmistakable signal to the armed robbers. After 30 years of mayhem the game was up.

People like Jimmy Moody still viewed themselves as soldiers of crime. That was the fantasy, the kudos, the delusion, the image and the ego trip; it was soldiers of crime versus the state and robbery was a dying art. From the mid-'80s onwards, 'going across the pavement' was seen as a risky profession for a criminal.

Some of Moody's acquaintances from the supposed 'good old days' were reduced to shoplifting just to get those adrenalin rushes – the 'buzz' – that were so relished a few years earlier. One of Jimmy Moody's oldest associates explained: 'Some of us still needed the buzz badly. But we were burned out, grumpy ex-crooks. The truth is we couldn't do anything else. Many old blaggers felt like they'd had a limb chopped off. We used to call them *the living dead*.'

'After all those successes of the '70s it was hard not to try and go back to it. The excitement of doing it and getting away with it was out of this world.'

Then, out of the blue, a team of younger criminals from Moody's manor pulled off the crime of the century.

At 6.25 a.m. on 26 November 1983, a gang of south-east London robbers well known to Jimmy Moody raided a Brink's-Mat security warehouse near Heathrow Airport, neutralised alarms and headed for the unit's vault where they found a carpet of drab grey containers, no bigger than shoeboxes, bound with metal straps and labelled with handwritten identification codes. There were 60 boxes in all, containing 2,670 kilos of gold worth £26,369,778. There was also hundreds of thousands of pounds in used bank notes locked in three safes. One pouch contained traveller's cheques worth $250,000. In the other was a stash of polished and rough diamonds worth at least £100,000. They'd expected riches but nothing like this. The Brink's-Mat robbery, ruthless in its conception and brilliant in its execution, had just landed them with the biggest haul in British criminal history.

The police eventually narrowed down their list of suspects to some of Jimmy Moody's most notorious gangster pals. Many were never caught, and most of those tens of millions of pounds were reinvested in everything from cocaine and ecstasy shipments to brothels and financing other major robberies. 'Brink's-Mat made the names and fortunes of many of today's most ruthless gangsters,' says one who should know. 'It's the stuff of legends . . .' Jimmy Moody would have loved to play a role in the Brink's-Mat heist, but his status as one of Britain's most-wanted men made him too hot to handle. Jason Moody remembers his father being 'green with envy' when he heard about the Brink's-Mat raid. (Years later, Jason played a small role as an actor in a Brink's-Mat TV movie broadcast in the UK in 1990.)

The release from prison of Jimmy Moody's old boss Charlie Richardson in July 1984 was a painful reminder to Moody that his years on the run were catching up with him. Jason explained: 'It really hurt him when all his old pals started getting out of prison. Here he was, on the run, watching his back every second of the day, and people like Charlie Richardson were out and enjoying real, unrestricted freedom instead of another form of imprisonment, which Dad was enduring.'

Jimmy Moody read in his favourite newspaper, *The Sun*, about how Charlie Richardson had been picked up from Wandsworth Prison in a gold Rolls-Royce and taken to a weekend of nightclub celebrations with family and friends. Moody heard on the grapevine that Charlie Richardson was a changed man. He'd taken an Open University degree in sociology and regularly wrote to broadsheet newspapers such as *The Guardian* and *The Times*. He'd also taken A levels, including one in geology, and had done stints preparing food for disabled patients at Stoke Mandeville Hospital, in Buckinghamshire. Richardson explained: 'I never carried a gun or a knife or killed anybody – yet when I was serving my sentence, murderers, child-killers and rapists, all sorts, used to come in and leave as free men before I could.' Moody would have dearly loved to have visited Charlie and talk over old times, but Richardson, who knew the police were keeping an eye on him, made sure that Moody was told to keep well away.

On 15 September 1984, Provisional IRA operative Patrick Magee arrived by train in the English south coast town of Brighton. Five years earlier he'd been assigned to England with Gerry Tuite and they allegedly planted some 18 bombs in 5 cities before Tuite's arrest. Magee checked into the Grand Hotel on the seafront for three nights with half board – at a cost of £180. He asked for a sea view, believing that a room on a higher floor would attract less security interest and might be closer to Prime Minister Margaret Thatcher, due in town for the Tory Party Conference. Thatcher didn't want to be on lower floors where disgruntled miners' leaders were staying.

When the bomb he planted in Room 629 went off early on the morning of 12 October, two people in adjoining rooms were instantly killed, yet miraculously the main structure of the hotel held together and the predicted collapse never occurred. The Prime Minister escaped unharmed, although a further four people were killed. Among the 32 injured were Norman Tebbit, Secretary of State for Trade and Industry and his wife Margaret.

Back in Kennington, Moody was still calling himself Tom the chauffeur and living in virtual isolation in his small council flat. In the aftermath of the Brighton bombing, he feared that if his activities in Ireland were known to certain security services, they would come after him with a vengeance. Shoot-to-kill might have already been the order of the day in Northern Ireland, but the Brighton bombing was seen as a declaration of war.

Jimmy Moody wished he was back in the good old days of the

Richardsons. The swinging '60s. Respect from all he crossed. The pick of the women. A free drink in every tavern. None of this politics bollocks, just good, clean crime, with a few hits on people who deserved it, but that was it. Now it was all very different. Jimmy Moody longed to walk down the Deptford Road with a few of his mates and bump into those old, familiar faces, who were the main men when he started out. Today the nearest he got to respect was when he had to threaten a bunch of yobs after they pushed past him on some shitty pavement somewhere. And even then he had to be careful not to start any trouble in case it alerted the boys in blue.

Moody became increasingly paranoid that the police or the Northern Ireland security services were after him. Following the Brighton bombing, British security forces believed more 'sleeping' bombs would be primed to explode at key targets, equipped with the sort of long-delay timing that had triggered the Brighton blast. It was a time of high alert in Britain, especially in London.

While Moody's family were delighted to have some regular contact with him, it wasn't an easy relationship. A classic example came when Jason took one of his first girlfriends over to meet his father at the flat in Kennington. Moody was cleaning a 12-bore shotgun in the front room and started pumping it in front of Jason and the young girl after they'd walked in. 'I think he was trying to impress this girl. Then suddenly he swings the gun around and points it straight in the girl's face, his finger stroking the trigger. We didn't know if he'd popped all the cartridges out or not. Then the old man pulls the trigger and it clicks – empty. He thought that was a right laugh. The girl was almost in tears.'

Two hundred miles north of London, Bernie Khan – the last member of the Chainsaw Gang still at liberty besides Moody – was feeling increasingly lonely in his Manchester hideaway. So when his girlfriend Pat travelled by train up to see him, Khan went to the city's Piccadilly Station to pick her up. Khan recalled: 'I'd just put her bag in the boot of my car when "bing" they're surrounding me. "Hands up." I stood there and rolled my eyes. Then one of them says, "Your name Bernie Khan?"' Khan later discovered that his girlfriend had been followed from the moment she walked out of her flat in the East End. He was eventually sentenced to eight years for his role in the Chainsaw Gang robberies.

For the first time in his life Jimmy Moody was beginning to wonder if crime really did pay after all. Here he was, constantly looking over his shoulder while the long arm of the law harrassed his beloved family in the hope of eventually recapturing him. To his loyal son Jason, Jimmy Moody was still a larger-than-life hero who was both deeply frustrating, yet extremely kind in other ways. Jason made a point of visiting his father's flat in Kennington as often as possible. Moody had turned the small flat into a virtual fortress. Jason recalled: 'There was a front door that led into a passageway, then into the living-room, bedroom and kitchen. The front door opened inwards so he'd have a big lump of four by four wood which would lean on the back of the door with a piece of rope attached, containing two nails either side of it. The rope was just tucked inside the letterbox so the police would have a problem kicking the door in. I'd stick my hand in the letterbox, pull up the string like a drawbridge and a note would be attached to that string. The note left by Moody would often say something harmless like 'Gone Shopping'. Jason explained: 'That always meant he was out, but most of the time he was in.' He also had a secret bell so he knew it was a friend calling if it rang. To find this bell you had to put your hand into the letterbox to press it. You never knocked because he'd know that was a stranger and not answer the door.' Just below the window of the living-room was a rope ladder for a fast escape.

The flat's bedroom had a scaffold pole across it, from which Moody did 30-minute pull-up sessions every day. There was also a wide range of weights. Moody slept in a single bed in the living-room because from there he could make a quicker escape if anyone burst in. Young Jason slept in a double bed next to the gym equipment. Moody kept three weapons under the kitchen sink at all times, plus a couple of other guns in various places around the flat.

Sometimes Moody and Jason visited a local café for a slap-up meal. Jason recalled: 'They had an offer where if you finished a plate of spag bol you got free afters. The old man would finish his own plus mine and both the afters, then go and drink six pints of bitter. He held his drink well and burned up most of the food training.'

Jimmy Moody also took his teenage son running. Jason recalled: 'He'd be on the bike with his hat pulled down for disguise and I'd be running alongside him and everyone would just think he was my trainer. He pushed me really hard.'

Then it would be back to the flat for hundreds of pull-ups on the scaffolding. Jason explained: 'He even had this mail bag stuffed with old clothes swinging from the ceiling. He'd really lay into that, wearing socks wrapped round his fists instead of gloves. I was quite a fit boxer at that time, but whatever I did in his makeshift gym he'd double it. He was as strong as an ox.'

After a work-out they'd play chess. Jason recalled: 'Chess was a very big part of our relationship. Sometimes we'd sit there for hours playin'. The old man would always make sure he was facing the window so he could see if anyone was coming up to the flat.' And, as always, he still cheated whenever he got the chance. Jason recalled: 'His favourite trick was to say, "Your turn to make the tea, Jason." Then he'd move everything around while I was in the kitchen.'

Moody – aka Tom the chauffeur – even started regularly drinking at a local pub. Jason explained: 'Everyone would say, "Hello Tom, how you doin'?" and the old man would answer, "Oh, I had a busy day today. I was at the fuckin' airport drivin these fuckin' Arabs around." Then he'd get right into character and start tellin' stories that were right over the top, but they seemed to keep the other customers happy.' No one ever questioned why Tom was never actually seen driving a car. Moody even claimed he'd fought in Korea, which made him seem a little older than he really was 'for good cover'. Jason explained: 'The old man was always thinking ahead just in case someone worked out who he really was.'

One time Moody, again as Tom, was in his local pub talking to another customer who claimed he was a close friend of that 'runaway villain Jimmy Moody'. Jason explained: 'This fella went on and on for ages about him without realising he was talking to the man himself. If he'd said one bad word about Jimmy Moody the old man would have given him a right seein' to.'

Back in his flat, Jimmy Moody spent a lot of time talking back to the TV. 'Sometimes things would come up on the telly and he'd go crazy and start shoutin' back at the screen,' Jason remembered 'It was a bit eccentric but he was lonely in that flat, away from his family and friends.'

Moody's two favourite programmes were *Match of the Day*, particularly when it featured his beloved Arsenal, and any old American cowboy films or TV series. His all-time favourite, *Rawhide*, was re-running at that time every afternoon.

About a year after Moody moved into the flat in Doddington Grove, a ten-year-old girl from the same block was brutally murdered. The police investigation was so intense that Moody had to move out of the flat and stay with an associate 'until the heat died down'. Jason saw the reaction in his father: 'The old man went totally paranoid when he heard the police were planning to knock on everyone's door, so we moved him out for a few weeks.' And Moody's hatred of child molesters soon boiled to the surface. Jason recalled: 'When a man was nicked for the murder, the old man told me, "Pity. I'd have liked to have sorted him out myself."'

On another occasion, Jason went clay-pigeon shooting with his father. Despite his reputation as a hired gun, Moody turned out to be a useless shot. Jason recalled: 'My mate who came with us said to him, "Fuckin hell, Jim, you is a bit rusty." He replied: "Yeah, but security guards don't fly do they?"' Moody later admitted he wasn't used to pointing a shotgun so high in the air. He preferred waving sawn-offs at waist height.

Jimmy Moody's self-imposed incarceration in that flat in Kennington caused him to become increasingly despondent. 'He could be very down at times and it was difficult to even communicate with him when he was in one of those type of moods. He was so frustrated by his life,' remembered Jason

Even the rope ladder Moody kept in the flat was nothing more than a symbol. Jason was concerned: 'I used to say to him, "It's not much use 'cause they'll surround the whole building surely, Dad?" He'd shrug his shoulders and smile. He knew what the score was.'

And Jason constantly worried that he might be responsible for his father's arrest. He recalled: 'I feared that if I was being followed, then it would be my fault if he got nicked. It was on my mind all the time. If the cozzers came callin', Dad wouldn't say "Fair cop, Guv," and go quietly. He'd rather die in a hail of bullets.'

Jason Moody suffered serious sleeping problems at his father's flat in Kennington. If there was the slightest noise he'd be up checking out all the windows, thinking it was the police come to get his father. Jimmy Moody had so much trouble sleeping he even resorted to earplugs. 'It was a risk in case someone did come for him, but he was wrecked without sleep,' recalled Jason. One of the saddest aspects of Moody's imprisonment in the flat was that he didn't dare have any photos of his family on display in case someone spotted them and it gave away his true identity.

In November 1985, a group of IRA inmates tried to blast their way to freedom from top-security Portlaoise Prison, in the Irish Republic, while staff were attending Mass. One inmate held prison officers at gunpoint as the group used duplicate keys to open the jail's seven security gates. Then they blew up the main gate with explosives – but the gates failed to open. Within minutes, Irish troops surrounded the prison and the 11 men – dressed in fake prison officer's uniforms – gave themselves up. The would-be escapees included Gerard Tuite, said to have become ringleader of all the Provos in the prison. It was even rumoured that Jimmy Moody was involved in helping organise the outside help for the escape. One British security services source insisted that Moody was involved. And one of Moody's oldest associates said: 'If money was involved then Jimmy would do just about anything. He might not have shared their ideals, but if they were paying him then Jimmy would have looked on it all as just work.'

Back in London, Jimmy Moody's status as a freelance hitman brought him into direct contact with many of the new, younger criminals whose main source of income was drugs. While Moody swore blind he hated drugs and anyone who used them, he still 'worked' for a number of south and east London drug barons. But Jimmy Moody's rumoured existence meant he was often blamed for murders he did not commit.

One classic example was the death of a couple called Peter and Gwenda Dixon, cut down by five shotgun blasts while on a walking holiday at a campsite, near Tenby, in south Wales. Police said they believed there was a link with the IRA because they discovered 100 lb of Semtex high explosive four miles from the murder scene. Detectives even released details to the media about a man known only as 'Mr Chartray', aged between 30 and 40, around six-feet tall with brown hair and possibly an Irish accent, who was staying near Tenby at the time of the killings. Chartray was never traced, but at one stage rumours started flying around that Moody had carried out the killing on behalf of the IRA. However, many years later, a local man was arrested and jailed for the murders. Jimmy Moody's involvement was nothing more than a myth.

Jimmy Moody was fairly careful to avoid most of the old faces in London, although he did keep in touch with Mad Frankie Fraser by sending Fraser Christmas cards to Parkhurst Prison and signing them 'Jim'. Fraser insists to this day he never saw Jimmy Moody from the moment he escaped from Brixton jail. Many other villains were living in Spain beyond the reach of Scotland Yard. But the Costa del Crime didn't appeal to Jimmy Moody, who still didn't much care for going abroad: different food, different language, different people. No, Jimmy Moody believed he was safest amongst his own people and that was the way it was going to stay. The heavy sentences handed out to the Richardsons, Krays and the Great Train Robbers had long since convinced him it was probably better to die than be taken alive and face the rest of his life in prison. The idea of going back to prison filled Moody with fear and trepidation. It was bad enough in that flat in Kennington, where he constantly paced up and down like those tigers he so adored, but the smell and fear of prison never left Jimmy Moody.

TWENTY

Costa del Nick

Around this time, Jimmy Moody was approached by one south-east London drugs baron to 'ice' a notorious supergrass, whose squealing to the police was threatening to break up two of London's most powerful criminal gangs in the mid-1980s. The man was being held in a specially built wing of a suburban police station 'for his own protection'. Explained one of Moody's oldest criminal associates: 'This bastard was leading the life of Riley. He had a colour telly, a stereo, a sofa, even a hair dryer. It was completely out of order for such a lowly piece of scum.'

Motivating Moody for this particular job wasn't hard. Moody's old associate continued: 'This grass was even allowed to have takeaway meals, booze of his choice and the guards were permitted to go and get him anythin' else he wanted.' The police nicknamed the grass's wing 'Costa del Nick', and the squealer boasted that his baby son was conceived on the bed inside the police station. In order to get close to his target, Moody followed the man's girlfriend when she made one of her regular visits to see him.

Moody planned to hit his target on a specific day when he appeared in court. He did a reconnaissance trip and found a perfect location along the route about a mile from Costa del Nick, but his plans went up in smoke when the squealer was committed to custody in a proper prison by an uncooperative magistrate. He was never returned to the police station. Moody hated failure – especially when it cost him a £15,000 fee.

Meanwhile, Scotland Yard continued to close down on the profession of armed robbery. When two old-time robbers called Ronnie

Easterbrook, 56, and Tony Ash, 49, attacked a wages van in south-east London and found themselves trapped by armed police, Ash was killed by a hail of bullets. The two men should have retired to run a pub in the country or set up an estate agent on the Costa del Sol. The police message to these old-style robbers was clear: they'd be shot dead if necessary, in order to clean up the streets. The armed robber was a dying breed.

Moody's decision to pull away from any work in Ireland probably prevented him from becoming another of the British government's alleged shoot-to-kill victims. Sources from within the secret services have claimed to this author that in the mid-1980s, the Tory government of Margaret Thatcher sanctioned the use of an SAS hit team to wipe out freelances like Jimmy Moody. The only reason Moody wasn't dealt with seems to be because once he was back in London no one had any idea where he was living. One security source explained: 'Moody was extremely lucky because he was on a list of targets. If he'd spent any more time in Ireland he'd have been a dead man.'

In the mid-1980s, Moody met a man called Nic Nicolades, a neighbour in Kennington, at his local pub. Nic later recalled: 'I thought Tom the chauffeur was a copper at first because he never seemed to do much drivin'.' But Moody and Nic, 25, hit it off and Moody even babysat for Nic's two young children. The men also dated a pair of sisters who lived near to them. Behind the scenes, the cautious Jimmy Moody was checking out his new friend Nic's credentials. 'He'd test me out by saying certain things and then wait to see how I would react,' recalled Nic. Once Moody had established that he could trust Nic, he told him his real name and the two men became close friends. Nic already had an inkling who Tom the Chauffeur really was from a friend who'd seen Moody in Kennington and recognised him.

One night Nic was walking home with Moody from a nearby pub when Moody stopped to have a pee in an alley. Nic recalled: 'Suddenly, these two coppers came along and questioned him. He apologised profusely and they let him go with a ticking off. From then on, whenever he was out and he saw a bobby on the beat, he would wish them a cheery "Good morning."'

By this time, Jason had left school, quit a good job in the City and was, in his own words, 'running around with some right dodgy geezers'. One day he went down to Brighton with a gang of East End tearaways and was involved in a fight in a pub. He was sent to prison for grevious bodily harm.

Before Jason's trial at Lewes Crown Court, in Sussex, police informed court officials they were very worried about potential jury tampering. Recalled Jason: 'I was in the dock with two others when the prosecuting barrister jumped up and said they weren't to give out any of the jury's addresses.' Jason insisted he had no knowledge of any intimidation of the jury. 'I didn't even twig it at first, then the other defendants asked me who my dad was and I realised the old man's name and reputation had created all these problems.' There was no proven evidence of jury tampering at Jason's trial.

Jimmy Moody later told his son Jason that he should consider his imprisonment as a warning for the future. 'He believed I had to get it out of my system. I don't deny I liked a fight at the time. I'd been a boxer and all that. It just happened and there was a lot of pent-up anger in my system.'

Jason Moody, Janine and mother Val continued to go to extraordinary lengths to keep in touch with Jimmy Moody. Jason would always be doubling back, making U-turns and circling roundabouts three or four times to see if he was being followed. 'If I was suspicious I'd abandon the plan,' he explained. Detectives also made regular dawn swoops on Val's parents' home in Poplar. 'We kept being raided. Police would turn out everything looking for the smallest scrap of paper – any hint about where he was hiding,' recalled Val.

Moody continued to avoid travelling by car whenever possible because he felt less vulnerable on a bicycle or on foot. But Moody – or 'Tommy Mann,' as he was still known in Kennington – did buy a driving licence from someone he met in a pub who had terminal cancer, just in case he 'needed wheels'.

Moody also took other more extreme measures to make sure no one identified him. He tried to erase the two distinctive tattoos of a geisha girl and an eagle from his forearms by pouring acid on them. Jason witnessed the outcome: 'The wounds got infected and both his arms blew up like footballs. He was in real agony. But he couldn't go to a hospital in case they worked out who he was.' Another time, Moody gashed open his arm so badly that a bone was virtually sticking out. Jason explained: 'It needed stitches so he threaded a needle, gritted his teeth and did it himself without anaesthetic.'

Moody couldn't even go and watch Arsenal in case his image was captured by one of the numerous closed-circuit TVs at the ground. And he still never allowed anyone to take his photo, in case it 'fell into the wrong hands'.

However, Jimmy Moody did risk the occasional round of golf at two east London public courses in Leyton and Hainault, with Jason and Nic Nicolades. They were not impressive golfers, however. Jason recalled: 'One time I went and hit the ball so badly it flew up in the air and hit me in the head. The old man thought that was a right laugh. Then he went and hit a ball so hard it smashed into a tree before bouncing back onto the green.'

But most of the time Jimmy Moody led a pretty mundane existence. 'If we went out for a meal, he preferred pie and mash,' said Jason. 'By this time if he needed clothes he shopped for bargains in the local markets.' And Moody always insisted on wearing one of his two flat, cheesecutter hats (dark blue and checked) whenever he was outside the flat. He continued to sit with his back to the wall and near the exit in every restaurant.

While most fathers would talk to their sons about football, Jimmy Moody preferred looking back on his most daring armed robberies. Moody still didn't mention that he had also worked as a hitman, but Jason already had a reasonable picture. He explained: 'Look, if my dad was asked to take someone out that was it – a done job. There was no goin' back. That was the sort of person he was.'

The hard, cold edge of Jimmy Moody was never far from the surface. When one of his son's friends committed suicide he offered little sympathy to Jason. 'The old man just shrugged his shoulders when I told him,' recalled Jason. 'He seemed to accept death as if it was nothin' special. Maybe that's how he got through doin' what he did.' Later, Moody wasn't much more sympathetic when Val's mother was diagnosed with cancer.

'Death was just a cold reality to Jimmy. He'd seen and caused so much over the years that he'd lost the ability to grieve for anyone, apart from his dear old mum,' explained one of Moody's oldest associates.

Whenever Moody ran short of money he'd go out and commit more crimes in order to survive – something that became a vicious circle that deeply affected him psychologically. Jason remembered: 'He'd often be pacing up and down and in a highly stressed state at the flat, mumbling to himself about what a bad situation he was caught up in. I'd walk out of that flat after a difficult session with the old man, thinking "Fuckin' hell. How much longer can he go on like this?"'

Moody sometimes got so paranoid about being captured that he'd stay inside the flat throughout daylight hours and then only venture out for a brisk walk at midnight. With two pump-action shotguns and a .38 always within reach, Jimmy Moody was ready and prepared to go to war at a moment's notice.

The Sun newspaper and terrestial TV were Moody's main source of worldwide news – although he always insisted he only bought the tabloid for the crossword, which he'd fastidiously finish by 11 a.m. every morning. He usually turned directly to the back pages to find out the latest news on his beloved Arsenal and claimed he didn't believe a word he read in the tabloid's news pages.

Even big-name robberies, which were once Moody's staple diet, started to pass him by. Jason explained: 'He spent two years casing one particular job and then this other team went and did it first.' Moody seriously considered another run at the money incinerator in Loughton, Essex, where he'd taken Jason on 'field trips' during the Chainsaw era. But Moody couldn't find a trustworthy enough team to pull it off.

It was inevitable that Jimmy Moody would start getting wreckless. 'He was bored and wanted some action. All that pacing up and down in the flat in Kennington was doin' his brain in,' explained Jason. Moody started turning up unexpectedly at the Phoenix Apollo restaurant in the East End, which had become a trendy nightspot for TV soap stars and the occasional pop singer.

Among the celebrities Jimmy Moody met while on Britain's most-wanted list was East End actor Ray Winstone, the undisputed hard man of film and television. Winstone, a tough character from a similar background to Moody, had once boxed for England and played gangsters long before it was chic to say 'geezer' in polite company. Winstone had no idea that the man he knew as Tommy was the legendary hardman Jimmy Moody.

Moody also encountered Page 3 models Tracey Elvik and Maria Whittaker, who never guessed his true identity. Then he became friendly with one-time West Ham soccer player Frank McAvennie, who was already on the slippery slope to drugs. He'd just rejoined the Hammers in a £1.25 million deal, but never recaptured his previous form at the club. A broken leg then kept him out of the game for almost a year. McAvennie was later convicted on cocaine charges.

One night at the Phoenix Apollo, Moody got within a hair's breath of being arrested when he upset a table of off-duty Flying Squad detectives out on a stag night. One of Moody's oldest friends explained:

'Jim – or Tommy as he was known – was a little the worse for wear and he started taunting these coppers from our table. It was a bloody nightmare. Two of them got up and came over and asked us to keep Jim quiet, but he simply told them to "fuck off" and offered one of them outside. We only just managed to persuade the coppers not to take any action. If only they'd known who he was!'

Jimmy Moody was also out and about in the bright lights because he wanted the London underworld to know he was still a good operator, someone who could be trusted with the biggest jobs. But in the process of doing that, he was also risking his own liberty.

On the evening of Friday, 22 December 1990, businessman Terry Gooderham, 39, and his girlfriend Maxine Arnold, 32, were at their flat in Shernhall Street, Walthamstow, preparing for an evening out with Maxine's mother, Violet MacNamara. But just before 7 p.m., the couple got a phone call and popped out, dressed casually in tracksuits. Gooderham didn't even bother to take his wallet or watch and Maxine left her handbag behind.

At four the next morning a police patrol spotted Gooderham's F-reg black Mercedes in a secluded car park at Lodge Lane, near Epping Forest – a spot regularly used by courting couples. The lights were on and the glass of the front offside window was broken. Moving closer to investigate, the officers discovered the horribly mutilated bodies of Gooderham and Arnold.

Police using dogs and metal detectors quickly sealed off the area and began a search for the murder weapon and other clues. They concluded that the killer must have muffled the weapon so the shots could not be heard. Within days, police established from forensic evidence that the killer shot the couple from the back seat of Gooderham's car. Friends of Gooderham insisted his death didn't have anything to do with his tangled love life – he had two live-in girlfriends based in separate homes owned by him – before it emerged that he owed in excess of £150,000 to gangsters. Police revealed they found a small quantity of cocaine in Gooderham's Mercedes, even though a post-mortem on both bodies did not find any traces of the drug. A week after the double shooting, a story broke in the tabloids, which suggested Terry Gooderham and Maxine Arnold were the victims of a gangland hit after he'd double-crossed a cocaine baron.

There were also claims Gooderham handled the gold from the Brink's-Mat robbery. Following calls to the police, an artist's impression

– resembling Moody – of a man they wished to interview was issued. As one detective later recalled: 'Jimmy Moody's name cropped up but we didn't even know for sure if he was dead or alive at that time.'

Although Moody and wife Val had been officially divorced since 1980, they still remained extremely close. 'His lifestyle destroyed the marriage but they still got on and loved each other,' revealed Jason. Moody didn't see Val too regularly in case the police grabbed him. Jason continued: 'Ladies loved the old man's company because he was a big powerful man and he'd walk in a room and everyone would immediately know he was someone special. But he really did have a special place in his heart for mum.'

Father and son also remained close. Jason explained: 'I really valued the time I had with him. In a normal family I s'ppose you see yer dad every day so you don't feel the need to have special chats with him the whole time. But with my dad I made a point of talking about all the important issues, just in case I never saw him again.' Moody only ever gave his son one piece of advice. Jason recalled: 'I had about 30 mates at that time and he'd say, "You'll be lucky if you've got two or three real friends out of that lot. A man can count his friends on one hand."' Later he'd be proved absolutely right.

But always lurking in the background was the spectre of crime – and of death. Jason never forgot the time he went to see his father in a pub with two friends and a girlfriend. 'We had a great night in the pub together. He really looked after us all and I felt very proud of him, but afterwards he said to me, "They're not gonna to say anything are they, son?" and I said, "No way, Dad." I'd pretended to them that he was just passing through on a visit to London.' But in the back of Jason's mind ever since has been the thought: 'Would he have done something to them if he'd thought they were a threat to his freedom?' 'The honest answer is I'm not sure,' said Jason.

Running short of cash yet again, Jimmy Moody accepted a cut-price contract killing job for a new gangster friend. He was hired to shoot dead the man's business rival, but was instructed the shooting should only go ahead after a signal was given by the man who had hired Moody. The setting was in the courtyard of an East End office building.

The man who hired Moody explained: 'Jim got hold of a rifle and was all set up in a window overlooking the courtyard. It was like something out of *The Day of the Jackal*. Anyway, the idea was I'd scratch my head, walk away from the target and Jim would do the business.'

So Moody teed up his rifle from his vantage point, squeezed his left eye shut and checked the exact spot once more as the two men came into view. Then he leaned the barrel on the windowsill, his forefinger stroking the trigger in expectation of what was about to happen. As the two men walked into the target area, Moody took a deep breath and squinted into the rifle sight to await the signal that would mean the end of one of their lives.

'But I never made the signal because this other fella paid up the money he owed,' Moody's customer recalled. 'Jim said afterwards that it was bloody lucky I didn't have an itchy head!'

Jimmy Moody was disappointed because he desperately needed the cash to maintain his lifestyle on the run.

TWENTY-ONE

King Jimmy

Despite his own run-ins with the long arm of the law, Jason Moody was becoming increasingly worried about his father letting his guard down and being spotted on the mean streets of south and east London. Jason explained: 'He was spending a lot of time with some of my dodgier mates. I had a club called Echoes in Bow at the time and he'd turn up unannounced some nights. I'd get a call from one of the doormen telling me a bloke was outside saying he was my uncle. Of course, it was the old man.'

As Jimmy Moody got out and about more, so he began bumping into a lot of old faces. One time Moody was in an East End pub and met fellow Chainsaw Gang member Alex Sears, who'd just got out after serving his sentence. It was an emotional moment, for both men had enormous mutual respect for each other. But as they hugged, Jason could see what was going through his father's mind. Jason explained: 'Sears had done his time. He was out. No more lookin' over his shoulder. No more fears about who was knockin' on the door. Meanwhile the old man was still servin' time.'

Moody's temper was becoming more unpredictable. One day, back in Kennington, Moody was with Jason when they got into an argument with four Irishmen around a pool table. Moody told his son to walk away from it because he didn't want to risk the police being called. Jason recalled: 'But by the time I got back from the toilet a few minutes later the old man was smashin' them to bits. He stabbed one up really badly with a little palm knife he had in his top pocket. Two others were hit over the head with pool cues. He was smashing the whole pub to pieces so I grabbed him and tried to pull him out. He chucked me off. I pleaded with him to get out. His face was black. He was gone in the head. He wanted to go back in there and finish them off. In the end, I calmed him down and we scarpered into a nearby council estate. The law turned up much later but no one knew who we were. What shocked me was that it took the old man hours to calm down. He totally lost it in there and I realised at that moment he was still capable of *anything*.'

The following morning Moody woke up with a sore head and fears that someone in that pub might 'put the finger on him'. Jason observed Moody's reaction: 'He didn't feel no remorse or anything. His only concern was whether the police might come after him.'

Jason has thought about this aspect of his father's character many times. He explained: 'He was so cold in some ways. I don't know where it came from, his mum was tough, but not like that. Maybe his real father, who he never knew, was the same. But when he lost it, you didn't want to be around him.'

There were other occasions when Jimmy Moody came to his son's rescue, such as the time Jason had a fight in a local villain's club which turned into a deadly feud. He explained: 'I'd given some guy a right seein' to and been chucked out of this club. I was furious. Then it got really heavy. They was after me. I heard the owner of the club was tellin' other people what he planned to do to me. They even kidnapped this mate of mine and forced him to say where I lived. I was well out of my depth so I went to see the old man in Kennington.'

The following night Jason drove his father into the East End. Jason recalled: 'The old man was whistling with pleasure. He was really gettin' off on the idea of wavin' his shooter around.' As Jason drove, Jimmy Moody checked his Remington pump-action sawn-off to make sure it worked and was properly loaded. Then he placed it carefully in his overcoat pocket. Jason explained: 'We knew this particular fella from the club always parked his car next to a bus stop, so Dad made me drop him at the bus stop.'

That's when Jason stopped in his tracks. 'I'm now thinkin' Jesus Christ! This is all down to me. But it was too late to back down by then.' Jason began circling the club in his car. Jimmy Moody stayed at the bus stop. Then their target and a group of doormen came out of the club. They spotted Jason as he got out of his car and he made a run for it. Just then, Jimmy Moody emerged from the shadows with the sawn-off clutched casually in his hand.

'Evening, gentlemen,' bellowed Moody.

The group of men stopped in their tracks.

Moody looked straight at them.

'You lot gotta problem?' he said calmly.

The men jumped straight in a Mercedes and drove off. Moody and his son followed them in a Granada from the top of Bethnal Green Road all the way down to the Mile End Road. But Moody insisted that his son pull up because he was worried the police might get involved. Shortly afterwards, Jason got a message from the same group of men to say they were sorry and if Moody kept out of their way they'd stay out of his.

Yet the police still had no concrete evidence Jimmy Moody was dead or alive. Moody encouraged his associates to put round stories that he'd been killed. He was still irritated by the IRA's refusal to put out a statement saying he'd died because, said one old friend, 'that would have made life so much easier for him'. But Jimmy Moody's liberty was still capable of being threatened by the most innocuous events. One day he was with his friend Nic Nicolades when they got stopped by police for driving in a bus lane. Nic explained: 'The cops pulled us over and Jim was in the back of my car where he always sat because he felt we were less likely to get pulled as I'd look like a mini-cab.' Nic spent five tense minutes talking his way out of trouble. All the while Moody remained glued to the back seat. Afterwards, he said tensely, 'My life nearly ended back there, all because you went in a fuckin' bus lane.'

Another close shave occurred when Moody and his son Jason stayed past closing time at an East End pub and two uniformed policemen walked in. Moody dived in a cupboard in the nick of time. No one else in the pub dared to ask why the man called Tom was so jumpy. Jimmy Moody even maintained a number of 'stash points' in local parks in Kennington where he'd hide money and a gun so that if the police were watching the flat and he couldn't go back there, he'd be able to survive.

Around this time Moody virtually adopted a neighbour's two-year-old son, taking the boy to nursery school and often looking after the child while his single mother was out at work. When the woman and her son moved abroad it broke Moody's heart. 'He loved that kid. It was so strange to think here was this fella who killed and robbed people yet he was a real softy with kids,' recalled one old friend. Another family in the same block employed Jimmy Moody as a babysitter. When the couple returned home late one night all the children were still up. The neighbour later explained: 'It was total chaos and there were toys everywhere. Jim was havin' the time of his life and couldn't understand why we were a bit annoyed about the mess.'

Domestic chores certainly took on a different meaning in Jimmy Moody's strange world. There was a time when Jason popped in to see his father in Kennington and Moody announced he had two shotguns 'that need to be put somewhere'. Jason offered to take them to a friend's farm in Kent. 'They were both wrapped in clingfilm and weighed a ton. Tryin' to get them into my car, parked a mile away as usual, was a nightmare. We covered them in blankets and somehow I got them to the car without being nicked.'

Most of Moody's neighbours in the block where he lived in Kennington found the big man called Tom very polite. But one elderly woman took a particular dislike to Moody and called the police after one shouting match about a broken milk bottle. Luckily, Moody's friend Nic was in the flat at the time and dealt with the police.

Jimmy Moody's biggest problem as a fugitive was always cash flow. He had a whole posse of crooks to pay in order to stay one step ahead of the law and everything was over-priced from the rip-off payment of £5,000 a year key money for the flat to splashing out at least £3,000 on yet another false passport, just in case he had to get out of London in a hurry. Yet Moody remained extremely overgenerous. 'Money didn't mean anything to him in that sense. He used to say, "What's the fuckin' point in hanging onto it? You can't take it with you, can you?"' revealed Jason. Moody was going through thousands of pounds some weeks.

Back at chez Moody in Kennington, the contract-killing armed robber still enjoyed playing ludicrous practical jokes, like throwing water over passing schoolchildren. He even stuck a kipper in his new friend Nic Nicolades's bed when he stayed at the flat one night. Jason pointed out: 'The old man had plenty of time to waste every day and used to sit there thinking up these jokes for something to do.'

Jimmy Moody was virtually hero-worshipped by many younger criminals who saw him as a fearless old warrior. One of those villains – a man called Frank, who is now an extremely powerful criminal, explained: 'Jim taught me how to prepare for a robbery. He taught me so many special things down to the minutest details. Without him I'd never have survived. We all looked up to him and many of us wanted to learn from him.'

Moody and many of the younger criminals he spent time with believed there was still a shoot-to-kill policy at Scotland Yard when it came to certain criminals and were obsessed with the phrase: 'Home Office approval was granted to kill'. Of course this all had shades of the IRA about it, but Jimmy Moody's paranoia was growing. He'd left a lot of problems behind in Ireland. He also knew that contract killing led to its own inevitable problems like the families of victims seeking revenge.

Moody's new young hoods weren't going to be much good for his future. They were fighting a vicious turf war over drugs, involving the deadly north London Yardies, the heroin-smuggling Turkish gangs of south-east London and a handful of other cold-blooded London faces and families. As one of Moody's oldest friends explained: 'Jim should have stuck to his own. These kids were cold fuckers who'd shoot their own mothers if they got in the way.' But perhaps that was the whole point; Moody may have come from a bygone era, but he was as cold and heartless as his new young friends and he'd already committed the crimes to prove it.

Moody enjoyed the stardom and adoration he received within that close circle of particularly dangerous young men on the streets of south and east London. As his young gangster friend Frank explained: 'At the end of the day Jimmy Moody got known for what he did best. People were terrified of him. When he lost his rag, that was it. In our world, if you are known as something you get everything.'

Yet this legend of London crime was still travelling most places by push-bike because he was convinced it was the safest form of transport. And Jimmy Moody remained in superb physical shape. Not only did he continue to train for two to three hours a day in his makeshift gym in the flat in Kennington, but he also continued to practise ju-jitsu.

God help anyone who crossed him.

Detective Chief Superintendent Bill Ilsley knew all about Jimmy Moody, but by the early 1990s he had so many responsibilities as the head of 3 Area Major Investigation Pool – one of 8 such teams covering the Metropolitan Police area of jurisdiction – that Moody's whereabouts was no longer the priority it had once been. A vast increase in crimes in south-east London had diverted Ilsley's attention away from veterans like Moody, whose liberty now depended more on the violence and criminal activities of others than his own behaviour. From 1988 to 1990 there was a more than 20 per cent rise in crime on the very south London manor where Moody was hiding. As Bill Ilsley warned at the time: 'The situation is getting to the stage that if we don't do something about it right now, there's going to be utter lawlessness out there.'

No wonder villains and police alike had come to dub south-east London the 'wild west'. By 1990, it was a law unto itself. As one west London villain explained: 'You notice the change the minute you get across Vauxhall Bridge. Everything seems different. The people have a different attitude. They're fuckin' hard and they know it. It's like that all the way to the borders with Kent.'

As such, south-east London was the natural home to a number of the ultimate professional criminals – hitmen. It was a booming arm of the crime industry. Multi-million-pound drug deals ensured that the stakes were now so high that one criminal thought nothing of splashing out £20,000 to have a rival permanently removed. Contract killings were a nightmare for detectives to investigate. As one south-east London detective explained: 'Domestic killings are generally easy to solve, but anything outside that, expecially involving pubs and clubs or criminal activity, then you really are up against it. No one ever wants to say anything because they are frightened of reprisals. It's the old south-east London thing: don't be a grass.'

A power struggle for control of the drug routes from North Africa to London, plus bitter reprisals connected to the distribution of the Brink's-Mat gold bullion from seven years earlier had cost at least seven criminals their lives over an eighteen-month period. At least four of those murder victims encountered Jimmy Moody. They were:

Car dealer Nick Whiting, who was found bound and shot dead on Rainham Marshes, in Essex, in June 1990. He was a well-known contact of major drugs dealers rumoured to have laundered some of the proceeds from the Brink's-Mat raid.

Brendan Carey, armed robber, who was shot dead in a pub in Caledonian Road, Islington, in July 1990. He was a close associate of another well-known criminal awaiting trial on drug smuggling charges.

Then there was Lionel Webb, an estate agent shot dead in Stoke Newington in March 1989. In his office safe, police found a vast consignment of drugs.

Lastly was Johnny Lane – alias John Gobba – who was found shot dead in Limehouse in December, 1989. He was a close friend of a well-known East End cocaine smuggler.

Scotland Yard watched all this increasing violence with bemusement. Most didn't like what was happening, while others were content to sit back and let the villains wipe each other off the face of the earth. No one ever proved if Jimmy Moody actually pulled the trigger on any of these murders, but his trademark was stamped all over them.

But Jimmy Moody – newly crowned hero to rich, young, drug-addled criminals in south and east London – was about to find himself drawn into an even more deadly gangland feud that could only ever have started on the manor where he grew up.

TWENTY-TWO

One-Way Ticket

It all kicked off in August 1990, when a group of men – including at least two members of a notorious south-east London crime family called the Brindles – went into The Queen Elizabeth pub in Walworth, south-east London and threatened owner John Daley and his brother Peter Daley, who'd known Jimmy Moody for more than 30 years. One of the group allegedly put a gun into Peter Daley's mouth. The Brindles, from Bermondsey, traced their criminal ancestry back to Tommy 'Tom Thumb' Brindle, a racketeer and crook in the 1940s, and they believed the Daleys were trying to muscle in on their drugs territory in south-east London.

The Daleys and the Brindles then accused each other of grassing up the notorious Turkish family, the Arifs, whose gang of armed robbers were jailed in November 1990. Then in March 1991, a cousin of the Arifs, Abby Abdullah, walked into William Hill's bookies, in Bagshott Street, Walworth, with his bull terrier straining at the leash. Minutes later, after Abdullah was identified by an innocent customer, a hitman squeezed off two rounds from his 9 mm Browning. Abdullah tried to use another customer in the betting shop as a shield, but caught a bullet in the back as he ran from the premises. He managed to stagger 400 yards to a friend's house on the Kingslake Estate, where he keeled over at the front door after whispering the name of his alleged killer. Soon certain quarters of the manor were alleging Abby Abdullah had named two of the Brindle brothers, Tony and Patrick. (Tony and Patrick Brindle were eventually charged with, but later acquitted of, the murder.)

The Arifs – despite being related to the Brindles by marriage – were incensed and swore revenge. Jimmy Moody got involved when youngest brother, David Brindle, charged round to The Queen Elizabeth pub because he thought the Daley's had set up the Abby hit to cause the Brindles problems. This time, though, the Daleys had Jimmy Moody alongside them and he proceeded to give David Brindle a severe beating with a glass ashtray and a baseball bat. The Daleys presumed that would be the end of their 'little problem' with the Brindles, but this was not the case. David Brindle – rumoured to be a member of a recently reformed Richardsons gang – started making threats to kill Moody and Daley. Jimmy Moody realised a beating hadn't been enough for the cocky young hood.

So at 10.45 p.m. on Saturday, 3 August 1991, two strangers walked into the saloon bar of The Bell pub, in East Street, Walworth knowing that David Brindle was inside supping a pint with his girlfriend and three associates. Moments later the raiders – wearing ski masks and dark clothing – opened fire. Tables were overturned and bar stools and glasses thrown as panic swept through the pub.

The two gunmen sprayed the room with bullets from a revolver and an automatic. One innocent bystander – Stanley Silk, 47 – was killed instantly. Barman John Plows, 36, defiantly threw a bar stool at the gunmen to protect his 15-year-old daughter Nicola. The stool hit one of the shooters in the chest who then staggered back before turning and blasting Plows four times in the stomach and legs.

Meanwhile, Brindle scrambled across the wooden floor before vaulting over the bar. As he turned his back one of the gunmen fired a bull's-eye right between his buttocks. The bullet passed through several internal organs and within seconds Dave Brindle was on the way to his maker. His 21-year-old girlfriend Fiona – who was five months pregnant and had just set up home with him – held him in her arms as he took his last breath.

Witnesses said the gunmen then screamed out, 'This one's for Abby,' which could have been a bit of mischief intended to link the shooting to the Arifs. When it was all over, the pub was filled with clouds of dust and the only noise was the groaning of people who'd been mortally injured. Barman John Plows, who was fortunate to recover from his wounds, explained: 'Everyone in the area knows who it was they wanted. There is a family which is like the Mafia round here. They are bad, bad people. It's a tragedy because all the other people shot just happened to be in the wrong place at the wrong time.'

The Brindles' mum Grace, 50, told reporters after the Bell shooting: 'My boys wouldn't hurt a fly.' She even insisted her 'lovely boys' cried when their pet budgie died and told how they helped old ladies across the road. Not many people believed her. Few witnesses had the courage to volunteer information to the police, who took a step back and began the countdown to the next inevitable hit. South of the Thames, sections of the underworld closed ranks. At the Brindle's south London house, a group of the family's henchmen shielded the family from unwanted callers. It was clear that the council of war being held inside the house was going to declare its right to revenge.

Moody's son Jason heard about the Brindle shooting when he was at his local barbers and saw the front page of the London *Evening Standard*. He recalled: 'I had a horrible feeling the old man was involved the moment I saw the story.'

Within a couple of hours, Jimmy Moody was on the phone to Jason saying he'd had to move and wouldn't even be able to go back to the flat in Kennington to collect his things. Jason felt a combination of anger, frustration and fear for his father. 'One side of me thought, "Fuckin' hell. What's he done?" I even had a bit of a row with him on the phone because I couldn't understand why he'd get involved in somethin' like this.'

Jimmy Moody knew the moment he pulled that trigger in The Bell that he'd never be returning to his flat in Kennington. Now he had one of the most dangerous families in the London underworld on his tail – as well as the police, Northen Ireland security services and probably a load more vengeful criminals besides.

With the heat well and truly on, Jimmy Moody made for the only safe bet he knew: his family. He hid out at his brother Dickie's flat in Dulwich, the same place where they'd been brought up as children. Dickie recalled: 'Jim was in a right state. He had nowhere else to go. He just knew he had to get out the way.' Dickie warned his brother it was a bit of an obvious hideout, but Moody felt it was the safest option. Dickie had had his run-ins with the law, but he'd not taken the same route into organised crime as Jimmy, which made him a 'civilian' in criminal terms, but it also made him completely trustworthy in Jimmy Moody's opinion.

Dickie soon withdrew £1,000 from his bank account and gave it to Moody. 'I knew he couldn't survive without cash. He'd been on the road for ten years by then and it had cost him a bloody fortune.'

Moody stayed at his brother's flat for three weeks. Every day, Dickie went off to work, leaving his increasingly despondent brother behind on his own. Dickie recalled: 'It was just me and him, a bit like when we was kids. But he couldn't stay too long because they were sure to find him eventually.'

Dickie wasn't surprised to discover that his brother was as fastidious as ever; 'He still washed his hands five times a day. Brushed his teeth at least three times. Everything with Jim was non-stop. He didn't like any mess in the house and was forever picking my shirts up off the floor. He was a neatness nut. He even made his bed up every morning. At least this time there wasn't a rope ladder, but he soon worked out a route over the back roof in case the Old Bill turned up. But he knew I'd cover his back whatever happened.'

Surprisingly, the police never once called at Dickie's home to see if Moody had even been in contact. Jason later explained: 'They sometimes don't come round because they want to watch you, but that wasn't the case this time. Maybe they'd already decided to let the Brindles do their dirty work for them?'

Brother Dickie remembers Moody's departure from the flat sadly. 'Just before he left we went over to the off-licence, got a few beers and came back and had a proper chat. Then it was time to go.' Dickie added: 'Jim was on a catch-22. The Old Bill knew he was involved in the Brindle thing and now everyone was after him. I was bloody worried about him.'

Jimmy Moody didn't want to get his older brother locked up yet again so he asked daughter Janine if he could stay at her flat in the East End. She later recalled that her father's presence was strangely rewarding. 'We started to get to know each other properly for the first time as adults.'

But Moody knew he couldn't keep putting his family in the firing line so he found himself a small flat in the East End. One morning Jason picked him up from Janine's flat and drove him to the apartment. The moment Moody got in his son's car they started arguing. Jason explained: 'I was angry about the way he'd been taking more and more risks. How he'd got involved with my dodgiest mates and now this Brindle business. But I'm not sure he cared any more.' Jason's frustrations continued to boil over as father and son drove to the flat that day. 'I wanted him to calm down, keep a low profile and watch his back. But here he was facing two murder charges [Brindle and innocent customer Stanley Silk], all the aggro of that IRA escape and the Chainsaw charges. He was lookin' at life in prison if they caught up with him, and there was no way the old man was up for that.'

In the car as they drove to Moody's new East End hideaway, Jason found himself wishing for the first time that his father had never escaped from Brixton. 'He'd have been out after about eight years, back with his family, a free man. Instead, he was caught up in this feud constantly watching his back and waiting for the ultimate knock on the door.' Jason was also angry because he felt his father's so-called old pals had led him into the Brindle nightmare. 'His old pals turned out to be a lot less loyal than the newer ones, I can tell you. They landed him right in it.'

Moody had also just heard on the grapevine that his flat back in Kennington had been raided by police, who'd found one of his fingerprints. Now the cops knew for certain that Jimmy Moody was on the loose. Jason says his father went noticeably downhill from the moment he knew the police had positively linked him to the Brindle killing. Moody was angry because he'd wanted someone to go to the flat in Kennington and 'clean it' of any evidence following the Brindle shooting. But the 'cleaning operation' was never carried out, which gave police their luckiest break for 11 years.

Still on that drive to the new flat, Jimmy Moody actually talked to his son about giving himself up. 'It's a thought ain't it, son? I've had enough of all this shit,' he told Jason. But he didn't mean it.

Moody's new home was 12 Mare Street, Hackney, a first-floor flat on a rundown '60s-built lowrise block. It had a tatty front room that was not much wider than the alleyways that surrounded the building. The move across London had cost Moody yet more cash, so he was desperate for work. Moody's new young gangster pal Frank teamed up with him on a debt-collecting mission soon after his arrival in the East End. Their target was two Eastern European mobsters based in the West End of London. Moody's partner Frank explained: 'Jim did a really detailed plan on how we'd handle it before we even got in the car. He'd done it all a hundred times before.'

Then Moody and his young sidekick travelled into the West End to find their targets. 'We grabbed the first geeza in his shop and took him back to a house in south London where we'd rented some space, tied him up and left him while we went and got the other bloke.'

Moody and Frank kept the two men prisoner for five days as he put into practise all the torture techniques he'd learned with the

Richardsons back in the '60s. His young partner-in-crime explained: 'We did it all in a sound-proofed basement. The pair of us didn't get much sleep and we worked it in shifts. I even fell asleep in the middle of torturing one of them. Woke up to find this geezer just staring at me and waiting for more torture.' The two men eventually agreed to pay up their debts.

But Moody and Frank failed to pick up work from any more firms in south and east London because of the 'Brindle problem'. Moody himself hated talking about the killing and people started trying to avoid him in pubs and clubs. 'They was treatin' Jimmy like he was a leper,' said Frank. 'It was well out of order and it was really gettin' him down.'

Jason and Janine saw more of their father after he moved into the East End because they both lived nearby. They found him somewhat distant and distracted by his own problems and he refused to talk about his future. Instead, Moody wanted to know about them. Jason recalled: 'I was thinking about becoming a stunt man at the time. He took a real interest in that and seemed very proud of me.' Jason had just made a brief appearance as a policeman in the popular ITV series *The Bill*. 'The old man thought that was a right laugh. I kept one of the uniforms and brought it round to show him as a joke. He said it was really lifelike and asked if he could he pop out for a while to hold up a bank. I think he was only joking.'

Daughter Janine felt much closer to her father after his move to the East End. She recalled: 'We used to go out and have a drink with him. In a strange way I felt proud of him just for surviving. We were closer than we'd ever been before.' Janine often visited her father's tiny apartment with bags of shopping and even cooked him special meals. 'He loved roasts,' explained Janine. 'Particularly roast lamb as well as pie and mash. Food was the way to his heart.' Food was his Achilles heel, seeming to soften Moody. After he'd eaten every scrap of available food, Moody would sit down in the tiny living-room area of the flat and talk to his daughter about her future. Her boyfriends. Her hopes. Her irritations.

To rub salt into his wounds, Moody was asked to Chopper Knight's coming-home party but couldn't go in case he got arrested. He sent Jason instead, who reported back to his father that everyone sent their regards. 'That sort of summed it all up really,' explained Jason. 'Everything had come full circle and now my dad was the one who was losing out big time. They'd done all their fuckin' bird and he'd still gotta face it all. To be honest about it, the old man was totally fucked.' Brother Dickie has a similar opinion: 'Jim knew time was running out. He wasn't getting any younger. It didn't look good for him.'

Over in Moody's old patch of south-east London, the word was out that the Brindles were terrified that the legendary Jimmy Moody was on the warpath and targetting their family.

TWENTY-THREE

The Net Closes

Jimmy Moody admitted to Janine that he was deeply depressed about having so little to show for his life. Thanks to the problems with the Brindles, he was now living in a tiny flat on Mare Street and occasionally working as a pub cellarman to pull in some extra cash. He was so worried about his security that he'd hidden some money and a gun in nearby Victoria Park in case he had to do yet another runner. If he'd been better organised when he'd left Kennington then the police would never have found the fingerprints that confirmed he was alive in London and involved in the Brindle killing.

Jason Moody summed up his father's life at that time: 'It was way different from what people think. His total worth was a few hundred quid. He didn't own a home, a car or have a girlfriend. He never went on holiday. He lived in a £40-a-week room. He walked everywhere or went by bus. His property consisted of a bed, a table and a chair. The sum total of his days as a wealthy bandit was a battered Rolex watch.'

Jimmy Moody was growing increasingly angry about the feud and blamed a lot of it on the Daley brothers. 'When the shit hit the fan they'd fuckin' disappeared. Nowhere to be seen just when Jim needed them,' said one old criminal associate. 'They're as much to blame as anyone.' At one stage, Daley contacted Moody to try and explain why everything had blown up. 'But by then it was too fuckin' late and Jim knew it,' added Moody's old associate.

Jimmy Moody recognised there were too many different waring factions involved in the Brindle feud, and that guaranteed a lot of people would get hurt. After years of committing relatively low-key, if deadly, crimes Moody had walked into the equilvalent of the gunfight at the OK Coral. He was so upset he wrote a letter to his solicitor which he hoped might help explain what happened and take the heat off him. Naturally, he insisted he was innocent.

Moody's letter is reproduced here in his own raw and rambling style, illustrating his emotional state at the time and his conviction that he would never be given a fair trial. Typically, Moody even claims an alibi for the Brindle killing – a traditional response of a hardened criminal who would never 'fess up' his crimes, sometimes even in the face of daunting evidence. Moody wrote:

> I'm making this statement to you in case of my future arrest and automatic frame up by the police on myself (or shoot to kill). Hopefully the statement will never be used.
>
> This is the story AND my statement today, 20 October 1991 (I'm watching New Zealand walloping the Canadians on the telly). I have just heard that my name Tommo at the start 'today James Moody', has gone into the kitty for the shootings of David Brindle and five others in The Bell public house Walworth some three months ago. I was involved in an incident with David Brindle a few days before his death. The police have now got a perfect patsy.
>
> They can make a motive out of this event. Motive/living witnesses/fair cop, guvna verbal/leaving my flat etc./not at home to answer questions so therefore must be guilty etc.
>
> Just because they have come to zero they have turned their case on to me. Enough publicity over this – NO EVIDENCE – and no future jury will automatically find me guilty of the other charges I escaped from Brixton Prison back in 1980 for.
>
> I left the flat because I can't answer any questions: £800 rent, £150 poll tax, £80 electric bill, court order to appear over the arrears, I would have left the flat anyway over being evicted.
>
> When the news got out that David Brindle was shot dead, I was in a Greek restaurant with some friends, I'm not going to name names because we all know what the police do to restaurant owners and witnesses who tell the truth for people like me – a wanted man on the run; their lives would forever be ruined. However, I remember the time D. Brindle was shot because a man called Dave came in to the restaurant about

midnight and mentioned it. Now it stood out because a few days earlier I was in The Queen Lizzi pub, Walworth, when David Brindle and his pals attacked an old man and his wife 'Peter Daley and Pamela Daley' (your old clients).

I went over and tried to stop the fight by throwing D. Brindle and pals out of the pub. David Brindle was then shouting out to his pals to get a gun; I went back inside the Lizzi pub and stood by the door. A minute later David Brindle, who had blood on his face and his shirt, come into the pub with one hand down his trousers shouting out, who wants to be shot first; his pals came behind him with a blue beer crate and bottles; they hit me on the neck and arm, I picked up a kids' baseball bat and lashed out at them, as far as I know I didn't connect. It was a case of pure self defence and nothing more. David Brindle and his pals run off away from the Lizzi pub (they threatened to shoot everyone and burn the pub). That's the incident in The Queen Lizzi. I went home to my flat in Doddington Grove, Kennington.

A few days later in a restaurant I heard David Brindle had been shot. So a few days after that I left the Doddington Grove flat (the name Tommo would possibly come to light).

The reason AND ONLY REASON I left the flat was for a few days while things cooled down.

I cannot, I CANNOT, stand a pull to be questioned about The Queen Lizzi incident.

I never went back to the flat because the police came to a stop in their enquiries with the Abby murder in Bagshot Street and switched to The Queen Elizabeth pub incident. The police had two names on their list.

Peter Daley and Tommo. Tom was the name I was using, everyone and everyone knew me as Tommo, NOT ONE person knew me as James Moody or that I was on the run, a wanted man.

The police are desperately trying to pin this murder on someone. Is it really possible that a man facing over 20 in prison on the run 10 and a half years would jeopardise all this over a pub fight!

WHAT MOTIVE IN MY CASE?

David Brindle is younger than my own son. David Brindle never hurt me in any way; threats were against everyone. I worked the door for years and heard this crap before when I turfed them out, BUT I don't go and shoot them later.

The police will automatically put bullets, guns, maps with unsolved murders and crimes on me now (while the cats away the rats will play?).

If and when I'm arrested for this unsolved murder, I James Moody am innocent.

(Also I will photo-stat this statement and leave several copies elsewhere.)

I WILL NOT BREAK DOWN and ADMIT ANY CRIME, FAIR COP, GUV'NOR ETC ETC.

I WILL NOT CONFESS TO POLICE, SCREWS or the usual child-molesting scum who line up in prison 'over-hearing' prisoners confess all and sundry to get off their own evil crimes.

I suspect the police will kill me. 'Shoot to kill.'

That way they can close the book and keep the public happy over the Brindle murder and the other unsolved crimes.

When they shoot me they will put a gun in my hand, tell the press, *The Sun* (their puppet paper) that I resisted arrest and my dying words were, 'Fair cop, Guv'na, I did it all,' signed James Alfred Moody.

[In bigger letters over one entire side of paper]:

I WOULD LIKE TO STOP ANY PREJUDICIAL PUBLICITY ON ME and MY CASE PENDING ADVERSE PUBLICITY. I BELIEVE IF I'M NEVER MENTIONED THEN LET SLEEPING DOGS LIE.

J. Moody

P.S. I hope I can write you another statement in ten months time 'ON THE OUTSIDE'

Jimmy Moody knew he was in deep trouble but refused to let it stop him getting out and about. One night Moody turned up at Jason's East End nightclub and nearly started a fight in front of a row of CCTV cameras because the doorman wouldn't let him in. Jason was furious with him for endangering his own safety and security. 'But he just laughed. He didn't give a fuck by then.'

Jimmy Moody was a changed man. He started to wander the streets of the East End most days. His favourite place of all was Victoria Park, just a five-minute stroll from his new home, a place that helped bring back many memories. The vast and varied faces of the East End, old and new, met in the local pie-and-eel-shops, on the run-down estates and even the more expensive private homes dotted around the green expanse. The park itself had first opened in 1894 to provide the poor of the East End with a green lung. The cast-iron railings, drinking fountains, duck pond and cottage-style park attendants' homes had remained to this day. The park even had its own three-mile circuit along the Regent's Canal towpath, then round the park's perimeter – shared by occasional joggers and serious runners like Jimmy Moody.

Victoria Park, like much of the so-called 'new' East End, was split down the middle. To the south was Tower Hamlets, with its '60s estates where despite recent investment, unemployment and high levels of petty crime continued to thrive. To the north of the park was South Hackney and Hackney Village, where affluent young families lived in townhouses worth several hundred thousand pounds each.

The world of Cockneys, recently arrived immigrants, City executives, even artists and musicians all found a place to meet in Victoria Park – jogging, walking dogs, keeping an eye on the children or reading a newspaper or book on one of the many benches. Crime was always around if you cared to look closely. Park visitors were known to have been mugged near the bowling lake and flashing was virtually a weekly occurrence. One time Jimmy Moody chased off a bunch of youths harrassing two young girls.

Other youngsters illegally rode motorbikes and burned-out stolen cars around the perimeter. Meanwhile, park workers struggled to clear the used condoms discarded around the railings and in the car parks near the entrance gates each night. But all the potential dangers did little to put Jimmy Moody off Victoria Park. He adored walking briskly through the green expanse most mornings to buy a newspaper – *The Sun* – from a newsagent on the other side of the park from his tiny flat. With the City of London's skyline rising on the horizon, it all seemed a million miles away from the East End he'd moved to so long ago.

Jimmy Moody's old Chainsaw Gang partner Bernie Khan bumped into Moody walking in Victoria Park one sunny, spring day in 1992, not long after his own release from prison. Khan recalled: 'Jim was walking along with his cheesecutter [hat] and his paper under his arm. Hitting his leg with the newspaper. Funny thing is my girlfriend spotted him first. She said, "There's a fella comin' along here. I bet you know him." I looked up and there's Jim.'

'How are ya?'

'Fine.'

'Nice to see ya.'

Khan later recalled: 'He said he was working as a doorman somewhere. I thought that must be a good job for someone on the hoof. But I never referred to him being on the run. You just don't talk about such things where I come from. You shouldn't. Only the arseholes do that.'

Khan saw Moody a second time in Victoria Park a few weeks later, which made him think Moody was living nearby. He explained: 'I didn't ask no questions again. Didn't introduce my bird or nothin'. We'd done all that earlier so we just nodded. That's the last time I ever saw him.'

Bernie Khan knew all about Moody's serious criminal activites. 'We all knew Jimmy was a hitman. Obviously, we didn't know which people he'd done. Even before the Chainsaw jobs he was known as a heavy fella. I would never ask him anything awkward. Villains just don't do that to each other. They can volunteer if they want. If I hear things I don't want to know I just tell 'em to stop rabbiting.'

Not long after that encounter with Bernie Khan, Jimmy Moody teamed up with a group of young robbers and raided the Ministry of Sound nightclub in Vauxhall. The gang got away with £40,000 after tying up the doorman at closing time and stealing all the takings. One of his oldest friends told this author: 'Jim did it partly for the money and also for the buzz after these youngsters had asked him if he'd help them.'

Jason Moody, who to this day does not know who else was involved in the robbery or what happened to them, was angry with his father for doing the Ministry of Sound job. 'It was like he wanted to get caught. I couldn't understand why he was taking so many risks.' After expenses, Moody made just £5,000 from the robbery.

Over at his tiny flat in Mare Street, Moody now kept just one handgun, which he also took with him for protection when he was on his bicycle or out walking. Moody still sometimes proudly flashed the .38 in its shoulder holster at Jason when they were supping a pint in a local pub. Daughter Janine was terrified of the gun. 'I wondered if that weapon was going to invite something bad to happen to my dad. I started being a bit scared of being with him. After all these years it dawned on me that someone was out to kill him and we might get in their way.'

By 1992, London police had a list of unsolved professional hits they wanted to talk to Jimmy Moody about.

Besides the ones already mentioned in this book, there was also the killing of John Patrick Lane, 44, of Wells Square, Bloomsbury, shot after he arranged to meet an acquaintance in an isolated spot in Narrow Street, Poplar. His body was later discovered hidden on waste ground half a mile away. His lower back contained numerous gunshot wounds. As usual, there were hints of a connection with a drugs racket, but no firm evidence was ever uncovered by police to back up this theory.

Meanwhile record seizures of hard drugs pointed to a vast upturn in smuggling into the UK. Drug barons were taking advantage of record opium crops and the break-up of Eastern Europe to flood Britain with heroin. Powerful Colombian cocaine gangs were setting up new routes into Europe through Russia. Removal of European border patrols in the early '90s also encouraged the new influx of drugs. But the Russian mafia were the most chilling new criminal element creeping into London in the early '90s. As one old-time East End villain later explained: 'These fellows were fuckin' outrageous. They're cold, heartless bastards and they scare the shit out of most Brit crims.'

The Russians and other Eastern European gangsters were carving out new routes for their smuggling teams. Albanian clans from the Serbian province of Kosovo were deeply involved and even imported female sex slaves for brothels. Then Poland got in on the act by becoming the most important producer of amphetamines to the EU – there was an enormous demand for the drugs in pubs and clubs across Britain. All these drugs fuelled the kind of paranoia that had sparked the Brindle feud in the first place. Now it was threatening the life of Jimmy Moody and many others.

In 1992, Jimmy Moody's daughter Janine gave birth to his one and only grandchild, a girl called Chayce. Moody was soon regularly taking her to his beloved Victoria Park. One day, Moody was out in the park with Jason, Janine and Chayce when he turned to his son and said: 'Jason, d'you think I'll ever see the day when she runs up the landing on her own and goes "Grandad, Grandad?"'

Jason replied, 'Don't be stupid, Dad. Course you fuckin' will.'

Jason later revealed: 'When he said that I had this feeling in my gut and it wasn't a good feeling. I nearly cried after Dad went home that day. Something inside me told he hadn't got long.'

A few weeks later the family were out in Victoria Park again and Moody was in an even more depressed state. Jason turned on his father and shouted in frustration: 'You're crazy. After all you've gone through, nearly 13 years on the run, and now you're mixin' with people who are at it and half your age. Your life's gonna go up in smoke if you're not careful.'

That reference to 13 years on the run sent a shiver down Moody's spine. As one of his oldest associates later said: 'Jim wasn't a superstitious bloke, but when he realised it was the 13th year he'd been on the run, he started to believe it'd be his last year. The more that year progressed, the more he talked about it. He just kept on about 13th year this and 13th year that.'

At his flat in Mare Street, Moody had a special code so that only his close friends and family knew if he was in or out. 'If you saw the badminton racket up at the window it meant he'd gone out,' explained Jason. 'If I had an important message I'd get in my car and drive round to see him. He didn't like using the phone.'

Jimmy Moody continued to wander the streets near his new home, greeting locals who now knew him as 'Mick'. After buying a copy of *The Sun* most mornings, he'd then head off to his favourite pub, The Royal Hotel, on the edge of Victoria Park.

Dickie remained very worried about his brother. 'Everyone knew what had happened with the Brindles. I could have got Jim out on a plane, but he wouldn't go. Then I heard the Brindles were looking for someone to do a job on Jimmy. It looked bad. I knew he didn't have long.'

Dickie even heard on the grapevine that one south London criminal had sent someone over to Ireland to find a hitman to kill one of the Brindles. The villains who helped Moody and Tuite after they fled Brixton 13 years earlier were also said to be recruiting hitmen in Ireland for certain 'jobs' in south and east London.

In May 1993, an increasingly desperate Jimmy Moody took a ridiculous risk by robbing a bank just half a mile from his East End home with his new young gangster friend Frank. The job netted them just a few thousand pounds and a starring role on the front page of the local newspaper, *The Hackney Gazette*. The newspaper featured a description of one of the robbers which exactly matched that of Jimmy Moody. Moody had been forced to go back to the streets because all the hitman contracts and bigger robbery targets had dried up as word of his feud with the Brindles swept round London. One south-east London criminal face explained: 'A lot of people were after Jim by this stage and most people didn't want to be seen anywhere near him.'

At the end of May, Jimmy Moody met up in Victoria Park with Janine and his now 15-month-old granddaughter Chayce. The child seemed to bring out a different, softer side to Moody, who adored throwing the little girl up into the air and then catching her in his arms as they played in the park together. Janine recalled: 'It was a touching sight – this bear of a man cradling such a tiny child.'

On this particular day, Moody went with his daughter and granddaughter to the lake in the middle of the park and fed the ducks. Janine recalled: 'He crouched down and held Chayce's hand while the ducks pecked scraps of bread from their hands. It was so sweet.'

Then Moody did something completely out of character: he allowed Janine to take some photos of him with Chayce, although he did make sure his face was not visible in case the pictures ever 'fell into the wrong hands'. Moody crouched back down towards the ducks and looked out across the pond, deep in thought. Then he turned towards Janine and said: 'When your time's up, that's it. When you're dead that's the finish. There is nothin' else.'

'What d'you mean, Dad?' asked Janine.

'Nothin'. Don't worry about it.'

'It was the first time I'd every heard him talk like this,' reflected Janine later. 'I didn't know what to say to him. But he was growing old and tired of life. It was obvious. He'd had to look over his shoulder all the time, knowing there was no future, and he was fed up of it.'

TWENTY-FOUR

Mission Impossible

Late on the evening of Saturday, 29 May 1993, Jimmy Moody travelled with his criminal associate Frank and two others in a black BMW Seven Series with blacked-out windows to his favourite pub, The Royal Hotel, on the edge of Victoria Park. They were greeted by landlord Joe Anderson, who took them in a side entrance to the back bar where they enjoyed a long drinking session before emerging at about six the following morning. Moody was in good spirits, although his friend Frank noticed that 'he seemed to have a lot on his mind. He wasn't totally with us, if you know what I mean.'

The group got in the BMW, parked next to Victoria Park, and set off into the hazy early morning sunlight. Frank later remembered: 'A couple of really weird things happened driving home. Jim's in the back seat as he always was and suddenly while I'm drivin' he grabs hold of me and kisses my forehead and says, "Yer know I love yer, don't yer?" I didn't think much about it at the time because we was very good mates and there was this special bond between us, no doubt about it. But then another thing happened a few minutes later which really did my brain in; we'd just turned into Jim's street when three pigeons smashed into the windscreen. It gave me such a scare I slammed the brakes on in the middle of the road. Afterwards, Jim looked at me as if to say, "That's not a good sign." But we didn't say a word and I dropped him further up the street.'

As Moody was getting out of the BMW, Frank leaned out of the window and said to him, 'Don't forget our meet tomorrow night.'

Moody nodded and headed off towards the stairway up to his flat.

The following morning Jimmy Moody's son Jason heard fresh rumours about his father's impending death. He immediately contacted Moody who, typically, refused to be worried. He couldn't see the point in hiding. They knew where to find him if they wanted him so badly. 'Bollocks,' said Moody to his son. 'If they come, they come. I'll be waitin' with a little surprise in store for 'em.' Moody made it clear he'd 'tear 'em to bits'. One associate explained: 'Jimmy didn't hide from anyone. He took the attitude that they were welcome to come after him, but he'd wouldn't run away from anything or anyone.'

So it was in that stubborn frame of mind that, at shortly after 7.30 p.m. on the evening of Monday, 1 June 1993, Jimmy Moody, dressed in black trousers and a black leather jacket, secured his exterior anti-burglar bars before shutting the powder-blue front door of his cramped, one-bedroomed council flat. With thundery showers threatening overhead, he descended the concrete steps to the deserted street below.

Moody's green eyes were shadowed by bushy black brows on a short, thick bulldog neck. He glanced in all directions while walking over the Grand Union Canal and down Gore Road, which took him onto a narrow thoroughfare leading directly to The Royal.

Thunder continued to rumble in the distance as Moody picked up his pace a little because he had quite a thirst on him. He was soon marching alongside his beloved Victoria Park, slapping the side of his leg with that day's copy of the *Evening Standard*. With his ever-present hat pulled down close to his eyeline, he looked like a man on a mission.

There were only a small handful of cars slung up in The Royal's parking area as Moody deftly avoided the traffic by nipping across the main road just as the huge, gothic cast-iron gates of Victoria Park closed behind him. Despite a fresh lick of paint, The Royal had certainly seen better days and, despite its name, had long since stopped taking overnight guests.

As Moody strolled confidently through the L-shaped main bar, the rubber soles of his immaculately polished black monkey boots squeaked on the bone-dry wooden floor. A clap of thunder broke the silence as two regulars looked up from their pints. Across the bar, a couple ignored all around them as they sat talking in whispers at a window table. Both were white. The man was between 25 and 30, 5 ft 10 in. tall, slim-built, with short straight brown hair and was wearing a dark bomber jacket and dark trousers. His partner was a 5 ft 5in., slim, brown-haired woman aged between 20 and 25 in a white top and dark trousers. From behind the bar, landlord Joe Anderson greeted Moody as he polished pint glasses with a checked cloth.

'Evenin', Mick,' Anderson said, happily playing along with Moody's *other* name. 'Usual?' continued Anderson, taking down Moody's personalised pint glass from behind the bar. It had the name 'Mick' written on it with blood-red nail varnish.

Moody nodded. He was known in The Royal as a drinker who didn't reveal much about himself. But then he wasn't the only one round those parts to keep a low profile. No one objected to anything Mick said or did, on account of his powerful frame and guarded manner. 'There was something about him that made you keep yer distance,' one regular later recalled.

Landlord Anderson's sister Sharon, who helped run the pub with her brother, commented, 'He was a fine man and seemed very caring. He talked about his baby granddaughter sometimes. He was devoted to her. He also got very upset when he heard stories about child molesters.' The man they all called Mick had been known to kick up a fuss when anyone smoked near him in The Royal. A couple of times, Anderson had broken up potential bar brawls. But most of the time, Moody kept a lid on his sparky temper. That night, he pulled open his copy of the London *Evening Standard* and began reading the sports pages as he supped at his pint, while the thunder rumbled away in the distance.

By ten o'clock, the occupants of The Royal had dwindled to four: Moody, nursing yet another pint while still leaning against the bar between the two entrances; Anderson (his sister was off-duty that night), polishing yet more glasses; plus the couple who'd been so engrossed in each other at that same table all evening. It was so humid both entrance doors remained open to the twilight.

Outside, a white Ford Fiesta drifted slowly by, turning unhurriedly into a space next to the pub. Its driver, a 5 ft 10 in. to 6 ft-tall man, aged between 30 and 40, got out slowly and began walking towards the main entrance to The Royal. Inside, the only hum of conversation came from the couple in the corner. Seconds later, the Fiesta driver appeared in the main doorway to Moody's right side. The man's steel-blue eyes snapped across from Moody to the couple seated by the window and then over to Anderson. Moody didn't look up because he'd learned long ago not to make eye contact with strangers.

As the man moved towards the bar, his black monkey boots –

almost identical to Mick's – gave off the same dry squeak on the polished wooden floor. He ordered a pint of Fosters, then placed two £1 coins on the bar and took his change without uttering a sound. Just then, another knife of lightning shot out of the sky to illuminate nearby Victoria Park for a split second. The storm from a few hours earlier returned.

'One . . . two. . . three . . . four . . . five . . . six . . . seven . . . eight . . .' Anderson only stopped counting when a noisy clap of thunder shook The Royal. 'Means it's only eight miles away.'

No one responded so Anderson went back to polishing his glasses. He later noted that there had been a strange, empty feeling in the pub at that moment. Almost what one might call an expectant hush.

Then, without touching his pint, the stranger – his lightly tanned face expressionless – moved away from the bar. He walked in virtual slow motion past Moody towards the lavatories, only to double back while reaching inside a pocket of his dark jacket. Then a sudden movement made his blonde, tousled hair flicker slightly in the breeze. Before anyone realised what he'd pulled out of his pocket, the first two shots rang out from his Webley .38 revolver.

'You fuckin' cunt.'

Those were the only words the stranger uttered as the first two bullets pumped into Jimmy Moody's back. As he turned and tried to reach his assailant two more shells pierced Moody's head and upper torso and he crumpled to the floor. The explosive sounds of that .38 sent everyone diving for cover. The stranger stood there for a second or two as the sweet smell of cordite wafted up his nostrils. There is no doubt those in the pub would have got a good look at him, but he knew that the sight of Moody's splattered head and upper body would help cloud their memories. Frightened witnesses always can get very confused – and that stranger had just created a pub full of frightened witnesses. If the police later tried to get a photofit from the descriptions provided by these punters they'd be sure it wouldn't be much use.

The killing of Jimmy Moody clearly had all the bloody hallmarks of a paid execution, except for one aspect. As a police detective later explained: 'The killer did a very strange thing for a professional by swearing at his victim while pulling the trigger. Hired hands don't usually betray such emotion.'

Moments after the shooting, two young women approached the left-hand entrance to the pub from the street. The killer calmly stepped across the room and slammed the door in their face. They ran off. Then, crossing the room, he calmly exited the way he had arrived, got into that white Ford Fiesta – registration number B190 CBO – with its two round spotlights and two square ones on the front spoiler, and drove off into that sticky, thundery night. The vehicle had been stolen the previous day from a car park at Chessington World of Adventures, in Surrey.

The young couple sitting in the corner of The Royal ran out into the night, which raises the question: why did they take off so quickly? A few moments later a cyclist pedalled calmly past looking directly into the pub. Many later speculated he may have been another member of the hit team, checking to see if the job had been completed.

Two teenage girls arrived in a red car and walked in the door to be greeted by the sight of Joe Anderson leaning over Jimmy Moody, whose blood was seeping across the wooden floor. The two girls turned around and walked straight back out. Anderson tried to make Moody comfortable by propping his head up with a folded jacket. Then he called the emergency services and one of Jimmy Moody's son's friends.

Over in Poplar, Jason Moody got a call telling him that his father had been shot. No one knew how bad it was so he called his best friend John, who rushed round to pick him up in a silver BMW. The two men then raced down to The Royal.

En route Jason rang his mother on his mobile and told her what had happened. They arrived at the The Royal just as the paramedics were wheeling Moody out to an ambulance. Jason recalled: 'I could see from the state of him that he was just hanging on.' Jason and his friend followed the ambulance to hospital and hooted frantically whenever it slowed down.

Back at the family home in Poplar, a distraught Val called her daughter Janine.

'Jimmy's gone,' said Val.

'What d'you mean, gone? Has he been picked up?'

'No, he's gone.'

Janine didn't need to hear anymore. She put down the phone, got dressed and headed round to her mother's house.

At the London Hospital, in Whitechapel, Jason Moody's friend John slung his BMW up on a kerb and ran towards the back of the ambulance as paramedics carried Moody out on the stretcher, but

Jason knew the moment he looked down at his father that he was dead. Feeling strangely detached and unemotional, Jason later described the events that night as 'like being in a dream. None of it seemed real.'

Thirty minutes later Jason Moody walked into the freezing cold hospital morgue to find his father lying on a slab of marble. He forced himself to look at the body because he had to be sure it really was him. Jason then looked across at his father's left wrist and saw the Rolex watch which Moody had always said he would one day give to his son. Jason took a long gulp and then gently removed the watch, surprised to notice how smooth his father's skin felt.

Then he put the watch straight onto his own wrist.

'Goodbye, Dad.'

Years later, Jason recalled: 'That was it. There was nothin' more I could say. I think he was relieved it was over. He'd never have done any more time in prison. He'd never have to look over his shoulder again. This was the only way he was going to go. I felt so relieved for him when he died. He just wasn't living a normal, healthy life. It couldn't go on like that. It was like he'd had cancer, so when it finally happened it was for the best.'

Val and Janine Moody were just arriving as Jason was walking out of the hospital. He told them he couldn't stay with them because he had something very important to do *immediately*. Janine and Val didn't ask any awkward questions because they knew exactly where Jason was going.

Jason's friend John drove his BMW to a point 100 yards from Moody's flat in Mare Street and parked the vehicle. Then he walked to the rundown '60s-built block. He explained: 'We couldn't tell the police where he lived. There were things in that flat which might have affected other people. I knew I had to clear it. But it wasn't easy.'

Janine's boyfriend Jed was positioned near the flat in another car as a lookout in case the police or any villains turned up. Jason didn't have any keys to his father's flat so he broke in by forcing a side window, which brought a slight smile to his face because his father would have been annoyed the flat wasn't harder to break into. Jason recalled: 'When I got in I could smell him. It was really disturbing. My dad's body wasn't even cold, yet here I was going through his personal affects and chucking anythin' that might be important in black plastic bin bags.'

'The lack of personal items told its own story. There were no photos of us, no reminders of the past. Everything had to be like that for the old man because he was on the run.' Jason left the flat after midnight that evening, exhausted and emotionally drained by the worst day of his life. He dropped eight bags of his father's belongings into a huge waste dump near Canary Wharf and went home to his mother and sister. The three of them stayed up crying and talking all night.

Jimmy Moody's closest young gangster friend Frank is still haunted by the events of that night and the previous weekend when they went for that drinking session in The Royal. Frank first heard the news in a phone call from his cousin.

'Somethin's happened to Jim,' said the caller.

'Wot? Has he been nicked?' asked Frank.

'No.'

Then there was a long silence on the line.

'Somethin' bad's happened,' said the caller.

'Wot? Heavy?'

'Yeah.'

'Is he dead?'

Frank slammed down the phone and immediately tried to call Jason, but his line was engaged. Close to tears he recalled: 'What doesn't make sense to this day is: why did he leave the flat when he knew we were supposed to have a meet and I was going to pick him up? Who got him out of that flat?'

Jason Moody fielded virtually non-stop calls from the south and east London underworld right through the night.

'So sorry for yer loss,' said one gangster.

'Such a waste,' said another.

'He was a good man,' whispered yet another.

There was no phone call from Jimmy Moody's great Provisional IRA comrade Gerard Tuite, who'd heard about the shooting on the radio. He recalled: 'I was really saddened but not that surprised. Jim's death was such a waste.' Tuite says he didn't contact the Moody family because 'in a scenario like that no one wants to know when a stranger calls.' However Tuite later made up for it by inviting Jason Moody to stay in Ireland with him and his family.

Early next morning, Jason Moody was woken up by four Scotland Yard detectives who hauled him into Stratford Police Station. 'They started asking me about all sorts of names. There were at least nine murders they couldn't solve so they decided my old man killed the whole lot. They put a lot of pressure on me to back their claims.' The police also wanted to know where Moody's flat was but Jason told them, 'I haven't got a clue.'

TWENTY-FIVE

Legacy of Fear

The whole of east and south London was abuzz with rumours about who'd 'iced' Jimmy Moody. His young friend Frank – who was with him just before he died – claimed in an interview with this author that police knew where Moody was based, but encouraged the hit to be carried out 'so that it was one more crim off the streets'. Frank explained: 'Jim was killed with Home Office approval. The police wanted him dead. Some in Ireland even wanted him dead. The spooks probably wanted him dead. And a whole lot of villains wanted him dead as well. I have a police source who saw the Moody file a few weeks after he died and I know they approved it. They let him be killed.'

Another source claimed Jimmy Moody was offered some 'new work' by the Provos shortly before his death and this may have 'encouraged' authorities to allow the hit on him to go ahead. The informant explained: 'Jim knew working with the Irish upset a lot of people. But it was just a job to him.' No one knows if Moody even seriously considered going back to work for the Provos.

At the end of the day, Moody paid the ultimate price for crossing swords with the Brindles of Bermondsey. As Frank explained: 'Murder was likely to occur. In our world, if you are known as someone like that you get everything, including a hitman on your doorstep. That's the way it is.'

Overnight, at least half a dozen east and south London criminals disappeared from their usual haunts in fear of reprisals and the long arm of the law. Some went abroad to places like Spain, Italy and Cyprus.

Others simply melted into the background in much the same way Jimmy Moody had done over the previous 13 years.

Moody's son Jason and many of Moody's younger gangster associates felt extremely dissillusioned by the police attitude. 'The Old Bill were over the moon at my dad's death,' claimed Jason. 'They were just happy to have got him off the streets.'

David Brindle's mother also rejoiced at the news of Moody's death. 'I'm glad Moody is dead. He got it the way he gave it out. That man was evil and I hope he rots in hell.'

Seventy miles away, in the sparsely populated county of Suffolk, Detective Superintendent Harry Wilkins, who had begun his own career around the same time as Moody had embarked on his, was working on the house he'd planned to retire to when a colleague rang suggesting he take a look at a corpse in an East End mortuary. Police genuinely believed that Jimmy Moody's own son Jason might have deliberately identified another man as his father to finally bring an end to Moody's life on the run.

So, less than eight weeks before starting his retirement, DS Wilkins found himself looking down at the man he'd been pursuing for 13 years. Wilkins later recalled: 'He was considerably older looking than his pictures. But it was the body of a man who kept himself in trim.' He spotted marks where Moody had used acid to try and to burn off those tattoos from his arms. DS Wilkins also couldn't help noticing the two bullet holes in Moody's back, a third in his head and a fourth in his chest. He examined the contents of Jimmy Moody's pockets, which included his house keys and £90 in cash.

Ultimately, there was absolutely no doubt this was the 18-stone cadaver of Jimmy Moody, whose escape from Brixton all those years earlier had made him one of Britain's most-wanted men. However, there were so many unanswered questions it was difficult for DS Wilkins to know where to start.

At the so-called 'Moody incident room' in London's Arbour Square Police Station there was little sign of activity and even less evidence of optimism in the days following Moody's death. Everyone knew about the Brindle feud, but trying to get any help from within the criminal community would be like trying to prise open a tin of concrete. Harry Wilkins knew the entire police operation would be quickly wound down if they didn't get a lead within the first 48 hours of the murder. He said. 'Moody's is a typical villain's story: a name to conjure with in his younger days – then it's over.'

Harry Wilkins knew only too well how back in the so-called good old days of the swinging '60s, old lags would openly chat about villains and what they were up to. A lot of it was exagerrated in exchange for a pint or two, but now and then it proved to be valuable info. That's what the Moody inquiry team needed in June 1993. Unfortunately, the new underworld was filled with cold-blooded millionaire criminals obsessed by their next drug deal and content to commission a hit on anyone who dared cross them. Drugs had pushed up the level of gangland terror, combined with tighter rules of evidence and an increasingly selective Crown Prosecution Service deciding who goes into the dock.

By 1993, even senior detectives like Harry Wilkins were discouraged from entering pubs in the quest for information. And it was that very rule which prevented detectives from solving the murder of Jimmy Moody.

As one officer explained: 'All the rules about drink/driving, consorting with the enemy. You have to fill in paperwork before you can even go to a boozer to meet the opposition. It's just not worth the trouble anymore. But if ever there was a crime which needed info from those types of fellows it was the murder of Jimmy Moody. No one's going to walk in off the street and say who did it.'

Police even compiled a bizarre, Cluedo-style reconstruction of Moody's deathscene in a desperate appeal for witnesses to come forward. Scotland Yard's graphic of the last few minutes of Moody's life was reproduced in London's *Evening Standard* in the hope it might prompt calls. More than 20 detectives were involved in the hunt for Moody's killer. They even set up a special hotline for information – *071 275 5424*. As one detective explained: 'The most important witnesses are the young couple. It may be that they were meeting secretly, but we are not bothered about that.'

Some newspapers even gave Moody a new nickname, 'Long Jim', as they reported a few snippets about his criminal past. The articles referred to several sightings of Moody during his 13 years on the run, but claimed they were either too vague or too late to be of any help to police. The media soon concluded that Moody had been killed as part of an ongoing vendetta between criminals.

Not surprisingly, police feared more tit-for-tat gangland murders would be sparked off by the Moody killing. Then questions started to be asked about why Moody wasn't tracked down earlier, following the discovery of his fingerprints in the Kennington flat raided by police after the shooting of David Brindle two years earlier. One senior detective summed up the police attitude when he said: 'Summary justice has finally caught up with Moody. The next few weeks will tell who ordered the hit and why. It will be a tense time as we wait to see if it will spark off revenge shootings.' Detectives let it be known they expected to reopen their books on several contract killings, including the David Brindle job.

A couple of days after his father's death, Jason Moody was summoned to meet various criminal faces who wanted to pay their respects to him in person and try to find out who was next on the list. These scenes were like something out of TV's *The Sopranos*. Jason explained: 'They had guns strapped under the table and were wearing bullet-proof vests and I had to sit there and deal with the grief over my dad while talkin' to people watchin' their backs. It wasn't easy. Thinkin' back on it, it was a fuckin' mad time and that's when the grief really hit me.'

Jason, his sister Janine and their mother Val even went down to Moody's caravan on the south coast to try and get away from the constant police and media harrassment. Jason recalled: 'We sat down there one night and looked at the stars and wondered how Dad was getting on, wherever he ended up. Then we all had a good cry.'

Daughter Janine found the grieving process very difficult to deal with. 'I couldn't grieve properly because of the way he was. The things he did. He hurt a lot of people. I know my dad wasn't an angel and I'm not painting him white. I know what he was about. I know what he did.'

Janine was finding it especially hard to cope with the banner headlines and endless rumours published in newspapers just after the murder. 'The lies about him really bothered me,' she revealed. 'I wanted to defend him. I think it's because I always felt he gave us protection. He was our dad and he did do these things, but we loved him and he was a good dad.'

His father's death sent a very serious message to Jason. 'I had to completely walk away from that world. The game was up. I had to get out before it was too late for me, as well.' Jason had run nightclubs and even done a stint as a bodyguard for the Saudi Royal Family, but it had all brought him into close contact with the east and south London underworld.

Jason held no grudges against individual policemen. He was even quite touched when detective Bill Forman, who'd spent years tracking Jimmy Moody during Operation Ohio, appeared on TV shortly after

Moody's murder and proclaimed Moody's death as 'the end of an era'.

A few days later, an unnamed policeman was quoted in one newspaper as saying: 'Moody was not the sort of guy you fight. You don't punch him or rough him up. You kill him.'

Jason sensed a level of 'respect' for his father from the so-called 'enemy'. As Bill Forman later explained: 'Jim Moody was a hard man, but he was an old-school villain with certain standards and that made him a whole lot better than many of the mad, drug-riddled bastards running around London today.'

A few days after the Moody shooting, Jason was out in the East End when he spotted a London *Evening Standard* billboard in front of a newstand. It read: 'DEATH OF A HITMAN – SPECIAL FEATURE'. Jason bought a copy of that billboard and has kept it to this day. 'It's a reminder and a warning not to go down the same road as my old man.'

Jason Moody's biggest problem was convincing criminals and police alike that he wasn't like his dad. 'People thought I was a chip off the old block, but I am not,' he explained. Jason was particularly disturbed when other criminals started trying to lean on him to provide some typical Moody-style 'services'. 'It was completely out of order. People had no right to think I'd do the same things as my old man.'

Some of Moody's criminal associates also tried to put Jason under pressure to order a reprisal killing, but he knew the violence had to stop. 'Sure, I was angry, just like any son would be whose father had been murdered in cold blood, but his death came about because of a spiral of killings. Someone had to eventually say, "no more," and that was the way I felt.'

London's *Evening Standard* even suggested one of Jimmy Moody's girlfriends held the key to his murder. Detectives claimed women had flocked to his bed and that he might have been executed by a jealous husband or boyfriend. One senior detective was quoted in the *Standard* as saying: 'He was an animal for the women, but that may have caused his come-uppance.'

Jason and the rest of the family laughed off such stories as a purile attempt by the police to further dirty the name of their father. And the police attempts to penetrate the wall of silence that surrounded the Moody murder continued. One detective explained: 'There are people who knew who he was when he was alive, who cannot give any motive for the murder. We need people to come forward.'

Detective Harry Wilkins believed the case was still wide open. He said: 'The killing could be related to anything from armed robbery to drugs. Those who live by the sword die by the sword.'

The attitude of the police to Jimmy Moody's life and death was perfectly summed up in a two-page feature article which appeared in the coppers' own publication *Police Review* just two weeks after the murder. Under a banner headline 'THE GREAT ESCAPER', the author of the article admitted that Moody's ability to survive 13 years on the run had raised serious questions about the police and their ability to hunt down supposedly dangerous criminals. The article said the police had expected Moody to be more carefully guarded once he was incarcerated in the high security D-wing at Brixton. So it was a surprise – and a measure of the respect felt towards Moody, even by the long arm of the law – that the *Police Review* article described in almost admiring terms how Moody, Tuite and Thompson had cut through the brickwork and then removed the rubble by placing it in prisoner's chamber pots when they slopped out.

The article concluded:

> Once initial efforts have been made and 'wanted' circulations noted, what does the service do to try to recapture people like Jim Moody? In the main, these efforts are likely to be left in the hands of individual police officers; when staff are transferred, the impetus fades. Some senior Metropolitan officers have begun to call for the formation of a team dedicated to tracing wanted serious criminals. It might not, they concede, be a welcome innovation in these cost-conscious times, but they feel sure that it would prevent people like Jim Moody escaping justice for 13 years. It should have been the police who brought Jim Moody to justice rather than an anonymous assassin.

Even Moody's close family and friends felt that the police assessment was fair and balanced. And many continued to ask the all-important question: 'Why did Jimmy Moody have to die in a hail of bullets?'

Jason, Janine and Val Moody revealed the other side of Jimmy Moody to the *Daily Mirror*'s chief crime correspondent Jeff Edwards in a moving interview shortly after his murder. They insisted he'd been a doting grandfather. Janine revealed to the *Mirror* how she'd last seen her dad when they went with Chayce to Victoria Park just a few days before he was gunned down

Jason refused to publicly deny his father's dark and dangerous past. He also admitted to the *Mirror* that he and his family had gone to 'extraordinary lengths' to keep in touch with Moody.

Val spoke about her very special relationship with her ex-husband. She said: 'It was impossible being married to a professional villain. We were apart so much. But even though we were no longer married there were still deep feelings between us.' Val added: 'Jim always expected to die violently but he thought it would be the police who shot him, not another villain. He always said "They won't give me the chance to get away again." I think it was his secret wish. He would have preferred to die rather than go back to prison.'

Many of the very same tabloids who'd fed Jimmy Moody with his diet of news and sport during 13 years on the run had a field day after his death reporting Moody's encounters with celebrities and page 3 girls. One paper described Moody as '6 ft 4 in. but anything but a friendly giant . . .' Yet most papers still managed to concede that Moody was a devoted father.

Two weeks after Jimmy Moody was shot dead, a body washed ashore in a sack on the morning tide at Sheerness, Kent. The victim – who had at least two shotgun wounds to his chest – had been dumped at sea about ten days earlier. The body was never identified but there were whispers in south and east London that the victim had links to the Brindles of Bermondsey.

TWENTY-SIX

The Last Goodbye

The Poplar coroner finally released Jimmy Moody's body for a cremation service on 19 June 1993, held at the vast, gothic-looking east London necropolis in Manor Park. A five-car funeral cortege containing close family and friends groaned under the sheer weight of the mountain of floral tributes as it drew up at the crematorium entrance. Several men with close-cropped heads and brick-outhouse torsos scanned the scene before Jason and the rest of his entourage emerged from their black limos.

When two of the minders spotted a group of journalists and cameramen at the gates to the crematorium, one man-mountain yelled at them, 'Keep back, right?' The press dutifully took one step back rather than risk any bodily harm. 'Well back,' growled the same minder once again. No one dared put a foot out of step from then on.

Janine was particularly upset by the press pack. She recalled: 'When we drove up with the hearse I thought, how dare they be here, and then they ran over and started snapping away. It stopped us from being allowed to grieve properly.'

Nearby, two fairly obvious plain-clothes police officers disguised as gravediggers watched the proceedings. Another pair of detectives cruised the narrow roads of the cemetery in a silver Sierra, anxiously scanning all the faces in the crowd and hoping they might spot someone worth arresting.

Val, Janine and Jason led about 30 mourners in a final tribute to their dearly departed husband and father. The mourners included a large number of faces in square-cut suits, dark glasses and the occasional gold earring. The service, conducted behind closed doors away from the prying eyes of the media, was conducted by Moody's parish priest, Father Seamus O'Boyle. It lasted barely ten minutes. Father Seamus later recalled: 'It was a rather bizarre occasion, but everyone deserves a proper funeral whatever they might have done while alive. But I was rather surprised the police bothered to try and pretend they weren't there. We all knew exactly who they were.'

As the mourners filed out of the church, Val, Jason and Janine clasped each other's shoulders and their minders turned and glared towards the waiting presspack. When everyone had finally dispersed, the floral tributes were there for all to see and cherish.

'Best dad in the world. We love you and miss you always – Jason and Janine.'

A friend of the family who signed himself 'Paul' sent a wreath inscribed: 'With the greatest respect to a very funny man in his own way.'

There were also a lot of cards to 'Terry', 'Tom' and 'Mick', which were some of Moody's many alias during his 13 years on the run. Jason explained: 'A lot of these cards were from "straight" people because he'd been decent to many ordinary people. It gave you an indication of how much he was liked in the normal world.' There were even a handful of cards from Moody's sworn enemy, the police, including some from the family-liason officers who offered the Moodys counselling facilities after the murder. There was no mention of David Brindle's death at the funeral.

Jimmy Moody's ashes were scattered in a special plot in the eastern corner of the cemetery. No one present that day dared mention the likelihood that at least one of his murder victims had been laid to rest in the same cemetery. Moody's ashes and the small tree planted in the same plot of earth was adorned with just a few scrappy leaves clinging to the ground. The inscription on the plaque was simple and to the point: 'May he rest in peace'.

Moody's daughter Janine said later she felt a strange sense of peace after his funeral. 'The life he was leading meant it had to happen one day. People used to wind him up and take advantage of him. They'd point at someone in a pub and say, "He's a grass," and Dad would go over and have a go at them. Then we'd all have to drag him off them. That's how he came to die, because people used him to have a go at others.'

As Janine looked at the other people who'd gathered to wish farewell to her father a strange, but perfectly understandable, thought went through her mind. She recalled: 'I did wonder if any of them there that day knew who'd killed my dad or maybe one of them had actually pulled the trigger? It was a difficult, terrible day.'

Janine was so shaken she attended bereavement-therapy sessions for more than a year after her father's murder. 'The counsellor always used to say to me, "You led such a strange childhood," and I used to get really uptight and my back would go stiff and I'd say, "What was strange about it?" She used to say it was so different from most people's. But we were still children and all that other stuff involving my dad was separate. He didn't actually put us in danger, but where I think that there were problems was that we had to accept him for what he was. Most of it went over my head and I never questioned what he said. Never. I think that's why I was so shattered when he died. At his funeral all the flowers from all these different names sort of summed up all his different personalities. It was terrible what he'd done, but I accept what he did. I loved him.'

The day after Moody's funeral, detectives finally located his flat in Mare Street. They weren't surprised to find it had already been emptied and wiped of all fingerprints and significant evidence of Moody's secret life. Detective Harry Wilkins admitted: 'Between Moody's escape and his murder, we have one big black hole – we have no real idea what he'd been doing, other than a bit of interior decorating: we found rolls of wallpaper in his flat.'

Police continued to visit Jason Moody. 'They were on my back all the time,' explained Jason. 'I didn't blame them in a way, but I also knew they didn't care for my dad and he didn't care for them, so why should I help them?' One detective even tried to provoke Jason into cooperating with the police by making a suggestion that he played some kind of role in his father's death. 'But I laughed that one off,' said Jason. 'What else could I do? It was an outrageous suggestion, deliberately made to exert maximum pressure on me.'

A year after Jimmy Moody was cold-bloodedly shot down in The Royal Hotel, the Richardsons and the Krays – with Mad Frankie Fraser in tow – finally made their peace when members of both 'families' visited Reggie Kray in Maidstone Prison. The name Jimmy Moody was still on everyone's lips, but none of them had been surprised about his death. As Mad Frankie Fraser wrote in his book *Mad Frankie*: 'He could be stubborn and obstinate, a good man but a loner. He'd be content to do his work and watch the telly knowing that every day was a winner. That's how he would look at it.'

As far as his death was concerned, Fraser summed up the underworld's attitude to Moody's death thus: 'Much as I knew Jim well, I can understand the feelings about David's death, and that it was one that had to be done. I suppose if someone who knew it was going off had really pleaded for him it might have made some difference, but I doubt it.'

Aftermath

In August 1994 two completely innocent citizens called Peter McCormack and John Ogden were shot dead in Cavendish Road, Balham, south-west London. The police believed they were killed by mistake because one of them bore a striking resemblance to the Brindle's arch-enemy Pete Daley, the man whose problems with the Brindles led to Jimmy Moody's death. A couple of days later another of the Brindle brothers, George, was shot and injured while visiting his parents' home in south London.

A few months later INLA hitman Michael Boyle, an armed kidnapper with lengthy prison terms behind him in Ireland, was hired for £25,000 from across the water to murder Tony Brindle. Boyle claimed he'd worked as an intelligence gatherer for the Provisional IRA as well as the INLA. In prison in Ireland he'd rubbed shoulders with some of the most notorious terrorists in the world, including Jimmy Moody's great friend Gerard Tuite.

In September 1995, Boyle's attempt to kill Tony Brindle failed in dramatic fashion when a police unit pounced on him after he started shooting at 39-year-old Brindle outside his Rotherhithe home. It turned out detectives had been shadowing Boyle for days. Following his arrest, Michael Boyle called a detective to his cell at Bellmarsh high-security prison in south-east London and revealed the names of his paymasters.

Boyle said the man who'd hired him on behalf of the Daleys was Irish gangster George 'The Penguin' Mitchell, who told him that Tony

Brindle was 'treading on a lot of toes' as he tried to expand his drugs cartel in south-east London. Mitchell had met Jimmy Moody on numerous occasions and also had strong links to the IRA.

Hitman Boyle also revealed that he'd earlier informed Dublin detectives when he was arrested on unrelated matters that he'd been recruited to shoot dead a south-east London gangster. The Irish police told Boyle to distance himself from the hit, but Boyle ignored them and made six return flights from Dublin to London between April and September 1995 to research his intended victim and study his movements. It was later alleged in court that Boyle had also been contracted to kill David Brindle's brothers Patrick and George before he was arrested for the attempted hit on Tony.

So for the moment the Brindles continued to thrive but they'd never forget their encounters with Jimmy Moody and the bloodbath that followed.

By the mid-1990s, silence within the London underworld had forced Scotland Yard detectives to virtually close their investigations into Jimmy Moody's death. After much intense work, including checks on at least four other murder cases, police told Moody's family they couldn't find a motive for the crime or the identity of his killer. Detectives still claimed they'd been unable to fill in many of the details about Moody's life since he'd escaped from prison 13 years earlier.

So the Jimmy Moody inquiry joined a string of other unsolved killings including those of at least seven possible victims of Moody himself. Detective Chief Inspector Norman McNamara said he and his investigation team had faced 'An inpenetrable wall of silence around Moody and his life. There are people who knew who he was when he was alive who cannot give any motive for the murder.'

Police insisted they couldn't connect Moody's murder to other gangland killings, or find enough evidence of the so-called feud that sparked all the killings in the first place.

Meanwhile, across the nation, night and day, police cars and helicopters whirl and wail as they go about the business of protecting citizens. But criminals still thrive. The war continues.

Postscript

JASON MOODY has left the East End far behind and settled down with his wife and three children in a quiet hamlet many miles from London. He is now a property developer and currently contracted to a film-production company, who have written a movie script based around his life with his father. Jason shares with his father not only very distinct physical looks but certain attitudes, which have at times greatly disturbed him. He explained: 'I'm fanatically fit just like the old man was. But my hatred of dogs is getting worse as I get older. I'm definitely getting less tolerant of smokers and I've never smoked, just like the old man. But I don't go around beating people up who smoke near me. Hopefully, I've taken on the good parts of my dad, not the bad ones.' Earlier this year Jason was yet again swooped on by police investigating an alleged crime which took place almost 20 years ago. Jason says: 'Some of them just can't let go.'

JANINE MOODY now lives happily in a house in Kent with her partner. Her second child, a son Jacob, was born in 1995. The apple of her father's eye – her daughter Chayce – is almost a teenager and often asks about the grandfather she barely remembers. Janine says she still greatly misses her father and that brother Jason has taken on that role for her. 'But unlike Dad, he's *always* there when you need him.'

VAL MOODY lives on her own with many memories – good and bad – of her time as the wife of one of this country's most notorious criminals. She is looking forward to a safe and happy retirement, but will never forget the most special man in her life, Jimmy Moody.

DICKIE MOODY still lives in the same council flat in Rosendale Road where he and Jimmy were brought up by their strong willed mother Rosina. Dickie – now in his early 60s – keeps himself fit and works as a plumber in south London.

GERARD TUITE is now a successful businessman in Ireland who drives a Mercedes and lives with his wife and two children in a detached house in a picturesque village 50 miles from Dublin. He insists his days with 'the movement' are over. He says that Moody's son Jason is now the spitting image of his father at that same age.

STANLEY THOMPSON, the master jail escaper, lives east of London and works as a builder. His eyes light up whenever he talks about the Brixton breakout and he says he'll never forget Jimmy Moody or the good times they spent together.

BERNIE KHAN, from the Chainsaw Gang, still lives in the East End but has long since retired from crime. He says those days as a master robber were the best of his life.

JOHN WOODRUFF, another of the Chainsaw Gang, proved beyond doubt in April 1997, that old habits die hard when he and a man called Billy Hickson each got 17-year sentences for a £300,000 series of robberies they hoped would set them up for a long and healthy retirement.

FRANK, the energetic young gangster who accompanied Moody on so many crimes during the last couple of years of his life, has graduated into the criminal Premiership after learning all the tricks of the trade from the ultimate 'Masterblaster'.

BILL FORMAN, retired detective, lives in quiet retirement with his wife in a neat semi just a few miles from the scene of the Chainsaw Gang's most daring robbery in Banstead, Surrey.

CHARLIE SNAPE retired in 1982 and lives quietly in a large detached house in the suburbs of south London

JIMMY MOODY died in that hail of bullets as thunder and lightning illuminated the East End on a steamy June evening in 1993 . . . or did he? Has he pulled off the biggest job of his life and fooled us all?

Bibliography

Donoghue, A. & Short, M. (1996) *The Krays Lieutenant*, Macmillan, London

Fraser, F. with Morton, J. (1994) *Mad Frank*, Warner Books, New York

Fraser, F. with Morton, J. (2000) *Mad Frank's Diary*, Virgin Publishing, London

Geraghty, T. (2002) *The Irish War*, HarperCollins Publishers, London

Kray, R. (1990) *Born Fighter*, Arrow Books, London

Lambrianou, T. (2000) *Inside The Firm*, Pan, London

McDonald, B. (2000) *Elephant Boys*, Mainstream Publishing, Edinburgh

Morton, J. (2000) *East End Gangland*, Warner Books, New York

Pearsion, J. (1972) *The Profession of Violence*, HarperCollins Publishers, London

Thompson, T. (1996) *Gangland Britain*, Coronet, London